Ch
and
cla
and
Na
the

imp
and
for
Jap
fur
of

a l
cul
wo
rel
de
ex

The trilogy *Quiet are the Mountains* consists of three novels: *The Mountain Village*, *The Open Fields* and *A Distant Journey*. The first was written in English in 1946 while the author was in Cambridge and was published to great acclaim in 1947. The other two were written in Chinese in 1984 and 1986 after Chun-Chan Yeh had had the opportunity to revisit the village region of his childhood, the background of the trilogy.

Quiet are the Mountains
The Mountain Village
The Open Fields
A Distant Journey

THE MOUNTAIN VILLAGE

Chun-Chan Yeh

faber and faber

LONDON · BOSTON

First published in Great Britain in 1947
by the Sylvan Press
Published in Hong Kong in 1984
by Joint Publishing Co. (HK)
This new edition first published in 1988
by Faber and Faber Limited
3 Queen Square London WC1N 3AU
This paperback edition first published in 1989

Phototypeset by Input Typesetting Ltd London
Printed in Great Britain by
Richard Clay Ltd Bungay Suffolk

British Library Cataloguing in Publication Data

Yeh, Chun-Chan
The mountain village.
I. Title
823[F]   PR94509.Y43

ISBN 0–571–14172–2

CHAPTER 1

When it was fine there was always a song in the valley, whether it was early morning or afternoon. Even when there was no one singing, the song seemed to be still lingering there, unwilling to go. The undulating mountains walled in the air which carried the song, and it could not go. It was a melody beginning with:

Aiyu, aiyu, ai-aiyu, ai-ai-yu, ai-yo-ho-ho . . .

and ending always with the same refrain:

This yellow earth gave us rice in spring.
And in autumn, soya beans and sweet potato.

It was a silly song, but people liked to sing it while working. When they started, it provoked a multitude of echoes from various directions. They vibrated in the air discordantly at first, but soon became confluent into a huge chorus. And then there was only one echo. The chorus grew bigger and bigger in volume until at last it came to a sudden stop, trailing in the air a feeble note, which sounded like a lullaby. It died out gradually as though the baby were falling asleep. The tranquillity meant midday or that the sun was about to set.

Then the many farm-hands, who looked like ants in the valley, moved up from their fields and formed a line on the path on the river bank, which also served as a highway, extending along the stream into the distant horizon in one direction, and to thick woods in the other. The peasants walked with leisurely steps, with hoes and spades on their shoulders, towards the dense cluster of trees. The first disappeared into them, then a second, then a third . . . and finally the last. They moved like a long snake that wriggles into a forest leaving no trace behind, or like a streak of evening smoke that vanishes the moment it touches the dark foliage of ancient plants.

These trees, which we called aspens and oaks and maples, enclosed a large space and served as a screen, through which we could see the outside world, the river, the mountains and the highway. Towards the back of the space stood twenty cottages or so, built of wood and stone. They were as old as the mountains, as the sky, as the ever-smiling white clouds, so old that no one could tell their age. Between the wooden doors and stone walls there was no difference in appearance, all being bleached white by the heat and cold, wind and frost. The only contrast to them was in the tiled roofs, which were pitch black. Joining together, they looked like a series of waves suspended in the sky. The oldest grandfather in the village used to say that they had always looked like that and that they would still look like that, no matter what dynasty came and what emperor went.

All doors opened on to the space, which was flat, hard and even, like a modern tennis court. There we would thresh and husk our grain and rice in the summer, gather to chat in the late afternoons, sit and listen to our village story-teller in the late evenings, and stare at the stars and Milky Way aimlessly on midsummer nights. To the right of the space, where it narrowed, stood the only building of any magnificence, our ancestral temple. Its tiles were glassy and green, and would often dazzle our eyes. Their reflections in the sun were very vivid. It was said that the reflections led up to the heavens and served as a highway for our ancestors to come back to us at festivals and to receive our offerings and homage. To the left of the village, almost inside the forest by the highway, lived our God of Earth and his plump, elderly wife, in a stone pavilion. He was a gentle mandarin. He sat all the time with the tapering fingers of his soft hands resting on his knees, his wife beside him in the same fashion, with a motherly smile on her face. But they were both very busy. They looked after not only our farming, but also our well-being and our ploughing cows. After having thus served us for a number of years, this god and his wife would retire without a pension, like the mayors in big towns, and then go up to the heavens to become saints, free forever from reincarnation, from living in our sorrowful world again. Our present God of Earth was said to be one of our great-grandfathers, who had been a scholar and a virtuous man. Every day in the late afternoon a family would go there to burn incense for him in a large iron urn, which stood on a stone table immediately below the altar.

In the distance beyond our village the river flowed gently to the west. We could not see its whole extent because of the trees on the embankment. But we could see the water. It shone all the time in the sun. When a breeze ruffled its surface, the wavelets would glimmer like stars smiling and winking at us through the gaps between green leaves. It was at this time, as on many other days, that I went out of the village and walked down the highway which sloped gently to the river, to have a look at our cow. A large strip of green pasture stretched up from the bank. All our ploughing cows and calves and oxen were there, grazing, butting each other or frolicking like pups. Alongside the grassland ran a sandy beach, about a quarter of a mile wide. The sand glittered in the sun like golden grains. Then there was the stream, forever transparent and peaceful. I liked to stir it up with my bare feet, and today I went to do it again. The fine sand at the bottom whirled upwards like a spiral of smoke, as I swung one of my feet, obscuring the clear water. And the water murmured, at first high and then low. But the graceful current soon rolled down the sand and clarified the frothing pool. Then it was quiet again as I stepped out of the water, and the drying sand on my feet smiled with the sun. And I remained standing by the stream stupefied. It had no end. Such a long stream of water!

'It is the longest river in the world,' Uncle Pan said one day. when he was brushing our ploughing cow on the pasture. 'It is

3

thousands and thousands of miles long, longer than all the highways in our country put together.'

'How can it be so long?' I asked.

'Just imagine how many miles you have to walk up to the Milky Way. The river starts its course from the Milky Way, see?'

'What is the Milky Way, then, Uncle?'

'It is the river in the heavens,' he said, still brushing the flank of the cow, which gave a kick as the brush touched her udders. 'That heavenly river, again, has no end.'

I thought of these words as I stared at the sand grains on my bare feet, which were still glittering in the sun. Then I lifted my head and gazed up the river towards the east. No end, indeed. And I heard a cow lowing, deep and heavy. It was our cow. She was looking dreamily in the other direction. She was often like that, mooing without a cause, staring hazily at the water which flowed down west rhythmically, day and night, always in its own peaceful way. So I found nothing new in that direction either, except that the stream made a slight bend round a terrace in front of the town. But beyond that it went on running again, straight to the distant horizon. However, at the bend there rose a song. Perhaps our cow was mistaking it for the call of an ox. That was why she appeared so foolish.

> Hai-ho, hai-ho, lololo, hai, lolo, hai-lo,
> Hoho, hu, hai-ho, hu, hai-hai-ho, lo-lo-lo . . .

It was a meaningless unison struck up by the coolies on the sandy beach round the bend over there. I did not know why they should hum it. It sounded silly. They were carrying heavy loads on their backs, their heads bent. As they plodded along the road leading to the ancient walled city up on the flat ground beneath a semi-circle of hills, they chanted ceaselessly these monosyllabic sounds as though to accentuate their weighty steps. The city, apart from numerous shops and houses, had a big Buddhist temple at its east end with a large square before it, to accommodate worshippers on festival days. The shops bought all sorts of things from 'The Big City', about a hundred miles down the river, and sold them to the villagers. The commodities were carried up on bamboo rafts. Every day there were flotillas of rafts, pulled up stream by trackers. They stopped at the bend for half a day or a night. While the coolies were unloading the cargoes, the raftsmen took their rest. There was a cluster of restaurants and tea-shops, and even a barber's shop on the terrace. The trackers, all browned with the sun and wind, would sit over their tea like foreigners, watching the coolies humming the senseless song. Sometimes they smiled at them like children. Sometimes they tried to smarten up during this brief interval of rest by having their stubbly chins shaved or their dust-covered heads thoroughly shampooed in the roofless barber's shop.

After the rafts had been cleared the trackers pulled them further upstream along the sandy beach to the towns away in the east, to collect local produce for 'The Big City' down the river. Then they would sing, too, like the coolie carriers, but a much sadder tune. The wind on the open river used to dilute the volume of their voices; so the song became feeble and consequently melancholy. Again, when they started their journey upstream, it was generally late afternoon or even dusk, so their shadows on the sand appeared terribly slender, weak as their song, and somehow they even looked ghostly and sad.

Now I saw a flotilla being drawn up against the stream. The water gurgled as the rafts came nearer and nearer in my direction. Our cow was following them with her stupid eyes, her ears stretched at the raftsmen's song. Perhaps she was again mistaking the song for the call of an ox. Suddenly the unison came to a pause. The flotilla had come level with me, while I was watching our cow.

'You lazy cowherd,' one of the men said to me, 'your cow is dreaming of her bed, her warm bed with the ox. And you're still idling here!'

The speaker, a sturdy black fellow, burst into a fit of laughter, which sounded a little queer on the still river. Then another raftsman said, 'Go back home, my boy. The cow is longing for her shed.' And he threw a handful of roast peanuts on the sand for me to pick up. Then they trudged away. They used to leave something on the beach for the local cowherds, believing that the goodwill thus earned would bring them happy dreams at night. Their only possibility of relaxation on the lonely river was to have good dreams.

I picked up the peanuts one by one then looked at the western hills. The swollen, blood-red sun was suspended just over the pine trees on the hills. From the marshy paddy-fields in the valley below rose a cloud of mist, which kept expanding as the night became dimmer and dimmer. Gradually it climbed up into the sky and paled the sun, which was sinking slowly behind the trees. And after the sun had completely disappeared the western hills became simply patches of diluted ink in the evening landscape of a classical painting.

I took our cow by the cord that ran through the soft bridge of her nose. She meekly followed me home. We walked leisurely along the bank. As we were about to enter among the trees that stood on either side of the entrance to our village, I gave a last glance at the flotilla. It was now entirely enveloped in the river mist. Only the senseless song of the raftsmen was still trailing feebly in the thick evening air.

And I entered the village. Life there had just begun when the outside world was about to fall asleep. All the farm-hands had come back from their work and were gathering on the square. The old people lighted their long pipes while the young folk were busy loosening the girdles about their waists and beating the dust of the field off their gowns. The baldpate Mao Mao was standing on a stone against a wall and narrating with gusto how he had greeted, like a perfect gentleman, She-crow, the eldest of the wine-maker's nine daughters in the neighbouring village, as he came across her on his way to the town. She-crow was a gigantic girl with a huge mouth, absurdly small eyes and a pair of large feet, which looked almost square. Mao Mao had been an orphan and was now a field labourer without land of his own. He used to say that he was head over heels in love with this girl, that he must marry her, that she would make an ideal wife as well as an excellent field labourer and that no one in the village should court her without his permission.

'Are you sure that you can win her heart?' asked Benchin, our Taoist priest. Benchin had remained always 'an old bachelor', although he knew how to write and read and even invoke ghosts. He had no land, and was as thin as a skeleton, and his back was crooked and his eyes were shortsighted. So no girl in the neighbourhood wanted to marry him. But Mao Mao for some reason, which no one could understand, regarded him as his potential rival.

'I'm a man of strong will, you see.' Mao Mao said. 'A man of strong will can always do things.'

'Yes, and your shining bald head is an attraction as well,' our priest commented with a senseless giggle.

Hahaha! All the bystanders sent out a wave of laughter. Uncle Pan was standing against an ancient elm tree. He had an odd habit of throwing his head back when he laughed. Now he hit his old head on the tree. This provoked another fit of laughter.

'Enough! Gentlemen, enough!' shouted Lao Liu, our story-teller. He was coming out of his cottage with a small drum, and a pair of castanets, and a drum-stand and a drumstick. 'Go in for your meal, gentlemen. I'll have to start right after supper and wait for no one, whether he be the magistrate or landlord. And I never repeat the same story.'

He was serious and frank in his statement. He never told the same story twice. None of our village could afford to lose the clue of his tales.

The crowd dispersed into their cottages.

We sat on benches at a low table in the middle of our sitting-room, a few feet away from the ancestral altar. O Ran brought out from the kitchen a large pot of noodles stewed with vegetables and sweet potato and onions. When she put it on the middle of the table, hot steam immediately rose up and gathered around the vegetable-oil lamp. We could not see each other's faces for a good while, so we waited quietly. After the steam finally dispersed, my mother ladled the stew into our bowls. We again waited till everybody had their bowlful. But O Ran could not. She was always the most hungry person in the house, because she worked all day long, now in the kitchen, now in the vegetable garden. So she started sucking the fluid food right away, making a rattling noise. 'Hasty eating hurts your palate' my mother said to her. But I knew she meant it was bad manners for a girl to eat that way.

Uncle Pan ate very quietly as though he was tasting the food only with the tip of his tongue, his head hanging mournfully. Looking at him, with his gentle appearance, my mother smiled. She seemed to have remembered something, but would not say it straight out. She watched to see how quickly Uncle Pan could finish his bowlful.

'Are you tired, Uncle Pan?' my mother asked at last, still smiling.

'A little, not much,' Uncle Pan replied, his lips pouted up, but he did not raise his head.

'Then why don't you warm yourself up with a cup of wine?' my mother suggested, stressing particularly the last three words.

Uncle Pan immediately lifted his head and beamed. 'Very good idea!' he said. 'I *never* thought of it!' I knew it was a lie. Every evening he would have a cup of wine during supper and each time he would say he had never thought of it. In fact, a green cup was always laid before his place at every evening meal.

He went to the row of wine barrels that stood beneath the ancestral altar, took off the lid of a newly-opened one and brought up a full cup of wine by means of a copper ladle. The liquor was home-made. Every autumn after harvest we asked the wine-maker from a neighbouring village to distil for us a few barrels of wine from barley. And Uncle Pan was the only person who consumed it. He used to say jokingly that had it not been for the 'exhilarating elixir' he would not have stayed with us for so long.

He was originally not a member of our family, not even a member of our village. He had come from the north, many, many years ago, when I was very small. Then two rival warlords were fighting civil wars in his province, and on top of that the Yellow River was swollen, flooding all the farms. He came with a batch of refugees to our village on his way to 'The Big City', where he hoped to become a rickshaw coolie. He suddenly fell ill and lagged behind. My father took him home, and my mother tended to him till he was recovered. Then he changed his mind and wanted to stay with us, farming our six acres of land. He said he might not make a good rickshaw coolie, because he was born a peasant. He loved land and the cow which ploughed the land. We had a beautiful cow. So my mother let him stay on and gave him the room next to the cowshed. He felt very comfortable, sleeping next to the cow. And he never thought of going back.

Now he held the cup up to the light of the oil lamp. The fire immediately descended on the wine, sending up a glow of weird, greenish flames. Uncle Pan contemplated it smilingly for a while. Then he suddenly blew it out, and sipped at the cup heavily and then heaved a sigh of relief. A kind of crimson began to creep on his wrinkled cheeks.

He began to talk. Words flowed out from his mouth like a brook from a sloping valley. And he gave many an emphasis to his words while narrating his tales, just as the stream runs against a number of stones in its course. And to illustrate his descriptions he made various gestures, which were different every evening. He had heard that such and such a peasant of a far, faraway village had caught an otter alive, that he had tied it by the leg to the handle of his hoe and that the tricky animal had managed to gnaw the rope to pieces and finally got clean away, much to the disappointment and amazement of the stupid farm-hand. He had also seen a townsman buying a hare from a wandering sportsman with a huge pile of silver coins. 'The sum must at least be two hundred and fifty three pieces, enough to keep me going half my life.' He stressed the numerals particularly as though he had counted the money himself. And so on, and so forth.

My mother kept on saying, 'Really? Really?'

'I never told lies in my life, ma'am,' he said firmly. 'They are as real as Mao Mao and me.'

And we finished all the stew imperceptibly, without knowing how much time we had spent.

O Ran then got up and tried to clear the table. But my mother stopped her, saying, 'I'll do that. Get yourself ready to go to the village square. Your lips are a little too greasy and your nose shiny.' O Ran blushed, but looked happy. She was one of Lao Liu's faithful listeners and would cry if she was a minute late. She rushed into the kitchen, her slender pigtail dangling on her back. After a moment she came out. She had washed her face and brushed a little oil in her hair, so it now shone smoothly in the half-light of the oil lamp. My mother glanced at her new appearance without comment, but smiled quietly at her vanity since nobody could appreciate her glossy hair in the darkness.

We went out, the three of us, Uncle Pan, O Ran and I. My mother warned O Ran as we crossed the doorstep, saying, 'Don't shed tears over the stories, or you'll have nightmares again.' 'Yes mother,' O Ran replied absent-mindedly. We were too anxious to get a space near our storyteller, so that we could hear distinctly the various kinds of tunes and voices in which Lao Liu spun his yarns.

Our villagers streamed out of their cottages and gathered around Lao Liu in a semi-circle, allowing him a space of about three yards in diameter to move about, for he had a strange habit: he liked to pace about round his drum-stand when he was narrating his tale in plain dialogue. He would sit down only when he was singing in verse. We sat in the back row, because we came a little late; Uncle Pan in the middle, I on his left and O Ran on his right. Next to me sat Aunt Chrysanthemum. She was a great friend of my mother's and very fond of me and O

Ran as she herself had no children. We also liked her very much, because she was very pleasant to look at. Although she was about thirty, she still looked as though she were eighteen. When she talked there was always a soft and amiable smile on her lips.

The old people lighted their long pipes. The tobacco in the bowls blinked nervously with the stars above, as though they were secretly carrying on some sort of love conversation. These signals attracted all our attention. Everybody seemed to want to decipher the codes with which they expressed their affections; and so all grew mysteriously watchful and silent. It was when we had entered such a stage that Lao Liu suddenly beat his drum and clattered the two halves of his castanets, fastened by a string between the thumb and palm of his right hand. The drum rumbled on and on for a good ten minutes, bringing our attention back from the stars to the story-teller. Then suddenly the drumming came to a dead stop. Lao Liu, under the influence of his strange habit, began to pace about round his drum-stand, attempting to compose the preamble for his story, which was generally in plain prose.

'Learned gentlemen and graceful ladies,' he said (in fact none of us were learned except himself and perhaps Benchin, our Taoist priest, but he was always polite like that), 'the story your humble servant is going to tell this evening is a brand new one, so new that your humble servant hasn't found a suitable title for it yet. But what does title matter if the story's interesting? It has a most significant origin. Please don't get excited when I tell you its source. When I was walking up and down the picturesque Hills of Three Devils in quest of the inspiration for a new story, I unexpectedly came across an old wandering monk, who in your humble servant's opinion, must have come from Tibet, because he wore an enormous yellow surplice, like a mosquito net, and a pair of long boots. He was sitting under an ancient chestnut tree, contemplating a viper about ten feet long, which was wriggling meekly before him but dared not approach his feet. Your humble servant immediately realized that he must be a holy man. As a story-teller your humble servant has always been keen on any revelation from the agents of the divine power about right and wrong on the earth. Your humble servant therefore approached this holy man for a story that might serve to enlighten our minds; and made it clear to him that in this Middle Flowery Kingdom of ours a story-teller was not only a beggar, but also a man with a high sense of morality. He gazed upon me with his all-penetrating eyes for a while and then suddenly he said, "Sit down young man. I know you have good intentions. I'll give you a story." Here it is.'

He paused, giving way to the roll of his drum, which rose to a crescendo until at last it sounded like distant thunder, foreboding a shower. The scintillating tobacco in the pipes had all died out, as though a mass of clouds was pressing overhead. Only the trail of a falling star that lashed down to the horizon in front of us brought us back to reality. I straightened my back and stole a glance at Aunt Chrysanthemum. She was craning her neck, staring at Lao Liu with her shining eyes, which seemed to have concentrated the energy and vitality of her whole body. Lao Liu gave us a complete surprise by laying the drumstick on the drum all of a sudden, causing a gentle twang, which radiated out like a wave. And he seated himself on the chair, keeping an unfathomable silence.

The quietness, however, was only an interval.

My humble self was named after the Flowers of May,
Reincarnated in a dewy morning in a scholar's family;
Dwelling by the brook with five weeping willows
I was taught classics and poetry and embroidery. . . .

It was no longer Lao Liu's voice, but an elegant soprano. The words sprang out from the lips of our story-teller like a string of pearls falling successively on an ancient lacquered tray, light and brittle and rolling with a ringing echo. The air vibrated with them and the vibration struck our ears with force and harmony. The square was so stilled by the singing, that the listeners seemed to be nothing but inanimate shadows, and the night seemed to consist of only a moon veiled by a mist of music and a vague hue of melancholy. The story was a tragedy.

The heroine, Flowers of May, was sadly cheated by a rogue, with whom she unfortunately fell violently in love. The young man was handsome and clever and well-versed in poetry. But he did not make good use of his gifts. He made friends with bad people when he was a boy. Instead of taking the Imperial Examination, he spent his time writing serenades and enchanted many a good girl with his rhymes. The present one was but the saddest victim, because he not only deserted her without mercy but also left in her heart a most beautiful but false impression, which she could not forget and which tortured her day and night.

'Now I want to call your attention to two things, as the holy man has asked me to do.' Our story-teller suddenly touched the drum with a twang, and the ringing pearls came to a standstill. 'First, the young man was spoiled by bad companionship. Secondly, the girl gave out her love too readily; in other words, she was too impatient!'

'But who knows that the man was a rogue?' Aunt Chrysanthemum murmured to herself with a sigh. 'Men are wicked!' she concluded. And then she took out her handkerchief and blew her nose and dried her eyes. Like all the women and girls present, she could not resist tears over the misfortune of her sex.

Lao Liu was really a master story-teller – a fact upon which my mother, who knew his history well, often insisted. He had learned his art through difficulties and superhuman ordeals. His father had been a landless peasant who could not feed him and had to send him to a monastery to be a lay brother. The abbot taught him to read and chant Buddhist psalms. He had the gift of a good voice and naturally made steady progress in his chanting. But when he had learned enough characters to read by himself he made excursions into old romances and legendary plays instead of holy books. One day the abbot discovered his collection of literature hidden under his bed. The religious man

13

gave him a kick on the bottom and showed him the door without saying a single word. He was not born a man to be purified of worldly emotions. Certainly he would have made a very bad monk had he stayed on. In fact he had a lot of romantic ideas, my mother stressed. For instance, he had tried once to be a female impersonator with a company, but failed to find favour with its masters. It was only when he came across a vagabond singer that he learned to spin yarns in tenor, falsetto and soprano. And as he had become a young man he returned to the village a successful story-teller.

He entertained our villagers till the moon tilted towards the west or the dew started falling. Many womenfolk used to return home with their eyes wet. My mother always came to fetch O Ran and me before the story reached its end, because the conclusion was generally sad. Indeed, Lao Liu was a sentimental soul, good only at tragedies. But tonight my mother came rather late. Lao Liu was already striking his sad note, winding up the history of Flowers of May's early life. O Ran was deep in her sobs, and could scarcely raise her head.

My mother held O Ran's head back, her face tilted upwards. The tears in her eyes shone with the stars. She was still shaken with sobs. Had it not been for my mother's strong grasp she would have slipped to the ground.

'You silly girl!' my mother said in a reproachful voice, 'how can you afford to shed tears every night?'

O Ran did not answer, but went on heaving with her sobs.

My mother helped her to stand up and added, 'If you go on sobbing like this, I will not let you come here tomorrow evening again. The story is simply a story. You shouldn't believe it so much.'

'But Lao Liu's tearful singing and lamentations are real,' Uncle Pan commented in sympathy with O Ran.

'Ah, that's why you let her stay here so long!' my mother said. 'You ought to have told her to go to bed a long time ago.'

Uncle Pan did not say anything more, but hung his head. O Ran passed her sleeve over her eyes to dry her tears and walked

14

unwillingly before my mother to the house. While we were on our way home my mother asked me in a low voice. 'When did O Ran start sobbing?'

'I don't know,' I said. 'Perhaps when Flowers of May began to think of committing suicide after her disappointment in love.'

'Suicide again?'

'Yes, but this one was done in a different fashion.'

'Tommorrow evening you both must stay at home,' my mother said in a louder voice now so that O Ran could hear. 'All these suicides are too bad for your sleep.'

But the next day as soon as we finished supper Uncle Pan again took us to the square. My mother did not raise any objection. She herself even came to join us after having washed up all the dishes. The story was a second part of the first one – it was a trilogy. My mother was sitting next to Aunt Chrysanthemum. The aunt kept on commenting in a whisper to my mother, 'Men are wicked! Men are wicked!'

'But Lao Liu is a nice man,' my mother said to her.

'Well, a bit too feminine and weak,' Aunt Chrysanthemum whispered in an offhand way.

'Don't you like that type?' my mother whispered back.

'Well . . .' Aunt Chrysanthemum could not finish the sentence.

Meanwhile Lao Liu went on with his tale, now in a tenor, when he took the part of the rogue, now in soprano, when he spoke on behalf of the heroine. The two voices sounded as though from two entirely different people. In our minds Lao Liu, indeed, existed no longer as one person but two characters; one feminine, quiet, beautiful and sentimental, the other masculine, clever, roguish and dangerously handsome. For this magic every family in our village gave him a picul of rice for a season so that he could go on coining stories without worrying about his livelihood. And this year, happily, the crop was good. Although the landlord Chumin, who lived in the town, took away a large percentage of the crop as land rent, yet the villagers could still save enough grain to cover the essentials.

15

CHAPTER 2

O Ran was a lonely girl, as lonely as Uncle Pan. But she did not come from such a distant place as North China. She came from a village about five miles away. Still, she was lonely, for her people were all dead. They had died so long ago that she could scarcely remember them. Her father was a poor peasant, and like most of the country folk of his kind, ended his life in an unexpected manner in a year of drought. It had not rained for a whole summer. The rice in the paddy fields was scorched to ashes. So there was a dearth which people later on remembered as 'the great famine'. There was no rice in the neighbourhood. But there was a large stock in the town, held by Chumin, the biggest landlord of the district. He doled it out to the distressed farm-hands in exchange for their land. In a few weeks' time he got hold of all the rice-fields in the region. Then suddenly a shower came down. It was a beautiful shower, which revived all the dead earth. O Ran's father went down to his old field and tried to plant some soya beans.

'You have no right to work here!' said Chumin's new tenant, a sturdy, dark young fellow, who had succeeded in obtaining the piece of land by offering better terms. 'It's now the landlord Chumin's property.'

'It is mine!' O Ran's father said. 'I have worked on it all my life!'

'You stupid fool, don't you remember that you've exchanged it for three piculs of rice? Don't you know that I have signed a contract with Chumin for this field?' the young peasant scolded him.

'How dare you! It's my land! . . . I inherited it from my father.'

Without more words he slapped the young farmer on the face with his large hand. The young man did not give in. He jumped on the assailant like a tiger, pounding his head with a big fist. O Ran's father was already quite old then. He could not stand the fighting and fell prostrate on the soil, which he claimed to be his by usage. His nose bled like two streams, and his mouth spat blood. In three days' time he died. His wife, scared by the dark landless future, hanged herself the following evening. O Ran then was only three years old.

O Ran was a beautiful child. My mother found her sitting stupidly on the doorstep of her cottage, when she went to offer a contribution to buy coffins for the dead couple. She immediately felt attracted to her and took her back home. In order to legalize her as a member of the household, my mother gave a small tea-party to our village elders, announcing that my elder brother was betrothed to her as her future fiancé when he grew up into a man. But according to the custom she was to be a servant girl before she got formally married. She started doing household duties under my mother's guidance at the age of five. As she grew older she really looked a beauty. My mother treasured her like a daughter, hoping that she would make a good housewife one day; a competent successor to herself in the house, so that she could retire complacently in her old age. She did not allow O Ran to do any hard work outside her house, lest her beauty should be spoiled. And my mother could afford to show such tenderness to a servant girl, because we were no longer dependent on the soil. My father, who was a poor schoolteacher in the market town, had found a job as a secretary in a firm in the new, prosperous cotton trade, in the metropolis. 'The Big City' down the river. He earned a better salary than he could have in teaching.

O Ran at first did not know that she was supposed to be a servant girl until she became my brother's wife. But as she

17

gradually came to understand human affairs, she began to realize her position and feel something wrong with her destiny. She sometimes became thoughtful and unhappy, particularly so when the autumn festival came, when young people went to pay visits to their distant relatives in other villages with presents. O Ran of course, had no place to go to.

This day was again an autumn festival day. In the morning she looked very pale. Her eyes were swollen. It seemed that she had not slept well the night before. As a matter of fact, I later found out that she had gone to the cemetery in the mountains at the back of the village the previous evening, to shed tears by the new grave of another servant girl, who had died of smallpox recently. She had know her very well, and they had often talked together of their loneliness and lamenting over their hard destiny. But my mother did not know that. She thought that O Ran was simply in a sad mood with the thought of the gay occasion as she had no relatives to call on. She gave her a day's holiday, and told me to keep her company for the day.

We did not know how to celebrate the festival. So, instead, we went for a walk on the river bank, because the sun was very warm. Many young people were out in the open too. Most of them were singing love-songs. It was a fine autumn day, indeed. The sky was very clear, and the breeze carried the smell of early cassia. Everybody was in the mood to sing.

But O Ran remained quiet. She looked only at her feet as we moved along by the river. She did not seem to have heard the songs, nor smelled the cassia flowers. We went on without a word as though attending a funeral. Suddenly a light gale swept along, ruffling her beautiful dark hair. Her face was covered with goose-flesh. Her legs began to shake and she slumped on a patch of grass on the roadside.

'I'm not feeling well,' she said in haste, panting. 'Take me home.'

I helped her to stand up and supported her to walk home with both my arms. Indeed, something was wrong with her. I felt her hands burning.

When we got home my mother put her palms over O Ran's head for a while. 'Too bad,' my mother said to herself. 'It is fever. Where have you been?' She turned her eyes to me.

'On the river beach,' I said.

'She must have caught a cold. The river wind at this time of the year is sharp and always steals into one's body through the pores.'

She put O Ran to bed and covered her with a cotton-padded quilt and, on top of that, all the winter clothes she could find. 'She ought to sweat so that the wind can come out through the pores again,' she said. Then she went to the kitchen to make a drink to accelerate the evaporation of the wind in her. She cut a piece of ginger and peeled some garlic and put them together into a small pot filled with pure water and cooked the contents over a gentle fire. After about a quarter of an hour she poured the water out into a bowl, which immediately sent forth a cloud of steam and a strong garlic smell. The concoction looked as white as milk. My mother took it to O Ran and said softly to her, 'This will put you right, my child.'

Hearing the voice, O Ran dreamily opened her eyes. Instinctively she sat up and looked at my mother deliriously. She had never disobeyed my mother. Even in her dreams she would answer her if her name was called. Without even giving a glance at the liquid she took the bowl from my mother's hands and gulped the concoction down, making a gurgling noise. Then she threw herself back into the bed again, her eyes closed.

We did not feel quite at home at the dinner table, where a seat was empty. We had never realized before what a difference O Ran made to our life. Uncle Pan declined to have his usual cup of wine, because he said he felt a bit uneasy about O Ran's illness. And as he had no liquor, his throat was parched. He could not tell tales like those about the otter captured alive, and about the pile of silver coins, with which the townsman bought a hare and whose exact number he knew by sight without counting them. The whole atmosphere was now cold.

My mother could not sleep that night. She went over to O

Ran's bed now and then, and each time remained standing there for a good while. She observed O Ran with an anxious air, her forehead puckered up and her eyebrows knitted. O Ran was unable to perceive her, her eyes being closely shut. Large sweat drops gathered on her forehead and shone in the light like tears. This immobility and insensibility, which now veiled her otherwise very earnest and enthusiastic face, pained me greatly, without my knowing why, and, it seemed to me, also brought more tears to my mother's eyes, which were already wet.

Towards midnight O Ran suddenly broke out into fitful groans, which sounded like the kind of inarticulate words she used to murmur in nightmares. But this was something different: she was panting and panting laboriously. My mother jumped out of her bed and lit the lamp and hurried to O Ran's bed. I followed her. O Ran was covered all over with sweat, which formed a veil of thin mist about her. She was in a terrible delirium. My mother shook her head and shouted in alarm: 'O Ran! O Ran.' O Ran slowly opened her eyes, showing the white and then closed them again. She could no longer make the usual quick response.

'Her trouble is not cold,' my mother murmured reproachfully to herself. 'The ginger-and-garlic concoction may have made her case worse. What can I do? What can I do?'

In great panic she fell mechanically on her knees before O Ran's bed and joined her hands together and prayed:

Ancestors, do have pity on her if she has by any chance innocently insulted you. Gods of the Heavens, do please forgive her if she has childishly invoked your names against some person she disliked. She hasn't got the parents to teach her how to behave. I'm the person responsible for any sin she may have committed. If she has to be punished, the punishment should fall on me, not her, who is an orphan . . .

My mother murmured on and on as though hypnotized. Meanwhile, O Ran's throat rattled. Each time the dry blunt sound came out of her lips, my mother's voice grew heavy, droning in the room like the monotonous incantation of Buddhist priests for the elevation of a dead man's soul. O Ran looked really somewhat like a dead person, because her face was pale as a stone and her lips livid, like the purple flower of May. I did not know what this was all about, because my mind could not think. I shifted my gaze now from O Ran to my mother and now from my mother to O Ran. They formed under the dim light of the lamp a picture, wooden and sombre, and also saddening and terrifying. At last I also fell mechanically on my knees beside my mother, making myself a part of the picture.

Towards dawn O Ran became silent and her face looked pale blue. My mother felt her forehead with her hand and muttered incoherently. 'The delirium is gone. But what is it? What is it? We must send Uncle Pan for the doctor. We must!' And she rushed out of the bedroom to call Uncle Pan.

Uncle Pan went to the village about three miles away, where lived a famous herb doctor, and returned with the medical man at breakfast time. This learned man was still in his indoor gown. Apparently Uncle Pan had managed to tell him the seriousness of O Ran's illness with the help of his usual famous gestures and emphasis in the voice, so that the doctor made the trip straight away without even dressing himself properly. After greeting my mother he went straight to O Ran's room without waiting for the bowl of meat-ball soup to wet his mouth, to which people in our district used to treat a doctor before he started examining the case, as a sign of respect to a man of a humanitarian profession. He took up O Ran's hand and felt her pulse. His brows immediately drew together and several horizontal lines stood out on his forehead and his eyes blinked thoughtfully. There was a deathly silence. We could even hear our breathing.

'She suddenly had a severe cold last night,' he said, putting O Ran's hand into the quilt. 'But now the fever is over. The pulse, however, still beats rather quickly, which is a very queer symptom indeed.'

'What is the matter, doctor?' my mother asked.

21

The medical man knitted his brows again and pouted his lips. 'I'm afraid I can't tell. It is certainly not typhoid, as it came with such violence; nor malaria, as the fever was not followed by a severe chill.'

'Can't you suggest what it might be?'

'I'm afraid I can't, madam,' the doctor said with an apologetic smile. 'My professional conscience forbids me to give any name based on guesswork.'

'Oh . . .' my mother murmured in soliloquy.

'But don't be afraid, madam,' the doctor added in a soft voice. 'The beat of her pulse is quite even, although faster than normal. There shouldn't be any danger to her life. If you let her rest quietly and put her on a diet of boiled water and diluted gruel, she probably will get well in a short time.'

'I will, doctor,' my mother said. 'I'll do anything if she can live.'

And the doctor took leave, refusing to accept any renumeration on the ground that he did not give any diagnosis.

After the doctor was gone Benchin, our Taoist priest, came to visit us. He sneaked in without knocking at the door. Even after he had walked into the hall he did not announce himself, but stood in a corner quietly, his small eyes blinking nervously at the door of O Ran's room. His furtive stare took me by surprise when I discovered him. He waved his trembling, bony hands to me in a friendly manner and approached me with his ghostly steps, light as a cat's, asking in a whisper, 'Has the doctor gone?'

'Yes,' I answered.

'Good!' he said loudly, 'he is no good.' And he walked straight into the room with hasty steps as though he himself were a doctor.

My mother was sitting on the edge of the sick-bed and feeding O Ran with water.

'Good morning, ma'am!' Benchin said. 'I've heard of O Ran's illness. I'm very unhappy about it. Is it serious?'

'It's nice of you to come, Benchin,' my mother said, putting another spoon of water into O Ran's mouth. 'The doctor said it was not very serious. But I'm worried.'

'Doctor?' Benchin said in seeming astonishment. 'What can he do?'

'Indeed he could not even give the diagnosis.'

'Of course he could not!' Benchin said with assurance in his loud voice. 'Let me have a look.'

Without waiting for my mother to make room for him, he pushed himself beside her and carefully adjusted his glasses over his short-sighted eyes and then bent low over O Ran, so low that his nose nearly touched her face.

'You see, her eyes are not normal,' he said to my mother. 'They stare at you without meaning anything. And they shut evasively as soon as you try to examine them. Do you know what this means?'

'Well, I don't know . . .' my mother said uneasily, glancing at the priest, who now looked as though he were a pathology specialist.

'This means that she is no longer the mistress of herself,' he answered himself. 'This means something else is directing her will.'

'What is this something else, Benchin? I don't understand you.'

'Well, if you want me to be frank . . .' he suddenly paused, waiting for my mother to speak. But she kept silent, staring inquisitively at him. This silence made him impatient and so he went on: 'Well, judging by my experience she is possessed by some spirit. It may be the wandering ghost of some man who died an untimely death. You know when a man dies by some accident, such as murder or drowning, before his time fixed by fate, his ghost is at large till he is reincarnated into an animal or a man again. During the period of wandering about he sometimes gets so bored that he would like to assume human shape once more. In this situation he often attaches himself to some innocent girl or boy and causes dreadful illness to the possessed.'

23

'Is that so?' my mother said suspiciously. She believed in gods and ancestors, but hardly ghosts. None of us believed in ghosts.

'Certainly it is!' the priest said, adjusting his old, rimless glasses on his small eyes again. 'It is the special branch of my philosophical research. With my own eyes I've seen ghosts in search of human bodies to possess, and I used to fight them to free innocent boys or girls from their merciless clutches.'

'Is that so?' my mother repeated the same doubtful question again.

'Certainly it is!' the priest answered with firm conviction.

There was again silence. My mother did not want to talk any more of ghosts, because it upsets us all, so Benchin could not go on with the conversation. He gave a last glance at O Ran, who was as quiet as death with her eyes closed, and walked out with a hopeless gesture, but murmured to himself: 'Poor girl, suffering from possession at such an early age. I must expel the wicked ghost from her.' As he was crossing the doorstep, he went on in a stronger voice. 'Yes, I must drive this heartless ghost out of the village! I must! It's a sheer insult to me for a ghost to cause trouble right under my nose!'

According to our grandfathers in the village, Benchin had been at one time reputed to be a master of wandering ghosts, for he was said to have been able to invoke various spirits, as well as gods, to subdue them. When anything went wrong with a family – which in the old days was generally believed to be the working of evil spirits – he was always invited to exercise his influence as a Taoist priest to put things right, and people paid him for his service with rice or money. But since the great famine, so many things had gone wrong with our villagers that even a dozen priests could not be of any good. People had lost many relatives through starvation, and on top of that all their land was taken away by Chumin. And with the land gone, they were at the mercy of the landlord. They had so much to worry about themselves that they had to forget altogether about ghosts. So

Benchin got no work to do, and therefore grew all the more bony and weak. As a result he could do no other work whatever, not even preaching. The vicious circle made him sink into such a hopeless state, both physically and financially, that even Mao Mao was sure that he could beat the priest over She-crow, although he himself was a completely illiterate peasant.

But this time Benchin seemed to be determined to remind our villagers of ghosts, and of his authority as the master of ghosts, thereby reviving his Taoist practice. In the evening he put on his Taoist holy garb, embroidered both on the back and in front with white dragons, and the dark square cape with a long black needle running through the top – paraphernalia which he had managed to keep in spite of his economic strain, as no pawnshop would accept them. And with his sacred wand, which bore his authority as the priest, he rushed officiously from his cottage to the pavilion of the God of Earth, his large dark surplice fanning up a gust of wind as he moved on. Our villagers, who gathered on the square to hear Lao Liu's story, thought he was mad, seeing him marching with such vehemence and energy and determination, as though he had just had a sound sleep and a good meal. He put on, with a deep frown and pouted lips, the air of a fighter, ready to engage in battle with the ghost.

He kneeled before the stone offering-table that stood below the altar of our God of Earth, with his small head held high and his crooked back straightened up as much as he could. A torrent of murmurs, long and even, began to rush out of his mouth, directed to our God of Earth and his motherly wife.

I, the faithful disciple of our master Lao Tzu, beg of you, in my capacity as the Taoist priest, to lift the possession of O Ran, to expel the ghost out of our village, and to chain the devil to the big oak tree on the other side of the river till his time to reincarnate into a dog or a pig is due. If you, God of Earth, fail to do this, I am afraid I shall have to make a report of your incapacity to our Master in Heaven. In your own interest you must co-operate with me by exercising your authority as the village god to carry out my orders against the wicked demon . . .

After that his voice came to a pause. An interval of silence ensued. Lao Liu, who had been waiting to start his story for the evening, thought that the priest had finished his performance, and with a sigh of relief began to beat the drum as a prelude to his narrative. But no sooner had his drumstick touched the surface of the instrument than a dry, splitting sound shot up into the air from the pavilion, grating on everybody's ears. It was again Benchin who was furiously beating his wand on the stone table like a madman. Simultaneously, he was calling on all sorts of names to revile and threaten the supposed possessor of O Ran.

If you don't flee away as you're told, my dear ghost, I will have no more mercy on you. I shall call upon the nine-headed bodyguards of the King of Hell to come to arrest you, to throw you into the pot of boiling oil, or to roast you over the infernal fire like a chicken, or to hook you up on the Mountain of Sharp Knives like a chunk of pork. Just imagine! You would never be able to get reincarnated again. Yes or no, you must make the decision right at this moment! I shall not wait any longer . . .

The beating of his wand on the stone table increased in speed in proportion with his voice, which again rose in pitch with anger that was fanned up by his imagination of the wickedness of the disobedient ghost. The grating, discordant noise drowned hopelessly all the musical tones of our story-teller. And so Lao Liu could not go on with his singing; Benchin's voice triumphantly increased in volume. It sounded proud, indeed. For the first time Benchin realized that he had at last gained prominence over our popular story-teller, who had so far made a much better living in the village. Indeed, that evening Lao Liu had to pack up his instruments and beg the audience not to be cross with his inability to carry on his job.

The sudden suspension of our story-teller's programme annoyed us greatly. We went back home with great reluctance and bitterness against the priest, whose solo was now splitting the quiet night air like thunder claps immediately overhead. We could not even sleep. At last Mao Mao, who had to get up very early in the morning to do his farm work, could not stand the noise any longer. But he did not want to interrupt the priest or start a fight with him, because he was afraid that any open insult would lead Benchin to compete with him over She-crow. He wanted to marry her as soon as possible, so he could not afford to have any untoward incident in the course of his wooing.

Mao Mao, however, succeeded in devising an ingenious scheme to deal with the annoying Master of Ghosts. While Benchin was in the highest spirits reviling the 'enemy of the village', having completely triumphed over our popular story-teller, Mao Mao sneaked up behind him on tiptoe with an old broom. He fastened the implement by a long string to the edge of his holy garb at the back. Then he quietly went away without our priest noticing it. Benchin kept on beating the table with his wand and his shouting grew louder each time he condemned the ghost.

Mao Mao was standing all the time under a tree at a distance, watching the priest. In the end he became tired and sleepy. But before he left the place he threw a handful of pebbles over the pavilion in order to give vent to his dislike of the unwelcome service. The pebbles fell over Benchin's cape like hail. Our priest thought this was an attack against him launched by an army of ghosts organized by the accused one. In great panic he suddenly took to his feet and ran in the direction of his cottage to save his dear life. The moment he started running the broom behind him began to trail on the pebbly ground like footsteps of the pursuing assailants. The faster he ran the louder it grated.

'Help! Help!' Benchin shouted desperately, at the top of his voice.

But no one came to his succour as everybody thought he

was mad, trying to rouse our villagers from their beds. At last Benchin's breakneck speed snapped the string and the grating sound came to a stop. But even so he mistook his own steps for those of the attacking devils. When he finally attained his cottage, he had already lost his holy wand and his priest's cape, and he had no more courage to recover them in the dark. Obsessed by disappointment and horror, he fell ill the next morning. And the illness kept him indoors for a good two months.

While our Taoist priest was afflicted by a mysterious sickness whose nature nobody except Mao Mao knew, O Ran's trouble gradually became tangible. Fed on the diet of water and gruel as advised by the herb doctor, she progressed quite satisfactorily. The fever did not develop although now and then she fell into delirium which generally did not last long. On the third day my mother began to discover the trace of some rash on O Ran's face. A kind of watery pimple appeared on both sides of her nose and on her cheeks. 'Ah, I did not expect it!' my mother exclaimed as she bent over her, examining her face. The pimples were pustules. O Ran had smallpox. It was an extremely dangerous disease in our village, of which many children died every year. But it cleared all doubts that had shadowed heavily upon my mother's mind. She felt relieved now and cheerfully told Uncle Pan all about it and asked him to help in taking precautionary measures.

Uncle Pan took from the attic a bunch of dried-up *ai*, a plant which gave out very good odours and which was said to kill all sorts of germs, and which we collected from the woods on the fifth day of the fifth month before sunrise. My mother lit it and smoked with it all the corners and dark nooks in the house. Many old mosquitoes and flies got smoked out and flew away through the windows, buzzing feebly, or dropped on the floor, dead. Meanwhile, Uncle Pan fetched a bucketful of dry lime powder and spread it all over the dark places, including the space under O Ran's bed. After all this was done, my mother sorted out a piece of new red silk and put it on the idol of the Goddess of Children, who stood next to the votive tablet on our ancestral altar. Then she burned incense before the goddess and prayed, her head hanging low, her hands joined together, murmuring that O Ran's life should be saved, that we would put more red silk on her head to glorify her kindness and benevolence when O Ran became well, that we would save more money to contribute to the fund for the erection of an independent temple for her.

After the prayer my mother took me to Aunt Chrysanthemum's cottage and asked her if I could stay at her house for the duration of O Ran's illness. She looked at my mother thoughtfully without a word at first. Then, lowering her eyes, she said, 'I'm rather afraid of people of the other sex, when alone. There has not been a single man in this house for years.' This remark made me notice that the room looked really chilly and quiet like a monastery. Her husband Mintun was the last man who had lived in it, but he had left the village shortly after they got married and had never come back since. My mother was worried. She touched my shoulder and was about to take me away to try some other neighbour. Suddenly Aunt Chrysanthemum lifted her head and said with a forced smile: 'But he is not a grown up man yet, is he?' She pointed to me. 'I remember him as a baby, who used to sit on my knees in the sun.' Then, taking me unawares, she held my head in both her hands warmly and pressed her lips on my forehead and added, 'I'll treat you like a big son. So stay with me!'

That evening I had supper with Aunt Chrysanthemum. It was a great supper consisting of scrambled egg, smoked ham and salted beans. And the food was delicious, because Aunt Chrysanthemum was a good cook. I had never had such a plentiful meal before.

'Where did you get all this delightful stuff, Aunt Chrysanthemum?' I asked. I was curious. Aunt Chrysanthemum did not farm land as there was no man in the house. Consequently she

29

did not keep pigs and hens, because there was no food for them. 'You see, we don't have such beautiful ham, even though we keep a pig,' I explained my curiosity.

'Ha! Ha! That's a secret,' she said laughing at me. 'You men only think about things in terms of land. I can get the food even without land.'

'But how?'

She burst into another fit of laughter. 'I *bought* it, see?' she said. 'I *bought* it!'

I dared not press further the question where she got her money as she did not seem to do any work, since she stayed all the time indoors. She did not even care to do her washing in the open pond by the side of our village, as most women did. She hated the cold water, which spoiled the tender skin on her slender hands. As I was reasoning within myself this way, she woke me up by adding:

'You see, the ham is five years old! It is a rarity, too.'

'Ha! That's a precious thing to have, Aunt Chrysanthemum. But why do you keep it so long?'

'In case Mintun comes back one day late in the afternoon or at midnight. You see, I must give him a feast to celebrate his *glorious* home-returning . . .' Suddenly she paused and became pensive, her eyes growing pensive too, staring at the vegetable-oil lamp. After a little while she started all of a sudden, and mumbled to herself, 'Oh, I must work. I must work.' And then turning to me, she went on: 'If you're tired, you can go to bed early. Your room is upstairs immediately above mine.'

'No,' I said, 'I'd like to sit for a while.'

'All right. If you feel like going to bed just go yourself,' she said. She did not want to talk any more. Something heavy was sitting on her heart, I could see that.

She moved to the spinning-wheel down at the end of the room, and seated herself on a stool in front of it. She began to spin, her right hand turning the handle of the wheel and her left holding a cotton-roll, as long as a squirrel's tail. The spindle turned as the wheel was turned, giving out a continuous hum,

30

dry, but musical. And a fine thread began to be drawn out from the cotton-roll like a thread of silk from a silkworm, and wound itself on the spindle. The spindle grew in size. In about a quarter of an hour's time it developed into a ball. Aunt Chrysanthemum took it off from the wheel. Then she started to make another one.

Aunt Chrysanthemum went on spinning, spindle after spindle, without interruption. Several times she yawned. Then she would only stop to rub her eyes for a few seconds, or to count the number of spindles she had finished. She would take a deep breath and then go on with the work. I was extremely interested, watching her quietly. She was so slight of waist and slender of arm that when she worked she looked as if she were dancing. Besides, the formation of the spindle-balls was itself exciting. I had not seen this for a long time. Since, a few years earlier, we had started buying machine-made cloth imported from the big town, there was practically no one else in the village who would work at the old-fashioned spinning-wheel.

At last Aunt Chrysanthemum heaved a long sigh. The machine ceased humming. She gave a glance at the spindles in the basket that lay beside her, and started counting, one, two, three . . . twelve . . . fifteen. 'Thank God, enough for tonight!' she said. She got up from the stool, spread out on the floor a large scarf, poured the spindles on to it, and wrapped them up into a parcel. Then she turned to me, trying to smile, and said, 'Don't you want to go to sleep? I am going to.'

'Is this what you do every evening?' I asked her as I stood up.

'Not only every evening, but every day, too.' And she gave me a faint smile. 'Goodnight.'

I could not understand all this, which confused me greatly. It was such a dull job, and unnecessary, too, since we no longer wove cloth ourselves. So I could not sleep well that night, thinking about this queer state of affairs. The music of the spinning-wheel seemed to be droning in my ears all the time. But shortly after midnight when I was tired and about to fall asleep,

something new further startled me. I heard Aunt Chrysan-
themum get up from her bed, making a rustling noise down
below. Then I heard her steps pacing up and down the floor.
She must be sleepless too. Queer aunt, I thought to myself,
taking a walk in the depth of the night. Was she afraid of ghosts,
living alone in this house all these years since she was twenty-
one when she got married to Mintun? But immediately I heard
her murmuring something:

'Ancestors, do guide Mintun to the right way of life, help him
to succeed in his career, and then send him home to me when
he becomes a great man. I have been waiting for him to be
famous all these years. I shall still wait for him. He is a man of
iron will, a man of ambition. He will distinguish himself one
day if you, ancestors, help him . . .'

So Aunt Chrysanthemum was praying, I began to understand.
She was praying for her husband, an ambitious man of whom
no one in our village had heard for ages.

The next morning Aunt Chrysanthemum asked me if I had
slept well the night before. I said I had. This answer prevented
me from asking her why she should pray so late at night and
whether this was due to the fact that she could not sleep,
thinking of her man. Later, however, I forgot all about it.

After a few weeks my mother came to fetch me, saying that
O Ran was now well.

I was very happy to know that O Ran was saved. The first
thing I did when I got home was to go straight to her room and
say something to her. But to my great disappointment, O Ran
was not there. I found instead a strange girl, thin and pale,
sitting by the window and idiotically staring out. Hearing my
steps, she turned round and fixed her eyes on me. Her lips were
moving nervously, but no words came out of them. Curious
and confused I also looked back into her face. Suddenly her
enlarged, glassy eyes started to shine, and in a minute several
tear-drops stood out on the rims. She burst into a fit of sobs.
'It's me! It's me, O Ran! Don't you recognize your old O Ran?'
she said. Yes, now I recognized her by her voice. But what a

different O Ran! Her face was covered all over with pock-marks, dense and big like soya beans on a plate.

CHAPTER 3

When O Ran had entirely recovered from her illness and started doing household work, Aunt Chrysanthemum told me that she wanted to give her a present. 'Poor girl, she must be feeling very bad,' she said. 'It is most distressing for a girl of her age to have pock-marks. I must buy her something to cheer her up. Would you like to go with me to town? You can advise me what to choose, since you know her taste well.'

I was flattered by the suggestion, because I liked to be with her, particularly for a trip to town. Many a young farm-hand had tried to keep her company but always failed. It was indeed a pleasure to walk beside her. As she never worked on the farm she had a nice pair of small dainty feet, and as she was light of waist she had the most coquettish and graceful appearance. So when she moved she looked nothing less than a perfect heroine in Lao Liu's stories. Once seeing her walking past on the village square, the story-teller remarked: 'She has a sort of undefinable alluring coquetry, intensified by her unconventional make-up. Together with her faithfulness to good principles, she makes an ideal wife as well as a wonderful sweetheart. O my! If only she would accept my . . . She needs a nice man to make her beauty perfect!' But she never cared for him, although he was the most elegant, the most artistic person in our village.

I replied to her invitation without a moment's hesitation: 'Certainly! I should love to go to town with you, Aunt Chrysanthemum.'

'Come in then, and wait for a few minutes,' she said and let

34

me into her cottage. 'I just want to put my hair in order. It won't take long.' And she walked to the dressing-table and started making herself up, neglecting my presence as though I were a mere baby. She tilted the mirror in such a way as to reflct her face in full. Then she backed a few steps so that her head was also shown. She had very rich hair, dark as midnight and glistening like black silk. She stood gazing into the mirror without a word. I stood behind her at a distance, marvelling at her silence.

She undid her hair and then combed it backwards. It was exceptionally long and fine, and streamed down her back like a brook flowing down a vale dark and overgrown with purple-greenish moss. She combed it on and on mechanically, looking into the mirror like an idiot. I was astonished by the mechanical movement. She was now behaving like a lazy servant girl, who always tries to while away a little time on the pretext of tidying up her hair. I swallowed a mouthful of saliva and my Adam's apple went up and down. She saw that in the mirror. And she started.

'What are you looking at me for, you little fool?' she said, her sensuous lips broadening into a smile without parting, her right hand still running the comb down her hair, over and over again, and her left hand supporting the flowing stream of the filaments.

'I don't know,' I said. 'You don't seem to be doing up your hair at all. You're simply combing and combing and combing.'

'What words!' she exclaimed with seeming surprise, her smile further broadening, showing a row of small, shining teeth. 'You're trying to read my thoughts, eh? You mischievous man!'

'Are you thinking of something?' I asked.

'Well,' she said, but soon refrained from letting the words out straight away. I saw her tongue rolled back against the palate and two blue veins bulging out beneath. 'Yes,' she confirmed my guess.

'What are you thinking about?'

'What makes you so interested in what I am thinking?' She pretended to be angry.

'Because I am so fond of you, Aunt Chrysanthemum,' I said. 'You are as kind and dear to me as my mother,'

'You're a good boy,' she said. 'I'm thinking of Mintun. He hasn't written to me for ages, you know.' And she let out a gentle sigh, which later on lapsed into a comment: 'Men seem to be really wicked. Don't you think so?'

I refused to confirm her statement, but said: 'But what makes you think of him while you're doing your hair? You can think of him at any other time.'

'Hahaha . . .' Her rolled up tongue relaxed and a peel of resounding laughter tinkled forth from between her teeth. 'What an idea!'

'Am I not right?' I asked. 'When one is doing a thing, one's mind should not be engaged in another thing.' I quoted a saying my mother used to repeat to O Ran when the latter grew lacka-daisical in her work.

'Say, you're a pedant like your father!' she explained seriously. Then she went on to correct me: 'You can never think when you are trying to think. You think only when you're doing something, because the work provokes thought.'

'What thought does combing provoke in you, then?'

'You're really a naughty man,' she said. 'It is a personal secret.'

'But you must tell me about it, Aunt Chrysanthemum,' I implored. 'It sounds so interesting!'

She remained thoughtful for a while. Then she asked, 'Well, you really want to know?'

'Certainly.'

'Well, as I've told you, I was thinking of Mintun. And it is not combing alone that makes me think of him, but you too!' she glanced at me with a smile. 'When we were newly married, each time I did my hair he stood behind me, staring at my hair and the movement of my hand, just as foolishly as you do, but he was a grown-up man, you know . . . He knew many other things . . .' She suddenly paused and her brilliant eyes turned

36

glassy, looking fixedly at the miror as though she were dreaming of something.

I was confused. What had Mintun to do with her hair? Besides, he was such a man of the past, being altogether forgotten in the village. I personally, for instance, had no idea of him at all. When he left the village I was barely five. I could not even picture to myself what he looked like. My mother mentioned him only once at supper to Uncle Pan in connection with Lao Liu, when he asked her:

'Can't Aunt Chrysanthemum love Lao Liu, who adores her so much?'

'Lao Liu certainly is a charming person,' my mother said. 'But I am not quite sure whether he will win her heart. She thinks too highly of Mintun.'

'But why? I understand Mintun went away shortly after their wedding and has never dropped her a line since. The silence is equivalent to desertion. She has no obligation whatever to him, even though he is still alive.'

'But she still loves him, I think, because he went away for her sake. You see, he was the sort of young man who likes good things. He knew that his bride was a beautiful woman, so he gave a grand party for his wedding just to humour her. Of course he had to borrow money from the money-lender for the occasion. After the marriage the money-lender forced him to clear the debt. He certainly couldn't do it. So the creditor took away all his land. This event shamed him, hurt his sense of honour in the very presence of his adored bride, you see. Thus he had to leave the village secretly one day early in the morning, while Aunt Chrysanthemum was still fast asleep. The message he left behind was so moving, although simple, that she could never forget it. He said he *would* come back one day as a *great man*, superior not only to the money-lender, but even to the landlord Chumin.'

'But why hasn't he written her a word all these long years?'

'Perhaps he hasn't succeeded in making himself a great man,' my mother explained. 'You see, it is not easy for an ordinary villager to get on in the big wide world.'

'Then he is fantastic.'

'I don't know.'

'I'm sure Lao Liu can conquer her heart, if he tries hard,' Uncle Pan commented, puckering up his old lips like an old lady-killer stating his own experience. 'You see, women are queer creatures. They need pressure before they yield. Lao Liu is certainly better and smarter than Mintun in many ways, I imagine. What he has to do is to exert pressure. Pressure, I mean!'

'Are you sure, Uncle Pan?' my mother asked suspiciously.

'Oh, I beg your pardon, ma'am,' Uncle Pan suddenly apologized, pale and uneasy, having realized that he was boasting to my mother, who was a *woman*. 'I beg your pardon! Don't mind what I said, ma'am. I am stupid!' And both his neck and cheeks reddened up like a lobster.

This conversation and the picture of old Uncle Pan's crimsoning face loomed in my mind as I watched Aunt Chrysanthemum before the mirror, who was now thinking of her ambitious husband, once a young villager by the name of Mintun.

As I was engrossed silently in thought, Aunt Chrysanthemum started doing up her hair, and finished this in a quarter of an hour. The hair was made into a coiffure towering on the back of her head. She passed her fingers several times over the top, glistening with natural lustre; and she heaved a sigh.

'He is a fine fellow, a man!' she murmured to herself, stressing the last word while looking into the mirror for the last time. 'I'll forgive him anything if only he comes back to me one day.'

She pulled out a small drawer in the dressing-table and took out a tiny case containing powder. She rubbed a piece of yellowish velvet in the contents and then rubbed the velvet on her exquisitely small nose. There were a few freckles on both sides of the slender bridge, so she powdered there more heavily than anywhere else.

'Now I am ready,' she said to me and smiled. After a second she added in a joking tone, 'Do I look like Green Jade?'

'Yes,' I said. 'But there is a difference.'

'What difference?' she asked curiously, her smile saddening a little and her glittering, even teeth concealed.

'Well, according to Lao Liu her eyebrows looked like the narrow leaves of the poplar tree, whereas yours have the shape of the new crescent moon.'

'When did you observe that?' she said anxiously, but her face brightened up with a new smile.

'When you were powdering your nose.'

'Ah, you mischievous man!' she cried, and her smile broke up into a fit of laughter. 'But I like that. I don't want to look exactly like Green Jade.'

Green Jade was the heroine in a series of stories, which Lao Liu had narrated to us successively for a week about a month earlier. She was beautiful and virtuous. Her husband was a soldier, who, during the invasion of the Japanese pirates in the Ming Dynasty, went to the sea coast to defend the country. On the eve of his departure he told his wife that he would not come back unless the invaders were repelled. He succeeded in carrying out his wish, but this took him a good twelve years. In the long years of fighting he was so busy that he did not even have the time to write to her, so that rumours had it that he was captured by the pirates and taken back to Japan to be a slave. Amidst all these apprehensions and evil tidings, many a suitor came to her, dandies as well as learned gentlemen, offering her a world of fortune and an ocean of love. But she turned them down one by one. At last when her passion for her heroic husband had grown to the 'bursting point', the long-awaited man suddenly turned up in the village with titles and decorations. 'Ah, just imagine the moment they met, you graceful ladies and learned gentlemen!' our story-teller concluded. 'They were as passionate in their love as though they had been only two and twenty!'

'Like Green Jade!' Aunt Chrysanthemum whispered to herself. 'Could Mintun have taken a military career?'

'How would you like a warrior for a husband?' I asked, having overheard her whisper.

'Well . . .' She suddenly blushed. She refused to answer my question, but walked with hesitating steps to the corner where stood the spinning-wheel, and picked up a parcel wrapped with a scarf. 'Let's go,' she said. And we moved out.

When we came out of the lane to the square we saw Lao Liu sitting on a bench in the sun with his back against the trunk of an ancient maple tree, facing the entrance of the lane. He was humming in undertones a little song, which soared in the air like a lullaby. As he sang, his head swayed right and left like a mother rocking a cradle. When he caught sight of Aunt Chrysanthemum, he immediately stopped singing and got up and smiled bashfully like a girl of eighteen. He was always somewhat shy before Aunt Chrysanthemum.

'Going to town again, Aunt Chrysanthemum?' he asked in a clear, tender voice, his face crimsoning.

'Yes,' she answered, glancing at him sideways.

Then there was an interval of silence, and we walked further towards the highway. Lao Liu followed us hesitantly as though he would like to take a walk and had yet not made up his mind. When we came to the edge of the village, he suddenly spoke again:

'It's a fine day, isn't it?'

'Yes, very fine,' replied Aunt Chrysanthemum.

There was another pause. And we came to the highway. Lao Liu was still walking irresolutely behind us. The sun was very bright, and the air warm. I felt my back slightly itching with the warmth. It was like July, although it was already late autumn. A row of migrating wild geese cackled cheerfully over our heads. Then abruptly Lao Liu came up on the right of Aunt Chrysanthemum and whispered to her with affection:

'May I help you with the parcel? I'm going to town too.'

'No, thank you!' she said in a dry voice. 'The parcel is very light. I can manage it.'

'Oh!' Lao Liu let out the monosyllabic sound painfully and remained silent. His face turned scarlet and shone in the sun like a ripened apple. Meanwhile his steps slowed down. He fell behind us again.

'Let's hurry up!' Aunt Chrysanthemum said to me, perceiving that Lao Liu had retreated.

We quickened our steps. When Aunt Chrysanthemum walked fast, she moved as though she were flying, for she was very light of build. I could not catch her up, and fell a few steps behind her too. As a breeze was blowing up against my face, I could smell the sweet perfume that was in the powder on Aunt Chrysanthemum's tiny freckled nose, and I could hear the rustling of her dress, which seemed to be scented too. I immediately became curious as to whether Lao Liu had discovered the same thing. I turned round. There! Lao Liu lagged far behind, tottering like an invalid. He now wore a very pale face.

'Aunt Chrysanthemum!' I shouted and ran up to her, 'Lao Liu seems very unhappy. Do you see why?'

'No, I don't,' she answered in a prosaic tone. 'Anyway, it is his personal business. Don't you worry.'

'Poor man, I'm so sorry!' I said, feeling that she had not been kind enough to him. 'He's such a nice man. He tells us such beautiful stories!'

'Yes, he's a great story-teller, but . . .' Aunt Chrysanthemum stopped as soon as she began.

'But what?' I asked with great anxiety.

'But he doesn't seem much of a man. He's too much of a woman.'

'What do you mean?' My curiosity grew greater.

'Don't you see that he sings like a girl?'

'Oh, I love that!' I exclaimed. 'He is extraordinarily charming when he plays the part of a girl.'

'That is because you're a boy.'

'But O Ran admires him.'

41

'That is because she is childish.'

'So you are grown-up?' I asked seriously. 'Don't grown up women like girlish men?'

She blushed. 'Well, I like men with ambitions,' she muttered uneasily. 'Lao Liu will remain forever a village entertainer and nothing else. He is not a bit like the heroes in his stories, who all had exciting careers. I adore those men . . .'

'But not the man who tells such fascinating stories about them?' I interrupted her.

'Oh, you naughty fellow!' she cried. 'Let's drop the subject. We are nearing the city.'

When we came to the city gate I gave a last glance along the highway. Lao Liu had disappeared. He had not followed us up to town. I felt very sad, because I remembered his face that was deadly pale after Aunt Chrysanthemum had refused his offer to help with the parcel.

We walked along a wide stone pavement, the high street of the town, and came to a big turning, where there was a cotton shop. We went in. There was a large stock of cotton and piles of spindles. They were heaped up to the ceiling. It was a shop that collected the material, and sold it to a native firm in the big city which provided foreign mills with the stuff through a comprador. A middle-aged shopkeeper with a harelip walked out from behind the high counter that hid him because he was so short. He was smoking a long pipe, and as his lips could not close completely, the smoke dribbled out from various corners of his mouth as though from a hill of burning cow-dung. It seemed that Aunt Chrysanthemum came to his shop very often, for he addressed her like an old friend, smiling a queer sort of harelip smile:

'Fine day, Aunt Chrysanthemum, isn't it? Well, what's new in the village?'

'Yes, fine day, Master Wang,' Aunt Chrysanthemum answered. 'Nothing particularly new in the village except that our Taoist priest had some kind of misunderstanding with a ghost.'

'What? With a ghost?' the shopkeeper said with curiosity and interest.

'Yes, something was wrong with his charm. The ghost did not obey his order and pursued him threatening his life. Poor man, he was in bed for a good two months.'

'Hahaha, good for him,' the shopkeeper laughed heartily, his harelip stretching out so tightly that it seemed to be about to split into several parts at any moment. I was very worried about him. But he did not seem to care much and went on laughing.

'Oh, do be kind to the poor man,' Aunt Chrysanthemum implored him, gaping at his queer lips. 'Seriously, what is the recent market?'

'Not very cheering,' the shopkeeper said, glumly.

'What do you mean?' Aunt Chrysanthemum wore a grave expression.

'I mean the prices of native yarns have gone down a little again,' the shopkeeper answered with a doleful face, which, together with his unconcealable protruding front teeth, looked rather unpleasant. 'Even so, there is no market.'

'Have the mills in the big city stopped working?' Aunt Chrysanthemum asked with anxiety.

'Yes, they have recently. That is why I've got such a huge store of cotton and yarns, which my old buyers down the river do not come to collect.' He pointed to the piles with his long pipe.

'Why? Are we going to live without clothes?'

'Why?' Master Wang questioned back, and began to suck at his pipe. 'Because of civil wars! We, living in this hidden corner of the world, have never bothered about such things. But people have been fighting them off and on all the time since the emperor was dethroned. This warlord against that and vice versa. I don't know how many are fighting one another now.'

'I've heard that this is a new dynasty – a republic they say? But don't people wear clothes in the new dynasty?'

'War, I mean, ma'am!' Master Wang sucked deep at the pipe and smoke wriggled out like several snakes from the apertures between his misshapen lips. 'They're now preparing a large scale war – so I have heard. And all the weaving factories in the big city down the river have closed down for this reason.'

Aunt Chrysanthemum nodded to herself and seemed to understand, but her face grew pale. For a long while she could not speak a word. She stared inquisitively at Master Wang as though she did not recognize his particular lips. The shopkeeper did not care about her, but went on sucking at his pipe. And the smoke continued to steal out from through the triangular openings in his lips and his large upturned nostrils, and finally veiled the whole of his flat face.

'Ah God!' Aunt Chrysanthemum cried out at last. 'How am I going to make a living? People don't want yarn!'

Master Wang blew the smoke about him away, and asked in a mild tone, 'How much yarn have you got? I'll try what I can do for you. As an old friend I won't let you down.'

'About two pounds.'

Aunt Chrysanthemum unpacked the parcel and took out several spindles of white yarn. 'They are superfine this time, Master Wang,' she said, 'because I spun them all by daylight.'

'How is that? Have you given up night work? Certainly the vegetable-oil lamp is not good for spinning.'

'Well, this young fellow has been with me for some days,' she said smiling, pointing to me. 'I have got to keep him company as a hostess.'

I knew it was a deliberate small lie. But Master Wang did not seem to care much about it. He said critically, 'No matter how fine it may be, it can't compete with the machine-spun yarn. Soon people will refuse to buy this hand-spun stuff. It is too expensive and does not suit the new machines, believe me. My buyers have told me to collect cotton only. However, since we are old friends . . .' He paused in order to suck at his pipe. Then he took up a spindle and examined the yarn by the light that came in through the door. He laid it on the counter and raised his head to look at Aunt Chrysanthemum and asked. 'How much do you expect for a pound?'

'Should not be less than the old price, I presume?' Aunt Chrysanthemum said.

'I am afraid it should,' Master Wang said, trying to pout his lips a little in the form of an objection, but failing. 'There is absolutely no market until the war is over.'

Aunt Chrysanthemum became thoughtful, staring up at the ceiling that was reached by the pile of cotton stock. Then she said decidedly, 'All right, Master Wang, pay as you will. I believe you won't let me suffer too much loss.'

'Of course not. I don't make any profit now. I only hope that I can keep the shop going so that I can always be of service to my old customers like you.'

And Master Wang paid Aunt Chrysanthemum the price he fixed for the two pounds of yarn. Without further words we walked out. As we came to the street Aunt Chrysanthemum commented with a gentle sigh: 'Those two pounds took me five days to spin, but it seems that the labour is not worthwhile.'

'Why don't you take to farming like the wine-maker's daughters?' I asked without much thinking, because at that moment I saw She-crow carrying a load of vegetables and selling them to housewives with as majestic an air as a regular mistress of a greengrocer's. 'They seem to make a lot of money.'

'Well, I've no land, in the first place, and in the second place . . .' Aunt Chrysanthemum paused and looked at her slender, tiny feet in a pair of purple shoes embroidered with a butterfly alighting on yellowish orchids. 'Well . . .' Words failed her.

By now we had come to a drapery shop. Aunt Chrysanthemum stopped for a while outside the door, rubbed a little powder on her nose again and then walked in. 'I think O Ran would like to have a practical present,' she said to me. 'I'll buy her a few yards of printed nankeen so that she can have an extra new dress for the New Year. What do you think of it?'

'Very good,' I said.

And she went straight to the counter and asked a young clerk: 'May I have a look at the blue nankeen printed with white flowers?'

The shop assistant sorted out the material from a pile and showed it to Aunt Chrysanthemum and said, 'Do you mean this?'

'Yes,' Aunt Chrysanthemum answered. And she felt it with her fingers. It was made of cotton, but by machine, so unlike the same material we used to weave at home by hand in the old days, the fabric being even and fine. 'How much a yard?' she asked.

'Thirty cents.'

'What?' Aunt Chrysanthemum said with surprise, her eyes wide open. 'A few days ago when I came here it was only twenty-seven cents a yard. How can the price jump up so soon, especially when the price for the native yarn has gone down? Isn't it made of yarns?'

'Yes, it is,' the clerk answered. 'Yet, it is not we that raise the price, but the military governor. You know there is going to be a new war between our provincial governor and the northern military lords. For this reason the foreign cotton factories in 'The Big City' have suspended output, so there is to be a great scarcity of the material. Again, for the same reason, the military governor has fixed a new tax on it, so that he can have enough funds to buy munitions. It's not our fault, you see.'

Aunt Chrysanthemum stared at the assistant speechlessly, marvelling at his easy flow of words. The young man looked back at us. He had a sincere face. 'I'm not lying, madam,' he added. 'We make only a modest profit and never tell tales to our customers.'

'Thank you, I understand,' Aunt Chrysanthemum said and lowered her head. Carefully, she took out the silver coins that were paid to her by the harelip Master Wang for her yarn and that she had cautiously wrapped up in a handkerchief; she counted them, again and again. 'Ah, they are not even enough for two yards of the material,' she exclaimed. 'What can I do?'

46

And she stared at the clerk again. After a few minutes' silence, she added. 'Could you show me some handkerchiefs?'

The clerk took out a case that contained handkerchiefs. They were also machine-made. Aunt Chrysanthemum selected a purple-reddish one and paid ten coins for it, the price of half a pound of native yarn.

'I hope O Ran likes it,' she said to me as we walked out of the shop. 'I'm sorry I can't buy anything for you for the moment. The rest of the money I have to use to buy a little rice and salt.'

When we returned to our village, Aunt Chrysanthemum went with me straight to my mother. To her surprise Lao Liu was sitting in our house, discussing something with Uncle Pan, his face downcast and his eyes sad. So he did not go to town,but came here instead, I thought to myself. And I discovered that he seemed to want to smile as he saw Aunt Chrysanthemum coming in, but his lips could not shape a cheerful expression. Aunt Chrysanthemum also appeared very uneasy; her cheeks had grown scarlet. She was never herself face to face with our story-teller except in the dark evenings when she could hide in the crowd, listening to his stories.

'This is just a little present to celebrate O Ran's recovery,' she said hastily to my mother, handing her the handkerchief. Then she immediately took leave.

'You see, she is embarrassed in front of you,' Uncle Pan said to Lao Liu after Aunt Chrysanthemum was gone. 'You must be courageous and aggressive just like the heroes in your stories.'

'Yes, she likes that type,' my mother supported Uncle Pan's idea. 'I know.'

Our story-teller remained silent, bashfully hanging his head.

'You see,' Uncle Pan went on like a schoolmaster, 'you are simply a man of theory, not of action. You know only how to describe other people's success, not how to act yourself. Look at Mao Mao. Even he knows how to win She-crow's heart.'

'What?' Lao Liu started.

'He is going to marry the wine-maker's daughter at last.' Uncle Pan said. 'He told me this morning in the field, happy as a landlord, that he had *definitely* got hold of She-crow's heart. *Definitely*, you see?'

'But how?' Our story-teller was dumbfounded by the news.

'How? That is exactly what you have to learn, my dear young fellow. Listen! Mao Mao conquered her by promising her several practical things. He promised her, for instance, that he would feed her always with white rice, would listen to her words like a younger brother, would work for her happiness like a horse, would stick to her like a baby to its mother, would never speak to any other woman or young girl without her permission, and would treat her always to smiles and never to fists. See? Just like that!'

'Pah!' Lao Liu let the sound out from his lips contemptuously and got up. 'That is not love, still less love-making.'

'Again theory, Lao Liu!' my mother remarked.

But our story-teller would not hear. He walked out with dejected steps.

CHAPTER 4

On the day of Mao Mao's wedding, everybody in the village felt gay over the event. Only the old bachelor Benchin, once the bridegroom's 'potential rival', refused to participate in the jubilation by shutting himself up in his cottage. As for us, we had something more to be cheerful about, which we did not entirely expect. My father and my elder brother turned up in the village, just after the happy ceremony was over. Their sudden return from 'The Big City', where they worked, was to us like a dream. It not only took us by surprise, but even stunned us into a state of stupor. We stared at them like strangers. We could hardly believe that it was a reality, had it not been for O Ran's abrupt, terrifying scream, which woke us up. O Ran had been staring at my brother, who was now a young man, and he had also been reading her pock-marked face curiously. Thus face to face with him, she became self-conscious and shrieked wildly in terror. Then she fled like a thief into the kitchen, hiding her face in both her hands.

'What kind-hearted gods sent you back home, and both of you!' my mother cried at last, amazement and joy mingled in her voice. 'You haven't written me a word about it!' And she instinctively joined her hands together. It seemed as though she wanted to fall on her knees and pray.

My father did not answer straight away, but stared back at her quietly. He was also seized with wonder and surprise. He did not seem to believe that this was his home. He had been away from the village for so long. When he left he had been middle-aged, but now he was old, with grey hair and wrinkled cheeks. As far as I could remember, during the many years of absence, he had come home only once to fetch my brother to be an apprentice in the firm – a generous gesture offered by the boss for my father's long years of dutiful service.

'What kind-hearted god sends you both back home!' my mother repeated the same words again, her eyes now dilated with happiness. 'You used to write to me saying that you would not be able to come back home until you got the *big bonus*. Have you got it?'

My father shook his head negatively, but he began to smile. The bonus was the only goal he strived to achieve in his old age. He would get it if he worked for six years successively in the firm without taking leave. It might be a very good sum of money, because the business between the native merchants and foreign mills was very profitable. My father was determined to work steadily for six years in order to get it, so that he could retire in the end without having to worry about finding a living.

My mother turned pale, seeing my father shaking his head, although he did it with a smile. He took up her hand and tried to smile much more cheerfully, saying, 'I will get the *bonus*. Don't you worry. I have come back only because of the civil war.'

'Civil war!' my mother shouted, her eyes becoming wild.

'Are you sure it is civil war?' said Uncle Pan with great surprise, he who had escaped from a civil war in his native place in the North.

'Yes, I am sure,' my father said quietly. 'So our firm has to be closed for the duration. Because it is going to be a big war. The warlords in the south and those in the north want to have a decisive battle this time.'

'It's not civil war, but an international war!' my brother's voice suddenly broke out, 'because both sides have been supplied with arms by foreigners.'

It sounded like a very complicated thing. 'Foreigners?' my mother asked herself. Then she fixed her stare inquisitively on

Uncle Pan, and the latter blinked his old eyes confusedly at my brother, who talked like a learned man. We did not understand anything about foreigners at all. But suddenly a voice shouted out outside as though to confirm the news about war:

'War! They have fought a big war!'

Simultaneously with the shout, there was a wave of furious barks. An old man dashed into our house, pursued vehemently by our watchdog, Laipao. He stood in the middle of the room, out of breath, waving a cane madly at the dog, and said to him as though to a mischievous brat: 'You illiterate animal! Don't you recognize me? Were you able to speak and learn like my pupils, I would teach you how to behave with this –' He showed Laipao the cane. But his hands were trembling. Laipao, however, was not cowed by the gesture. Instead, he jumped on him and pulled at his cotton-wadded old winter gown. It was so worn out that wadding hung out like festoons.

'Uncle Peifu!' my mother cried in an excited tone, 'what wind blows you here at this particular moment?' Then, turning to Laipao, she shouted, 'Get away! Don't you see that Uncle Peifu is not a beggar, but a great scholar and master of the school in town?'

Laipao seemed to understand my mother's words. He gave a suspicious stare at the old schoolmaster, then whined maliciously for a while at him and finally trotted away.

'Tell me what wind blows you here,' my mother repeated. 'You come just at the right moment to meet your old friend.'

'War! War makes me come here!' Uncle Peifu shouted, busy putting back into the gown the cotton that was pulled out by Laipao. Then, raising his head, he jumped up. He took my father's hands into his. 'Ah, Yunchi, when did you come back? Why didn't you tell me beforehand, so that I could welcome you? It is such an exciting event!'

'The war, as you said!' my father said excitedly, 'The war sent me back home even without my own knowledge!'

'It seems that the war is a jolly good thing,' Uncle Peifu

51

said, baring his toothless upper gum. 'It brings us old friends together. Ha! Ha!'

'We must have a drink to celebrate the unusual occasion!' my mother said cheerfully.

Without waiting for instructions Uncle Pan had already dashed to the barrel. He fetched a huge jug of barley wine, and poured out a large bowl for Uncle Peifu.

The schoolmaster lowered his head and sipped at the drink. After a sip, he inhaled a long breath as though he wanted to suck in the air about the bowl, which smelled of wine, too. 'Now I feel better,' he said. Lifting his head, he gave my father an amicable glance, saying, 'Well, let's forget about the war at the moment. Do please tell me how you have been getting on all these years in the big world outside.'

'As usual. And how about you?'

'Worse than when you were at school,' he said with a sigh. Before my father went to the big city, he had been a teacher at Uncle Peifu's school. 'If I were a little younger, I would give up this hopeless profession and find a new job with some business firm like you.'

'What do you mean? Don't you get enough rice from your pupils for instruction?'

'Rice! Yes, I get for each urchin half a picul of broken rice, and I've got to look after him for a whole year. You know, the middle-class parents are stingy by nature. They want good education for their children, but no rice for the tutor. I'm nearly starved. Now that the Imperial Examination is abolished, they simply have no respect for learned old scholars, you see?'

'I don't understand you, Peifu. The landlord Chumin used to be the patron of education. Can he let things go like that? He himself has children to be educated, hasn't he?'

'Landlord Chumin! I don't want to hear his name!' he said angrily, but, perceiving that he was being carried away by emotion, he lowered his tone. 'Yes, he gives me one and a half piculs of rice every year for his three children as tuition fees. He never fails to do that. Yes, he is kind . . .' Suddenly he restrained his voice. He could not go on. It seemed something was choking his throat. His eyes sent out angry fire, his face was red, and his lips resentfully pouted up. Then, to our great amazement, he threw back his head and poured the whole bowl of the strong wine into his throat. And the fire that he had suppressed by force of reason kindled up. His cheeks became blood-red, as though he wanted to fight somebody.

Laipao sneaked in again, and started sniffing at the feet of Uncle Peifu, whose toes showed through the worn-out socks.

'You illiterate animal! Do you want a lesson?' Uncle Peifu got up and threatened him with the cane.

Laipao started whining, goggling at the old schoolmaster maliciously.

'You want a lesson? Yes?' Uncle Peifu shouted again. And he wielded the cane in the air like a magician, with vigour and ferocity.

His eyes began to look delirious and his unsteady head began to swing to and fro and his legs began to shake. In a minute he slumped into his armchair helplessly like a piece of wood, his cane dangling from his hand and his head hanging on the arm of the chair. Meanwhile, he murmured as though he were in a dream:

'Landlord Chumin, you old fox! You always threaten me with withdrawing your three snotty urchins whenever I try to suggest that you should increase the fees. And yet you never for a moment refrain from working me hard, you want me to teach your hopelessly stupid children not only classics, poetry and calligraphy, but also how to behave like young gentlemen . . . You even asked me to teach them such nonsense as foreign devils' science and mathematics and English, which I have never bothered to look at . . . You even prompted the parents of my other pupils to cut down the half picul to one third. You want me to die. I know . . . That's why you also make a private slave of me . . . You old fox, you forced me to write eulogistic poems for your dirty birthday, to sing in praise of your generosity and kindness and public spirit and hospitality, which have never existed; to make a speech in front of your guests praising you as the patron of my school, of learning, of education . . . Landlord Chumin, you heartless wizard, I know you've a lot of land in the country and own several big shops in the town. Still I hate you . . .'

We were completely flabbergasted at the spectacle of Uncle Peifu now accusing so ruthlessly Landlord Chumin, who was the richest and most powerful man in the neighbourhood, and we were trembling because in ordinary times we did not even dare to mention his name. Most of the peasants in the district were at his mercy, because they lived by farming his land. As Uncle Peifu raised his voice each time he mentioned the landlord's name, Uncle Pan's face turned pale and became convulsed with fear. He cautiously tiptoed to the door and shut it and stood with his back firmly against the opening, so that no noise could escape.

'He is very tight,' my father said to my mother, pointing to Uncle Peifu, who now looked ghastly, with eyes closed.

'He swallowed the whole bowl of wine at one gulp and he has such a poor head. Poor man, he can't have tasted any drink for years. Give him a little cold water, will you?'

My mother went to the kitchen and fetched a bowl of water. My father poured the water into Uncle Peifu's mouth. Gradually Uncle Peifu opened his eyes and steadied himself up. At last he sat up properly in his chair with his back straight.

'What's the matter with you?' he said to my father, who was still standing close beside him with the bowl in his hand. 'Is there anything wrong with me?'

'No,' my father answered, 'you've finished up your wine a little bit too quickly – that's all.'

'What?' Uncle Peifu asked, turning pale again. 'Was I tipsy?' His eyes were now wide open, alarmed.

'Thank God! You're all right now,' Uncle Pan let out a sigh of relief and opened the door. 'What words you've said.'

'Did I say anything dreadful?' Uncle Peifu's dilated eyes now grew wild. 'I mean, did I say anything about Landlord Chumin? I've been dreaming of him lately, funnily enough!'

'Yes, you did!' Uncle Pan answered.

'Really?' Uncle Peifu's face was now deadly pale.

'But not much about Chumin,' my father added in great haste.

'And nothing offensive,' my mother echoed, winking at Uncle Pan.

'Yes, nothing terrible, thank God,' Uncle Pan said, looking back at my mother.

'I'm so glad that I did not say anything terrible about Landlord Chumin.' Uncle Peifu said, heaving a sigh of great relief. 'He's very touchy indeed. Oh, of course, every rich, benevolent man is touchy sometimes. I rather like him being easily offended. He is so charming when he is a bit angry. His eyes sparkle with a sort of fire, which kindles a kind of warmth in your heart . . .'

'Let's talk of something else, Peifu,' my father interrupted him, while my mother raised her hand to her lips to conceal a smile. 'I know Landlord Chumin is an interesting man, since I was also in the same school with you for a few years. But I haven't anything to do with him now, although he does operate a cotton shop in the same street in 'The Big City', almost next door to me.'

'I am so glad that you don't have to earn a living with him!' Uncle Peifu said, heaving another sigh. But soon he corrected his words with an apology: 'Oh, I'm sorry, I don't mean that. I simply mean that it is so much more interesting to work in a shop owned by an entirely different person. It's so much fun to have new experiences with a new boss.'

'Oh, do let's talk of something else,' my father said in a solicitous tone. 'You were shouting something about the war before you came in. What is the latest news about it?'

'Say! I've nearly forgotten about it!' Uncle Peifu said, gently tapping his old head with dissatisfaction. 'The war is over!'

'So soon?' my father asked, greatly surprised. 'At the time I left 'The Big City', the war was just beginning.'

'Believe me, it is over,' Uncle Peifu said. 'Chumin's messenger, Sweet Potato, returned from the big city only this morning. He said it was over. You know, Sweet Potato is an honest, reliable chap. You've often asked him to carry your letters home. He never tells lies, believe me.'

'Yes Sweet Potato is a very dependable person,' my father said. 'But how can such a big battle end in such a hasty way? I am confused.'

'I understand something was wrong with the ammunitions of the attacking Northern Army. They collapsed after the first combat.' He suddenly lowered his voice and his eyes began to blink nervously. 'A part of the vanquished troops are moving this way to the North. Landlord Chumin said that their morale is so bad that they are worse than bandits. They have already looted several towns down the river.'

'Are they going to pass through our town?'

'They must, because it is on their way.' Uncle Peifu reduced his voice further to a whisper, assuming a mysterious air. 'Landlord Chumin has asked me to do a big job, a very big job.' And he spread out his hands to show how big it was.

We were all mystified by his secretive whisper and sweeping gesture.

'You see, Chumin is really a genius,' he went on, changing his air of mystery into one of importance as he looked into our puzzled faces. 'He has thought out a way to keep their hands clean when they pass through the town. He wants to give them a splendid welcome party on behalf of the local people so as to bolster up their self-respect. When they are well treated, they will be ashamed to harm the town. Just make a guess: Who is going to do the key job of welcoming them?' Uncle Peifu goggled mysteriously at us.

'Landlord Chumin himself, of course,' Uncle Pan said, 'since he is the chairman of the Chamber of Commerce.'

'No! Remember, it must be done by a learned man, a man who knows how to talk elegantly. Besides, he is rich. Suppose one of the officers suddenly discovered his wealth and held him for ransom. Of course, this is only just a supposition. It will never happen, I am sure. But rich men are always cautious.'

'Do you mean that you . . .' my mother said with hesitation.

'Exactly, exactly,' said Uncle Peifu proudly. 'That is why I have come here. I want your help, Uncle Pan.' He touched Uncle Pan's shoulder like an old pal, and went on, 'You must join the welcoming party as a representative of the farmers. I'm going to ask Lao Liu as the representative of the intellectuals and Benchin as the deputy of the ecclesiastical world. You're going to be paid for the job – just a few hours of course; and it will be very good pay.'

'Could it buy me a few bottles of drink?' Uncle Pan asked jokingly.

'Oh, more than that. Chumin has promised to pay a large sum to each representative.'

'You must make sure that he pays, because sometimes his words turn out to be dishonoured cheques.'

'I'm sure he will. To be frank, it is he who suggested your names to me. He can't let me down like that. Oh, I must go and see Lao Liu and Benchin. Do come, Uncle Pan. We shall have a delicious feast and old wine too. Everything will be exceptionally good, because it is meant to flatter the officers and to intoxicate their wild hearts.'

'In that case, I'll come, Uncle Peifu,' Uncle Pan said sympathetically. 'I'll do anything for you.'

Uncle Peifu got up from his chair and said goodbye to us. At the door he turned round and added that he would let us know the time when the troops would arrive.Then he disappeared outside the door. But in a moment he hurried back again. He had forgotten his cane. He said to my mother by way of apologizing, that without the stick he could not think and deal with such a difficult situation as the pursuit of watchdogs. 'So it is not only an emblem of education,' he said, 'but also a good companion. Oh, speaking of education I am reminded of another important thing, that is, I have to get a representative of the younger generation for the welcoming party. Would you like to join us?' he asked me.

I looked inquisitively at my mother, unable to make an answer. She remained thoughtful for a while, and then said that if Uncle Pan went I could certainly go.

Uncle Peifu came across Laipao at the door again. The dog was suspiciously scanning him with its unfriendly eyes. Holding his cane firmly in his hand, he moved gingerly towards the village square. When Laipao at last gave him up, he slipped quietly into Benchin's cottage. Attracted by the promise of good pay and a grand feast, our priest agreed to act as the representative of the ecclesiastical world. Then Uncle Peifu called at Lao Liu's studio. Our story-teller was thrilled by the idea of meeting generals and warriors, returned from a 'heroic battle'. He loved to have fresh experiences with such people. He thought he could get some new inspiration for war stories.

The news of the arrival of the Northern Troops finally reached the village. We therefore proceeded to the town to welcome them as the representatives of the local people. Lao Liu was in his New Year best. Benchin had his three-week-old beard shaved clean; and had put on the impressive black Taoist cape for the first time since he had had the trouble with the ghost. Uncle Pan threw away his old three-foot long bamboo pipe. He had bought a packet of cigarettes, and in order to look fashionable, stuck one between his lips. But it choked him and made him cough several times, because the smoke somehow went straight into his nostrils.

We stood on the terrace before the city gate, waiting for the coming of the defeated troops. Uncle Peifu, as chief delegate, towered in front of us. We saw on the city wall many colourful posters, bearing slogans, all written by Uncle Peifu himself in classical calligraphy, such slogans as: 'Welcome to our ever-victorious army!' 'Best wishes to you, our people's army!' 'Our humble place is honoured by your presence!' 'You are to us like

water while we are like fish to you: we can't live without you!'
Uncle Peifu wagged his head as he now read them again, as
though they were immortal lines from the poetry of the T'ang
Dynasty.

About an hour later a cloud of dust rose on the highway in
the distance. Then, one after another, men in uniform emerged
into our view, marching in one line in our direction. We lost no
time in lighting the fuse of a long string of fire-crackers, which
hung from the top of a tree to the ground. The jubilant cracking,
interspersed with the whirr of rockets, sent the ground, as well
as the air, spinning. There was a kind of festive vibration in the
atmosphere, which we could only feel. For years since the great
famine we had not employed firecrackers, even to celebrate New
Year, to such a degree.

As the troops drew near to the city wall, we marched down
the terrace to receive them. Uncle Peifu walked ahead. As soon
as the officer in command of the army, who rode on a horse
in front of the line, came within talking distance, Uncle Peifu
performed a deep, graceful bow, as became a man of good
upbringing and learning. We followed suit. Benchin, in order
to compete with Uncle Peifu in gracefulness, bent his already
crooked back in an acute angle, so that his Taoist cape fell on
the ground – an act which startled the officer's horse. The animal
suddenly trod on it with one of its forelegs. But our priest dared
not stop it, for fear of spoiling his posture. At last the officer
said: 'Stand up, please gentlemen!' We stood up. But it was
already too late for Benchin to salvage his valuable cape.

'We, on behalf of the local people, extend to you our hearty
welcome, sir,' Uncle Peifu said to the officer, with another bow.
'We have heard of your arrival and consider it our greatest
luck to have the opportunity of meeting you and your heroic
warriors.'

Faced with Uncle Peifu's deep, reverent bow and the correct
recital of his speech (which, as Uncle Peifu later on confessed,
was Chumin's version, composed under the influence of his
'inspiring ideas'), the officer knit his brows into a frown and

wore an air of uncertainty and hesitation. As Uncle Peifu remained bowing, waiting for his reply, he at last turned round to his mercenary troops and said, 'Brothers, we must this time behave really like a *people's* army to this friendly town. Not a single blade of grass should be touched.'

'Thank you very much, sir, you're really a people's general,' said Uncle Peifu and he straightened up his back. 'We have a little wine ready to wash the dust off your lips and a few dishes to please your palate.'

'That is most kind of you,' the officer said.

We went together to the temple, where the feast was prepared. The soldiers were staying outside the city, resting on their hams, their rifles lying beside them. Tea and refreshments were served to them. And in order to keep them in good spirits three huge barrels of barley wine and a large basket of dried beef were put at their disposal. They were altogether only about a hundred men, so the drink was more than enough for their consumption. They all looked tired and haggard. Apparently they had fallen out from the main army and had no one to care for them. Seeing the wine they tuned up a song, a northern peasant song, which sounded sentimental and sad. Hearing the melody Uncle Pan said secretly to me as we walked to the temple with the officer and his subordinates, 'They are peasants from the north. I know the tune. People used to sing it while working on the fields. I'm sure there must have been a great flood from the Yellow River again, otherwise they would not have become mercenaries.'

'That is how people go to the army?' I asked in a whisper.

'Yes, the flood devastates their land. Sometimes, of course, when there is a civil war on the spot, they can't work and then they have to go to the army too, in order to earn a living.'

'Oh.' I could not offer any other opinion, because I had never seen any war.

We finally got to the temple. The table was already laid. Wine bottles and tea sets stood on a small table nearby. The officer and his guards sat on one side of the table and we on the other side. As it was a long table, we could all sit face to face with our guests. The food looked beautiful and smelled delicious, and was prepared by Chumin's personal cook. The officer seemed to enjoy it immensely, because he did not talk much, but kept on eating and drinking. But after three jugs of wine he began to chat in a more friendly tone, his face now red.

'You see,' he said to Benchin, who was staring curiously at him like a fortune teller, always interested in a stranger's face 'It's not our fault that we *borrow* some money or valuables from the common people on our way back home. It's theirs. They always avoid us as though we were poison. They regard us as bandits, knowing that we were defeated. They should treat us as you do.'

'Yes, yes,' Uncle Peifu said. 'Yours is a people's army, I know.'

'How right you are!' the officer said in a heightened voice, swallowing another cup of the strong wine. 'And the defeat isn't our fault either, but the Japs'. They sold us rusty rifles and old bullets which they had captured from the Russians during the Russo-Japanese War in Manchuria a quarter of a century ago. Our commander is a gentleman, who relied on the Japs' words. He did not examine them on the day of delivery. But when we found out that the weapons did not work at all, it was already too late.'

'Too bad! Too bad!' Lao Liu commented sympathetically, shaking his head violently in disgust at the dishonest Japanese. 'Too bad! Too bad!'

'But never mind,' the officer added consolingly, 'we haven't paid the Japanese yet. We'll never pay them as we've lost the war.'

'Very good, I like that,' Benchin said. 'All foreigners are no good. They don't believe in friendship, don't believe in ghosts and don't believe in the Taoist priest! They believe only in one thing: making money. Don't you think it awful?'

The chat went on till four o'clock in the afternoon when the officer's ADC, a hairy, gigantic fellow, reminded him of the time, saying that they ought to take leave or else they would not be able to get to their HQ in the north in time. So the officer stood up and expressed his appreciation of the rich meal and the good will of the local populace as demonstrated by the 'appropriately selected delegation'.

'If we were not in a hurry,' the officer added, 'we would like to stay here *for a few days* in order to have a complete rest.'

'What a pity that you've got to go straight away,' Uncle Peifu said courteously. 'We've been getting on so well! But *don't* let us deter you from your important journey, anyway, although we very much wish you to remain here for a few more days.'

Then we walked out and went through the street to join the soldiers outside the city wall. The street was now completely empty, and the doors of all the shops were shut. There was not even a cigarette stall. Only a few straying dogs were wandering about, sniffing at the legs of butchers' stools or staring at us with malicious and curious eyes. A gust of chilly wind swept over from the other side and blew into the air a few pieces of waste paper that lay abandoned in the rubbish dumps at the deserted corners. They whirled above us, wailing like homeless children, and gave us a sense of desolation. The officer suddenly looked around with suspicious eyes and asked Uncle Peifu, 'Where are the people that you represent?'

Uncle Peifu turned deadly pale at the question, his lips livid and his hands trembling. 'They are all staying indoors, sir, celebrating this day of your arrival as a holiday,' he stuttered, significantly eyeing Lao Liu for help.

'Then why should they shut their doors?' the officer asked again.

'It's due to the peculiar custom of this district, sir,' Lao Liu explained, trying to help Uncle Peifu out. 'When we observe a holiday we keep strict silence.'

'I don't like it,' the officer said. 'Tell them to come out to celebrate it together with us.'

'Well . . .'

Without waiting for a reply he walked straight to a linen shop that belonged to Chumin, and knocked at the door several times.

There was no answer from inside. Getting impatient, he began to kick it with his hobnail boots. The door only shook a little but refused to open. Then his ADC came to his help, hammering at it with a fist. The silent door now began to rumble like distant thunder, which made all the representatives shiver with fear. At last the door opened. A small apprentice appeared from within, shaking all over like a tiny mouse in front of a cat.

'Your Lordship,' he squeaked, 'please don't kill me, I'm only a poor apprentice. My master Chumin hasn't paid me my last year's pocket money yet. My purse is as empty as my belly today. I haven't had anything to eat since last night.'

'Where is your master and the shop assistants?' the officer shouted at the boy at the top of his voice, as though he wanted to swallow him up alive.

'They've all fled away, knowing that Your Lordships were to come. Your Lordship, I'm only a poor boy. Please don't kill me!'

The officer did not answer the apprentice, but looked round the shop searchingly. There was not much stock left behind the counter. Most of the valuable stuff had been evacuated. The officer turned round and said to Uncle Peifu, 'So you also regard us as bandits, eh?'

'No, no, sir,' Uncle Peifu babbled.

'Don't argue!' the officer shouted, off-handedly giving a slap on his old face. 'I know everything!'

He and his ADC and guards dashed to the city gate, and shouted to the soldiers: 'Come in brothers! Help yourselves to anything you can lay your hands on!' All the men reacted as though electrified and poured into the street like a torrent. Shouting, screaming, kicking and the slamming of doors created pandemonium. Taking advantage of the general confusion we took to our heels to the countryside. Several times Uncle Peifu fell to the ground and hit his head on stones, and his nose bled. Benchin, with his stiff, crooked back, could not run at all, but let himself roll down the hill into a dry ditch outside the city walls, where he was covered by the marshy grass. Uncle Peifu finally found a huge pyramid of cow-dung and pushed himself into it like a scaly ant-eater. Lao Liu and Uncle Pan and I, however, managed to flee home.

The soldiers spent the whole afternoon looting the town. In the evening they burned a number of tables and chairs to make fires. Early next morning they left with a message pasted on the door of the city gate to the effect that if their commander won another battle and became the governor of the province, in the future, they would certainly come back again to punish the bogus representatives of the local people and the 'deserve-hanging schemers.'

Several days later Uncle Peifu came to visit our village on a crutch. He had twisted one ankle when he was fleeing from the troops, and it had not quite recovered in spite of the many doses of herb medicines, which he prescribed himself. The cane that was always with him now hung by a string on his girdle at the waist. As he hopped along it dangled to and fro like the wand of a vagabond magician. He went first to see Benchin, who had twisted his back, and then to Lao Liu, who could not tell stories for many evenings as he could not move his leg after running home at breakneck speed that day.

'I am sorry that things should have turned out in such an unexpected way,' Uncle Peifu used to Lao Liu the same apologetic words he had used to Benchin. 'The defeated troops are even worse then bandits. They have looted absolutely everything. Landlord Chumin's linen and rice shops have not a single chair left!'

'Good for him,' our story-teller said, massaging his stiff legs. 'He should not have asked people like you and me to do the nasty job. We don't want to rent his land, do we?'

'Well, well,' Uncle Peifu muttered doubtfully. 'Well, yes. Oh no! Yes! Oh no!'

He kept on saying 'yes' and 'no' for a long while and could not make a decision about his attitude towards Chumin. Finally he gave it up and hopped into our house. Seeing Uncle Peifu for the first time on a crutch, Uncle Pan could not help smiling and said, not without resentment in his tone, 'A fine job, eh? To be the chief representative of the people, eh? Let's pray God that we may not be elected again.'

'Don't joke, Uncle Pan,' Uncle Peifu said seriously with a frown. 'I simply had to do it.'

'I know,' Uncle Pan said. 'But I don't have to . . .'

A voice from outside interrupted Uncle Pan: 'Say! How about the pay which you promised me?' It was from Benchin, the 'representative of the ecclesiastical world.' He tottered in on a walking stick like a centenarian. 'Because of the injury inflicted on my back I shall not be able to take the service for many days to come, and you saw with your own eyes that that damn horse destroyed my holy cape. What do you say to that? I don't demand any compensation but only the rightful pay you have promised on Chumin's behalf.'

Uncle Peifu knitted his sparse eyebrows together into a sorrowful frown and his lips trembled fitfully, producing a few inarticulate words: 'I'm sorry, Benchin, that I've got to break my promise. Chumin refused to pay a single coin on the ground that we didn't do the job well enough. We didn't, did we? I cannot even claim the expenses I have spent on the herbal medicine.'

'It is really most unfortunate, Benchin,' my mother remarked. 'If Chumin does not pay, Uncle Peifu can't do anything.'

'You're right, absolutely right!' Uncle Peifu said to my mother while looking at the Taoist priest, and was almost moved to tears by her sympathetic words.

'But, Peifu,' my father said, 'what are you going to do, now that one of your ankles is twisted?'

'Teaching! Of course, teaching! The war is over. No more defeated troops to pass through here. Landlord Chumin has reopened his shops. I must re-start my school. Teaching is my job.' And he swung the cane into the air with his left hand and the cane swayed back and hit his twisted ankle. He made a grimace of pain.

'Will you get the same children back to the school after this terrible event?'

'Yes, of course. The rich people can't afford to let their children go uneducated. But, unfortunately, this time Chumin insisted on cutting down the half picul of rice to one third and he got it.'

'How can he do that?' my father asked in surprise. 'Half a picul of rice for the education of a child is little enough already.'

'You are right,' Uncle Peifu agreed, his eyes burning with suppressed anger, which, however, was quenched by tears. 'But what can I do? He said that we failed in preventing the defeated troops from looting, so that he suffered great loss. He made it plain to me that if I did not agree to the cut he would withdraw the children from my school. I simply can't bargain with him, I am so old.'

My father did not make any more remarks, but shook his head dejectedly. The silence was oppressive. Uncle Peifu began to feel uneasy, and a little later he took his leave. Benchin followed him closely, still demanding the promised pay and a small compensation for the loss of his holy cape.

A long time after their departure their quarrel seemed to be still lingering in the air. My father gazed confusedly into the direction in which the limping old schoolmaster and our hunchbacked Taoist had disappeared. He was speechless. His eyes looked dreamy. He seemed to be thinking of something, something about the future, past and present, something vague and undefinable. Suddenly he started, and became vigilant. He said to himself in a determined voice:

'I must get the *bonus*!'

'What do you mean?' my mother asked, shocked by his abrupt burst of speech.

'I must go back to the firm immediately, now that the war is over.'

'Won't you stay till after the New Year, which is not far ahead? You haven't been home long.'

'But I must go. I mustn't forfeit the *bonus* by the interruption of service. This is my last chance!'

'Does the *bonus* matter so much to you?'

'Much! Much too much! If I don't get it this time, then I have to work on in the firm for another six years and they may not let me do it, as I am already old. And I can't be a schoolmaster again, like Peifu, as you see.'

'Aw –' My mother swallowed her voice, and remained silent. She understood what my father meant. Just then my brother came in from outside, with a cabbage in his hand. Apparently he had been to our vegetable garden.

'Has he to go back to the big city with you, too?' she said pointing to my brother.

'He still has three months to finish his apprenticeship,' my father said. 'Perhaps he had better go.'

'How about his marriage, then?' my mother said. 'He is now grown up. O Ran has mastered the art of house management. She should now be the mistress of the house. I am ready to give up every responsibility to her.'

'I will not marry her!' my brother broke out bluntly.

'Why?' my mother asked in an alarmed, wild voice. 'What makes you think of that? I've brought O Ran up carefully and dutifully for the house. Don't you want to live in this ancestral house of yours?'

'Because I don't love her!' my brother replied also in a wild voice. 'Besides, we are so different in our *world outlook*.'

'What do you mean by your *world outlook*? Where did you learn this new language? Are you a foreigner? Weren't you born in this old village?' My mother became mad with fury.

My father tried to mediate, saying to her: 'Don't mind much what he says. He did learn a lot of new ideas from the evening class of the Workers' Trade Union, where he went regularly. But when he gets older, he will come to himself.'

'But I'll not marry O Ran in any case!' my brother insisted firmly.

'Why? Isn't she your betrothed? Do you want to break away

67

from the tradition of our village?' my mother questioned him furiously. 'Or is it that you don't like the pock-marks on her face? But that is destiny! You're destined to have a pock-marked wife!'

'But I *will not* marry her, pock-marks or no!'

Suddenly a scamper was heard from the inner passage leading to O Ran's room. I knew it must be O Ran, who had been eavesdropping. She had of late become very nervous about herself, and would always try to overhear any discussion on her future. I thought she must have been greatly hurt, having heard her looks unfortunately mixed up with a family quarrel. I went to her room and tried to find some kind words to cheer her up. She was sitting speechlessly at her dressing-table, looking like an idiot into the large mirror, while two streams of tears were coursing down her rugged cheeks.

'Don't weep, O Ran. My brother was simply joking,' I said.

Hearing my words she burst into a fit of sobs. I could say nothing more. Words simply failed me. I stared at her like a fool, and discovered to my astonishment that some of her pock-marks were as big as peas.

Early next morning, both my father and my brother left the old village for the big city, one to continue the long-term secretarial work for the sake of the bonus, the other to finish his apprentice-ship. At their departure my mother's eyes were wet, because a few weeks later it would be New Year, which is our festival of family reunion. But she managed to restrain the tears and even said in a cheerful tone: 'Good luck! We shall have a huge celebration together for the next New Year!' She meant by that to cheer my father up, who was also sad: to suggest to him symbolically that he might get the bonus before then.

CHAPTER 5

As New Year drew near, every family in our village began to get busy. We started preparations not only for our own family reunion, but also for that of our gods. Six days before the festival, the Small New Year would take place – the New Year of the gods when our God of the Kitchen, who also acted as our God of the Household, would go up to Heaven to join his immortal relatives and at the same time to make a report to the Supreme God about the family he ruled. Every family tried to get the best possible present for Him before He went so that He might make favourable reports about them. Never before had we talked so much about the things in the town and their prices. The little walled city three miles away seemed to be a part of our life, without which we simply could not start a new year.

My mother and Uncle Pan were particularly concerned with the gifts we could buy from the market. Both sincerely wanted to offer the best thing to our God of the Kitchen, because both had a wish. It was not only a good report about us that we desired, but unprecedented blessings that the Supreme God might kindly confer on us after his reading of the report: my mother wished that my father, by some miraculous chance, might be able to get his bonus the next year, practically two years ahead of time; while Uncle Pan expected a 'daughter', a new calf from our ploughing cow, whom he had grown as fond of as a sweetheart. The hard-working animal had been pregnant for several months, and might give birth to a baby at any time now. Uncle Pan had a centuries-old superstition, supported by his personal experience as a peasant, that if a baby was born before the Small New Year, it would grow up healthy and beautiful. This belief had been proved true. Many a baby animal, delivered after the Small New Year, could hardly survive the snow that would fall continually for weeks in the early spring. He secretly prayed that some divine influence might help to accelerate the arrival of our new calf.

Before making the trip to the town, he tried to make some inquiries about the best things available and their prices on the market. He wanted to inquire about this from Mao Mao, who was the first person in the village to have tried to do the shopping. Mao Mao had been particularly enthusiastic about it, because he needed special blessings, too. His wife She-crow had grown rather fastidious about food of late. He was not quite sure whether she was trying to put on airs, now that she was no longer a maidservant at the beck and call of her prolific, hardworking father, the wine maker, or whether she was simply pregnant. He wished it to be the latter. But, unlike Uncle Pan, who prayed for a 'daughter', he wanted a son, who could be his help on the farm in the future. For this he could do nothing as a simple mortal. Only God can change the sex of the baby in the womb. And, like Uncle Pan, he had also a superstition: he believed that a greedy woman could bear only girls. Although She-crow was not obviously greedy, yet she did have a quite impressive capacity for food and was extremely fond of eating, to such a degree that she even called eating her hobby, her pastime.

Uncle Pan asked Mao Mao to have a smoke with him – he had recently made a new pipe out of bamboo root – in the sun in front of our house.

'Tell me what you have bought in town for the New Year, Mao Mao,' he said, offering Mao Mao his new pipe for a trial.

'Nothing!' Mao Mao said; his resolute voice made Uncle Pan start. 'Absolutely nothing!' Mao Mao's eyes were downcast. Since he had married She-crow, he always looked at the ground as though something heavy were weighing on his head all the time.

'Then what did you go to the town for?' asked Uncle Pan, confused.

'To buy presents for the God of the Kitchen.'

'But you just said that you bought nothing.'

'Yes, nothing, absolutely nothing.'

'What do you mean? You are talking of things like a philosopher, always in an abstruse way. Do you learn this art from your wife? You were such a straightforward chap before. I am puzzled, Mao Mao.'

'I bought absolutely nothing!' Mao Mao insisted, further complicating the puzzle.

'I still don't understand you. I still want to ask you: what did you go to town for?'

'To buy things.'

'Now! Now! Are you trying to joke with me as though with your wife? I know, young men are always like that. They like to talk absolute nonsense with their women face to face in their warm beds. I know. I know. You are only trying to show off to me, knowing that I have never tasted such a delicious life.' Uncle Pan became sentimental, but he forced out a laugh in order to look strong.

Mao Mao blushed at the outburst, and his eyes were even more downcast. He babbled out:

'It is very simple to understand, Uncle Pan. There is nothing to buy on the market. The passing troops have looted most of the valuable things. Those left were damaged by the fire they set to the shops. A few articles that are displayed on the stalls cost five times as much as before. I cannot afford to buy them. Soon we shall have no salt to cook with, because its price is fantastically high, too.'

'Is that so? The shopkeepers are too greedy then!'

'They always are. They want to get as much out of us poor peasants as they can.'

'So you made a futile trip, eh?'

'But I did take the opportunity of seeing my landlord. You see, this year is nearly at an end. I wanted to find out when I could renew the land contract.'

'When? Did you settle it?' Uncle Pan felt interested in the affair as every farmhand in our village was, although he did not have to rent land from Chumin.

'Any time. But he raised the land rent by twenty per cent more.' As he said 'twenty per cent' he nearly burst out weeping.

'That is absurd!' Uncle Pan shouted, his eyes goggling. 'Then all you can get for yourself is only twenty-five per cent of the whole crop. Didn't you haggle with him about that?'

'I did. But he said he had suffered so much loss in the looting that he must make it up by other means. It is true that he had terrible damage done to his shops. He said if I did not accept the terms he would give the land to other people.'

'Did you accept them?'

'I have to, Uncle Pan. I want to rent a little more land.'

'How can you, on such terms! Are you crazy?'

'Well . . .' Mao Mao could not go on. He lowered his head sadly and stared at the ground like a fool. After a moment of silence he muttered, 'As I said, I have to. You know, She-crow . . .'

'Ah, yes! I understand!' Uncle Pan shouted, interrupting him, 'she has a large capacity for food. I know, I know! She eats much more than you do; no, more than any strong farmhand; no, as much as three or four field labourers. I know, I know!' Uncle Pan let his words flow out as loud as he could, as though trying to console himself that he fortunately had not found a woman to marry.

'What are you talking about, Mao Mao?' at the far end of the village She-crow suddenly called out. She was drying clothes there. 'Are you again talking about me? Mao Mao! If you can't feed me, you had better let me go. I can find a much better husband than you. Once a high official from the magistracy courted me, kneeling before me for three hours. Without interruption, understand, a solid three hours! Didn't I tell you that in bed the other night? Answer me, please. Didn't I tell you?'

Mao Mao did not dare to answer, but he grew deadly pale. His broad shoulders started to tremble and his legs to shake. He stood up, and he said to Uncle Pan apologetically, 'I'm sorry, I've got to go. I thank you for the smoke. It is a very nice pipe. I enjoyed it very much.' And he walked unsteadily towards She-crow as an obedient child to his mother.

At that moment my mother walked out. Apparently she had heard She-crow's words and was interested to see how Mao Mao would react. She was always nervous that they might start a row that way – but it was interesting that they had never quarrelled. When she reached the sunlight, Mao Mao had already gone to She-crow, and started helping her meekly to dry the clothes. But she suddenly shouted out: 'Look, Aunt Chrysanthemum has come back from town!'

When we turned our eyes to the highway we really did see Aunt Chrysanthemum walking gracefully back in our direction. It was surprising to realize that she had gone to town and now returned when it was still early in the morning. Generally she would make her trip to town rather late in the day, because make-up would take her some time, and she could hardly come back so soon. But immediately we understood why. She wanted to be the first to choose the best present in town, too. She always made the best offering to her God of the Household for the Small New Year, because she wanted to have a particular blessing, not for herself, but for a man, whom she adored and dreamed of most nights.

In a minute she had arrived. To our surprise she had bought nothing. She carried with her only a parcel of spindles, which she had spun.

'I don't understand! I don't understand!' she shouted in a wild voice. Her face looked haggard, and there was a veil of confusion in her eyes. We had never seen her, so graceful and gentle, in such a desperate and untidy state as she was in today.

73

'I don't understand! I don't understand!' she repeated, looking at my mother as though for some help.

'What is it, Aunt Chrysanthemum?' my mother said, taking over from her the parcel of spindles, so that she could have a little rest.

'Every little thing they sell in the town is unbelievably dear,' Aunt Chrysanthemum said in an unbecomingly hoarse voice, as rough as if she wanted to pick a quarrel, 'while everything we country folk produce costs nothing!'

'What do you mean, Aunt Chrysanthemum?' Uncle Pan asked.

'I was trying to buy a tiny piece of red silk for my God of the Household,' she explained, 'can you guess how much they ask for it? They wanted to charge me half a dollar – five times as much as before. On the other hand, when I tried to sell the yarn I have spun for days and nights, Master Wang offered only one-third of its previous price. And yet he was not very keen on the transaction. Oh, how am I going to live!' She lapsed into a self-pitying exclamation.

'How can that be!' my mother remarked. 'It's just a racket!'

'It is!' Aunt Chrysanthemum shouted righteously. 'And they even shamelessly confessed that they had to do it in order to make up the loss they had suffered at the hands of the passing bandit troops.'

'Yes, I know,' Uncle Pan put in a comment. 'Mao Mao has just told me the same story. It is only too bad, when we have to buy things for our god.'

'It is bad indeed . . .' Aunt Chrysanthemum's voice suddenly went down, almost to a whisper, her head bent, thoughtfully staring at her feet. 'I don't know what present I can give to my good old man for his journey up to Heaven . . . I shall be very unhappy . . .'

'It is really embarrassing,' my mother said, staring at Aunt Chrysanthemum quietly. She knew that the aunt was expecting, as in every other New Year, that the household god would guide Mintun's heart towards her and lead him back to her one day. She realized that Aunt Chrysanthemum lived entirely in a world of hope and expectation and that good presents to the god gave food to her hopes. 'We haven't started buying anything yet,' my mother went on. 'Perhaps we shall have to go to the county city up in the mountains for shopping. It is a much bigger town. The merchants there ought to be more honest.'

'Good idea! Good idea!' Uncle Pan commended my mother cheerfully. 'I haven't been there for a good while. Oh my! I love the old millet-wine shop there. The smell always tickles me beautifully, let alone the actual elixir!'

'You always think of drink, Uncle Pan!' my mother said. 'The shopping this time is a very serious thing.'

'I know, I know. If you send me there to do it, I promise I will not drink. I promise, on my word of honour!'

'Perhaps you really ought to send Uncle Pan there to do the shopping,' Aunt Chrysanthemum remarked to my mother. 'The town here is no good.'

'And I can sell the yarn for you there for a much better price, Aunt Chrysanthemum, I am sure,' Uncle Pan said quickly, echoing Aunt Chrysanthemum's idea in a cajoling voice, which made her blush with embarrassment.

'All right, then,' my mother said. 'Perhaps that is the only thing to do. You must go tomorrow, Uncle Pan, or other people will have chosen all the best things.'

'I am glad that you have made such a decision,' Aunt Chrysanthemum said to my mother.

'Trust me, Aunt Chrysanthemum, I will sell the spindles for you for big, big money! Don't you worry about the presents for your god,' Uncle Pan said light-heartedly for the moral support she had given him in favour of the journey.

'Thank you, Uncle Pan!' Aunt Chrysanthemum said, her eyes beaming with new hope. She left the parcel with Uncle Pan.

Early next morning Uncle Pan made the journey to the county city, which was about fifty miles away, carrying with him all our hopes for the next year, including those of Aunt Chrysanthemum.

*

Three days had elapsed since Uncle Pan's departure. My mother began to get worried as he did not come back. On the fourth day Aunt Chrysanthemum called several times to inquire about him. She was very anxious, because the Small New Year was drawing steadily nearer. Her anxiety made my mother much more nervous. And on top of that our cow began to show signs of fatigue. She sometimes refused to eat, and we did not know how to make her eat. She lay on her belly, munching feebly and slowly; a thick cluster of froth gathered about her mouth like a huge white flower, and her sticky saliva trickled out and hung down like a transparent string. Sometimes she gazed at people passing by, longingly and helplessly, as though in search of Uncle Pan. Sometimes she rubbed herself on the ground as though she were itching somewhere and in need of scratching and brushing. We could not help her, because we were not familiar with the various peculiar parts of her body.

And it was the fourth day. Still Uncle Pan did not come back.

On this day, every now and then, my mother went to the edge of the village and gazed towards the path leading up the hills to the county city in the distant mountains. There was not a single shadow on the road that resembled Uncle Pan. Each time she was disappointed she murmured to herself the same question: 'What has made Uncle Pan stay in the city for so long?'

The day ended in the usual way. The village grew dusky before the sun actually set, because the mountains around warded off its light. And then the homing crows soared in circles several times above their nests in the bare trees, croaking mournfully, the echo bringing more gloominess to the village. As they got tired at last they squeezed themselves into their nests. And then it became quiet and finally dark.

That night my mother could not sleep a wink. She was listening for any sound outside, which might be Uncle Pan's footsteps. But it was still, because there was no wind. In the absolute quietness, Laipao did not even utter a single bark. Uncle Pan was not returning. And the next morning would be the fifth day of his absence. The day after the next would be the New

Year of the gods. I heard my mother saying to herself in bed, 'I must send Mao Mao to look for him if he still does not come back tomorrow.' She was worried not so much about the presents for our God of the Kitchen, as about Uncle Pan, an old man.

The next morning, when it was still dawn, she got up and dashed out to look for Mao Mao. As she lifted the bolt of the front door, I heard a cry of alarm and surprise from her: 'What! You came back last night? Why didn't you knock at the door?'

I rushed out to join my mother, and saw her looking into the face of Uncle Pan, who stood against the wall like a mummy, his lips tightly shut. He did not stir, although my mother's stare was so sharp, wild and cutting. He looked just like an idol of Buddha, his face composed, dead and wooden. His eyes were open, but they were immobile too. They did not even seem to shine.

He seemed to have no ears. He remained as deaf as a stone.

'Has any evil wind blown on you?' my mother asked again.

He did not say yes or no.

'Did you meet any ghost on your way home in the darkness?' My mother's sharp, shrill tone split the air. She was desperate and frightened, because she now thought of ghosts which she never had believed in before.

But Uncle Pan's lips were as irresponsive as if sealed.

'Very strange, indeed. Uncle Pan has lost the faculty of speech,' she said to herself, her voice lowered to a whisper. Meanwhile, her mystified eyes were looking at the old man contemplatively, as though he were a magician, a quaint fakir from afar.

I noticed at that moment that Uncle Pan's long gown was hanging loose about him like Benchin's surplice, as his familiar girdle was gone. His hands were empty.

'Have you been robbed by some highwayman at a mountain pass?' my mother said, studying his strange appearance.

He did not nod or shake his head. His eyelids did not move. His body did not budge.

At her wit's end my mother made a step forward to him, and

looked straight into his dull eyes. Still, he did not make any response. At last my mother took hold of both his shoulders and shook him by them violently, as though he were the trunk of an old tree. He stumbled backwards and forwards as he was shaken. But as soon as my mother took her hands off he remained standing bolt upright against the wall again.

'O Ran! Fetch Benchin, please! Uncle Pan is possessed by a ghost, a very malicious ghost, which has taken away his soul!'

My mother did not only believe in ghosts now, but also was convinced that Benchin had the power to exorcize evil spirits.

At my mother's call O Ran dashed out from the cowshed, an empty tin in her hand, with which she had been feeding dish-water to the cow – a routine which she followed every morning. But instead of taking my mother's order she shouted back to her, out of breath: 'Ma! Our cow is giving birth to a baby! Our cow is giving birth to a baby!'

This piece of news functioned like holy water from Heaven after a long drought, endowed with much more magic power than the service of our Taoist priest, Benchin. It virtually brought life to the dead. Uncle Pan's eyes began to blink. His lips began to tremble. His legs began to move. Then, all of a sudden, he scampered to the cow-shed like a young goat. He had never been so swift and agile in movement. He did not only come back to life. He seemed even to have recovered his youth; no, his childhood.

The cow was struggling on the floor, which was paved with dry sand. The forelegs of the baby stuck out grotesquely from her womb. The mother cow was in pain, because her eyes were bulging out deliriously, burning with fire. Seeing Uncle Pan, she became quieter, and her eyes became immobile, radiant with the fluid that was welling out. As Uncle Pan came near to her, she wagged her head; and as she closed her eyes in order to let Uncle Pan caress her, two streams of tears trickled down her cheekless face.

Uncle Pan squatted beside her and held her head up and

looked into her tearful eyes. They stared at one another for a long time.

'Don't weep, my dear woman,' Uncle Pan said in a tender voice, while his other hand caressed her belly. 'It won't take you long. It will take you just a minute. Be patient.' And he puckered up his old lips like an old granny and went on cajolingly, wiping her tears with his sleeve: 'Be a good woman. Lie quietly so that the baby won't get hurt. Yes, like this!' Our cow became really quiet, lying on her flank against Uncle Pan's knee.

My mother was watching them stupidly all the time, standing wordless in a corner. After a little while the cow suddenly became restless and started panting heavily. Without a moment's thought my mother instinctively fell on her knees, her hands clasped together, and began to pray God for the safety of the cow. We all instantly turned pale, realizing that this animal, who had worked on our six acres of land all her life, was now facing a crisis. Without knowing why, O Ran kneeled down beside my mother like a fool, and I in front of the cow.

A great silence ensued. It stilled Uncle Pan's senseless babble and my mother's prayer. The cow held her mouth wide open. She had difficulties with her respiration. We knew she was gasping. We all held our breath. There was an intensity in the air, which brought about a primeval tranquillity. We felt something was about to burst in the room at any moment. And the dreadful thing happened: the mother cow was closing her eyes. Like a dying animal at the last stage of its life, she helplessly let her head fall flat on the floor, as though she had fallen into an eternal slumber. The child was born.

With great relief we stood up to examine the baby. It was extremely nice-looking. Its ears were as tender as young bamboo leaves, and its eyes as delicate as the kernels of the apricot fruit, and its belly, still thin, give it a very graceful figure. It was a girl, as Uncle Pan had hoped, a girlish cow, and appeared embarrassingly shy. Uncle Pan fetched a piece of an old cotton quilt and dried her carefully with it. She did not stir at the touch, as though she understood that he was her mother's great friend, her faithful companion on the farm. 'I love you, my baby!' Uncle Pan said, tenderly smoothing her hornless head.

O Ran brought in a jug of soya-bean juice, and poured it out into a basin. Uncle Pan held the liquid to the nose of the mother cow. She sniffed at it instinctively, still with her eyes closed. A little later, she lifted her eyelids and gazed at the milk-like juice with a knowing nod and then sipped at it. But soon she remembered something. She turned round. Her baby was lying close by her side. She gave up the drink and started licking the girl. The baby kept her eyes half open, soothed by the touch of her mother's long, soft tongue.

'This little cow will be yours, Uncle Pan,' my mother said with a smile. 'And she shall be called Miss Pan, to carry on your name.'

'Thank you, ma'am,' Uncle Pan said with a cheerful grimace. 'That is the most proper thing to do.'

'Then let's go and burn incense to our gods for the safe delivery, for the exceptional beauty of the baby's looks.'

'Yes, we must,' Uncle Pan said.

And we went into our hall to perform the service of thanksgiving at the ancestral altar.

After the service my mother heaved a sigh of relief. So did Uncle Pan. The child was born, just one day before the Small New Year. This lucky coincidence seemed to forecast a happy year to come. Both my mother and Uncle Pan looked at each other significantly for a long while, and they smiled a contented smile in spite of themselves. Uncle Pan was the happiest man in the world, indeed.

'But Uncle Pan,' my mother said, 'do tell me what has happened to you all these days. I was terribly worried about you.'

Uncle Pan's radiance immediately gave place to pallor. His lips began to twitch nervously, but he could not let out a single word. All he did was to stare at my mother like a fool. Then, embarrassed he hung his head.

'You must tell me what has happened to you, Uncle Pan,' my mother insisted, 'or I'll go on imagining things in a terrible way. Did you come across any highwaymen?'

Uncle Pan looked up. My mother's face was overshadowed with suspicion and anxiety.

'No, ma'am,' Uncle Pan talked at last.

'Then what is it that held you up?'

'Well . . .' Uncle Pan could not go on. His face went now red, now blue.

'Well what?' my mother asked in a persistent voice. 'Don't hesitate to tell me everything, Uncle Pan. It is not your fault if anything's gone wrong.'

'It *is* my fault, ma'am,' Uncle Pan said, raising his head. 'If I had taken your advice, there would have been no such incident.'

'What incident?'

'Well, it is a long story,' Uncle Pan heaved a profound sigh, like Lao Liu starting the narration of a tragedy. 'It happened against my will, *absolutely* against my will.'

'What do you mean by *absolutely*?' My mother could not help breaking into a smile, amused by his dramatic emphasis of the adverb.

'When I got to the county city,' he said, 'I discovered to my great astonishment that the town was emptier than ours. I was told that a much larger army of defeated troops had plundered it when they were passing through. They even went to the villages. They took away practically everything, even the cows for ploughing and sweet potatoes. All the village people in the neighbourhood have become destitute. Ma'am, how can there be a market under such circumstances? So Aunt Chrysanthemum's yarn began to worry me. I couldn't come back home to return it to her. You saw it yourself, ma'am, she was so helpless when she gave it to me. So I paced up and down the street and did not know what to do with it. Then a dark fellow with squinting eyes, who was following me all the time, suddenly spoke to me, "Old Uncle, what are you worried about?" See? The fellow had a very sweet tongue.'

Uncle Pan paused to clear his throat. Then he went on:

'I said that I was worried about the yarn of a neighbour, a beautiful woman. The fellow burst out into a fit of laughter, saying, "Do cheer up, old Uncle. There are so many nice creatures in the world. We cannot afford to worry too much about them. Let's go to the old millet-wine shop and have a cup together." See? He mistook my trouble for sentimental affliction.'

'But did you go?' my mother interrupted.

'Well,' Uncle Pan lowered his eyes and blushed, 'well, I did not want to, but somehow I could not resist . . . You know what I mean. So I went with him to the shop. The fellow ordered two cups of wine and two plates of peanuts to accompany the drink. He seemed too kind to be a friend. I said to myself secretly, "Uncle Pan, be careful with your money!" So I dug my fingers into my girdle to see if the money was all right. It was safe. Then I finished the drink. After that I wanted to go. But the fellow stopped me, saying: "Do please let me treat you to another drink! All men within the Four Seas are brothers, old Uncle." See? His tongue was so sweet!'

He made another pause to clear his throat again.

'So I had another cup of wine. It was a much bigger cup. It was really wonderful stuff, by the way. The more I drank the more I liked it. So I said to him, "Since you've been so kind as to give me a cup, you must let me treat you to one." See? I meant to be polite, but he really accepted it. So I had a third cup. Then suddenly I somehow felt my head turning. It seemed that I was flying into the clouds, that I had grown two large wings, that I could flap them easily and happily like a bird. It was a very nice feeling, ma'am. I was so happy, as if I were having a nice dream. You know, I haven't had nice dreams for years. I liked the dreamy feeling. And I had another cup. Then I felt my neck soft as wool, so that it could not stand up. At the same time I felt my head as heavy as a block. So I closed my eyes and fell into a sleep.

'When I woke up, I gave a yawn, a very big yawn, with my arms spread apart. I felt a little chilly. To be frank, ma'am, I felt something wrong with my clothes. When I looked round I found my girdle gone. And when I looked on the table, Aunt Chrysanthemum's parcel of yarn had also disappeared. And that dark fellow, too, had vanished. I began to realize that he had stolen the yarn and my girdle, which contained the money for the shopping. He left even without paying for the drinks, for the barman demanded cash from me.'

'Didn't you protest to him that he should be responsible for the theft, since it took place in his shop?' my mother said, her face pale.

'Of course I did. Ma'am, I am not so stupid. But . . .' Uncle Pan suddenly fell silent.

'But what?'

Uncle Pan's lips began to tremble. Uneasily he lowered his head. At last he managed to add:

'But the shopkeeper said that he had thought the dark fellow was my friend and that he did not ask for pay beforehand because he thought I was a gentleman. He said that he treated all his customers as gentlemen. He said that I should have known there were thieves and pickpockets everywhere since the looting of the town, because everybody was destitute. You know, he was a clever fellow. He knew how to talk. I could not argue with him. So I gave him my inner jacket for the drinks.'

'But how could you be so absent-minded, Uncle Pan?' my mother said in anger. 'Tomorrow will be the Small New Year. Our God of the Kitchen is going up to Heaven to report his duty to the Supreme God. We haven't got a single present for him yet. What shall we do then? And it is so late . . .'

Just then a voice from outside interrupted my mother. 'Uncle Pan! I have heard you're back and your cow has given birth to a beautiful baby. Congratulations!' It was from Aunt Chrysanthemum, who was now stepping in with a broad smile, so broad that the fine skin about her small nose wrinkled up, squeezing the powder off and thereby showing the freckles.

My mother immediately put on a smile to welcome her. But Uncle Pan still held his head low, and his whole body started shivering with fear. Aunt Chrysanthemum looked at him calmly, and she became suspicious of his silence. After a moment she asked: 'Uncle Pan, have you sold the yarn for me?'

Uncle Pan looked up, without a word. Aunt Chrysanthemum's smile was now replaced by pouts. Her brilliant eyes began to be veiled by a film of tears, which made them more radiant, but sad. She had, of late, grown very sentimental over her difficult plight arising from the general depression in town.

After remaining wordless for a while and secretly watching Aunt Chrysanthemum deep in thought, Uncle Pan became fidgety and restless. His lips trembled nervously like two pieces of tinfoil in the wind. He wanted to say something, but had not the courage to bring it forth.

'Aunt Chrysanthemum,' my mother said, trying to explain the situation for Uncle Pan; 'something untoward has . . .'

'No!' Uncle Pan suddenly burst out, interrupting my mother's words. 'No! Nothing untoward has happened to me, Aunt Chrysanthemum. I've *sold* your yarns, and for a good price too! Wait a minute. I'm going to fetch you the money.'

And Uncle Pan dashed into his room. In a moment he rushed back, with a tiny bundle in his hand. It was something wrapped up in rags. He undid it carefully, layer after layer, until at last a few notes showed out, side by side with a few silver coins. 'Here is the money,' Uncle Pan said to Aunt Chrysanthemum. 'That is all I could sell your yarns for.' And he handed it to her.

Aunt Chrysanthemum's sad face broke into a smile. She took the money and in order to show that she had complete confidence in him, did not count the sum. 'Thank you very much, Uncle Pan,' she said and at the same time nodded to my mother. 'You've helped me greatly, both of you. I must go. I haven't prepared anything for our God of the Household yet. All of us are in a terrible hurry for this New Year, aren't we?' And she left, her steps nimble and light as though she were dancing.

'Is it your own money?' my mother asked Uncle Pan after Aunt Chrysanthemum had gone.

'Yes, ma'am,' Uncle Pan answered in a depressed tone. 'I've saved it since our cow was pregnant. I meant to buy a silver bell for the baby cow.'

'Oh, my poor Uncle Pan!' my mother exclaimed. 'I'll buy you a silver bell as a New Year present, then. Don't you worry about the pick-pocketing any more, Uncle Pan. Let's forget about it.'

'You're so kind to me, ma'am,' Uncle Pan said, almost breaking into sobs. 'You've always been kind to me. I'm a foolish man, ma'am, hopelessly foolish.'

And his legs began to shake violently. It seemed that he wanted to fall on his knees. But somehow he turned round and dashed into his room like a thief himself. He threw himself on his bed, burying his head in both hands, his chest rising and falling with heaves.

In the evening of the Small New Year we had nothing to offer to our God of the Kitchen and the Household, who was going to depart for the Heavens for a short rest. My mother was very unhappy, because she had been hoping that the god would make a good report about our household to the Supreme God so that the latter could bless my father with success in his business. But she was not quite sure what kind of version the god would give of us now. Perhaps he might say to the Supreme God that our kitchen was not clean enough, that we used too much foul language in the house, that we did not wash ourselves regularly, that we had not been kind enough to our neighbours, and many other bad things. Any unfavourable account of us might incur punishment from the Supreme God in the form of illness or frustration.

'We must ask for forgiveness and understanding from our Kitchen God,' my mother murmured to herself, her head low.

But after a moment of thoughtfulness she lifted her head and added, 'It will be much nicer if He doesn't make any report at all. Let's hope that He is lazy this time.'

Then she became thoughtful again, staring at the ground, her hand fingering her hair. Suddenly she added, 'Oh no, our God of the Household is an energetic god!' And she beckoned to O Ran who was coming out from the kitchen, and asked her in a whispering voice: 'O Ran, have we still got some barley sugar?'

'Yes, mother,' O Ran answered, 'we've still a lot. But it has melted away into molasses and is very sticky.'

'Good!' my mother said, and further lowering her voice, added, 'Bring it out, will you? I want to offer it to our God of the Kitchen before He goes up to the Heavens.'

O Ran took it out from a cupboard. My mother put it on a green plate, iridescent with ancient glaze, and placed it on the altar in the kitchen. After having kowtowed three times she remained on her knees, and, bending low, started to pray:

O, our most venerable God of the Kitchen and Household, we are most grateful to you for your service to us during the past year, guarding us from pestilence and catastrophe, from crime and sin. We are glad to see that at last you can have a break in the Heavens, enjoying the food of nectar and the company of saints. But we are sorry, O, our most venerable God, not to be able to offer you the things you need for your journey, owing to the unforeseen miserable circumstances we are in. All we can present to you is a little barley sugar, which, I am sure, you would take without bad feeling, so kind you have been to us. O, our most venerable God, accept our best wishes, and Happy New Year to you.

After the prayer my mother remained bowing before the altar for a good quarter of an hour. Then we left the kitchen and sat in the living-room quietly, waiting for the god to eat our offering – the melted barley sugar. By midnight we thought that the god must have ascended into the heavens. We yawned. We thought of going to bed. But before we said good-night to one another my mother remarked regretfully: 'I hope our god will not discover our trick. The sugar is so sticky that his lips and teeth will be stuck with it into such a mess that he won't be able to make a report at all. However, this is only an emergency measure. We should not do such a thing to an old man like him next time.' And she heaved a long sigh.

We went to bed with troubled consciences, hoping for the best.

CHAPTER 6

One evening, towards the end of the second month of the year, as we were chatting by the fire, we heard an outburst of barking. The watchdogs seemed to be attacking somebody. Their yelps vibrated in the air like the lamentations of some wronged ghost. Uncle Pan, who was puffing at his long pipe, became restless. He stopped sucking and listened with great attention to the noises. They went on for a good quarter of an hour. Gradually they lapsed into whines and then diminished to spasmodic whimpers.

'I seem to hear footsteps outside,' he said, getting up. 'Cases of stealing cows have been frequent lately. I must have a look at ours.'

Our cowshed had a separate entrance, although it was attached to Uncle Pan's bedroom. Since he had had his pocket picked in the county city, Uncle Pan had become thief-conscious, nervous all the time about burglary. He knocked the tobacco ash out of his long pipe, and then tiptoed to the door. Having quietly lifted the bolt, he walked out, leaving the door ajar. For a moment there was quiet, because most of the dogs had flocked to him and were sniffing at his feet. He was standing under the eaves, looking around in silence. A few minutes later he coughed. There was still no particular sound. And he walked to the edge of the village, followed by Laipao, to see if there was anything in the trees.

As he disappeared into the darkness a new wave of barks arose. We heard Uncle Pan calling out: 'Who is that?' But there was no answer. We were suddenly seized by a chill that made our hair stand on end.

We kept an awed silence, listening with fear for what might be happening outside. A gust of wind blew the door open and put the lamp out. We shivered, not with the icy gale, but with the sudden ghostly darkness that enveloped us. We could see the night, as deep as the sea. There was no moon, no star. In the room the only noise was our breathing, which we could perceive distinctly. We seemed even to hear the beating of our pulses. Amidst the primitive hush the door creaked. Somebody was closing it. Then footsteps: one heavy and the other light. And somebody was striking a match. A weird flame trembled in the darkness, travelled to the lamp, and there was light. It was Uncle Pan who gave us the light. Behind him stood a stranger, a young man.

Uncle Pan turned round after he had lit the lamp, looked at my mother with a timid eye, and said apologetically, 'Ma'am, I've brought this young gentleman home.' He pointed to the stranger. 'He was trembling in the woods. He was starving. He said he hadn't had anything to eat for two days, he had travelled many miles, he was tired and exhausted. He said he was a friend of Mintun and your elder son, so I took him in. He doesn't look like a thief. Are you a thief?' He turned to the stranger and addressed him.

The young man did not answer, but shook his head.

Uncle Pan remained motionless but his eyes blinked nervously at my mother. She did not exhibit any surprise or fear, but studied the stranger quietly, scanning him from head to foot. The visitor was quite young. Perhaps he was barely twenty-two. His face still had a babyish look, with his rosy cheeks and chin, and he had long hair, which had apparently not been cut for weeks. Nor did he seem to have been shaved. However, there was not much beard there: only a few sparse whiskers stuck out. His long neck with a protruding Adam's apple, which was very pointed in shape and on which the skin was terribly thin,

89

gave the impression that he had really been starved. He hung his head all the time, rather shy.

'Young guest, sit down, please,' my mother said at last, in a mild voice.

Uncle Pan woke up from his coma and moved a chair for the stranger. 'Sit down, young man,' he said, showing his gum in a broad smile, where the front teeth were missing. 'Ma'am is a kind woman. When she says a thing, she means it. Sit down, young man.' He pulled the stranger down to sit on the chair. He was happy that my mother did not reproach him for bringing in the unknown man in the dead of night.

'Young guest,' my mother said again as the stranger seated himself in the armchair with his chin resting on his hand and his elbow on the arm of the chair, 'tell me your honourable name and the honourable place you were born. You don't look a local villager, I can see that.'

The young man raised his head and let his hand rest on the arm of the chair. He gave a suspicious glance at my mother. He was thinking of something, and was also swallowing saliva, for his pointed Adam's apple was moving up and down. Then he said, 'Ma'am, I have no name. I have forgotten where I was born. But can you give me something to eat and drink? I am awfully hungry and thirsty.'

'Certainly we can and with great pleasure, too,' my mother said, and, turning to O Ran, who was stupidly gaping at the stranger, she added, 'O Ran, we still have some noodles, haven't we? Warm them and make a pot of tea! Quick! The guest needs food.'

And O Ran went to the kitchen.

The stranger lowered his head again, his chin nestled in the palm of his right hand, and closed his eyes. He did not want to talk. His long, straight hair spread over his forehead, which was broad and smooth; and the end of his long gown fell on one side, showing his trousers and feet on the other. His trousers were long and tight, unlike the kind of loose, roomy lower garments we wore in the village. They must be a part of some uniform, probably student's uniform, for he looked very much like a student. He had on a pair of straw sandals. The toes showed out of his worn-out socks.

'Poor boy, he can't possibly be a thief or a bandit,' my mother said in a whisper to Uncle Pan. 'He is too young and too gentle for that. He still needs a mother's care!'

The stranger seemed to have dozed off, for he did not move a bit. He did not even lift his head to look when my mother made this remark about him. He was genuinely tired.

O Ran emerged from the kitchen, holding a large bowl of boiled noodles in her hands. She placed it on the table and then went back to fetch tea. Uncle Pan shook the stranger lightly by the shoulder. The young man started, got up and made for the door as if in great haste to escape, still rubbing his dreamy eyes with his fingers. But Uncle Pan stopped him, saying: 'Where are you hurrying to? Want to go to a lavatory? The food is ready for you.'

The stranger stared back for a moment at Uncle Pan, who looked sincere and simple as always, and said quickly, 'I am sorry! I am sorry! I was just having a terrible dream.' Then his gaze turned to the table. The noodles were sending up a cloud of steam, which veiled the feeble light of the oil lamp. 'Thank you for the food, friend. You are a real comrade!' he said. And he seated himself on a bench at the table. The terror that had shadowed over his youthful face now disappeared. He rolled the noodles on the chopsticks and, holding his face upward, his mouth wide open, let the food slip on to his tongue. Then he sipped the soup, making a gurgling sound. After that he gave out a sigh of satisfaction. 'Good food!' he said. 'It warms me up.' Indeed, a few drops of sweat began to stand out on his forehead.

'Perhaps a cup of wine will help you get rid of the fatigue,' Uncle Pan said. And without waiting for an answer, he fetched him a cup of barley wine. In order to warm up the cold atmosphere he held the wine to the light of the lamp, and the light immediately descended on the cup. A flame of tremulous green began to dance on the surface of the liquor. 'See? It's good old wine,' Uncle Pan said, blew off the flame, and handed the cup over to the stranger.

The young man sipped hard at the cup, producing a dry noise. 'Good stuff! You're really my comrade, you're so understanding!' He became talkative and lively.

'Tell me, young guest, your honourable name and the honourable place where you were born,' my mother repeated the old question again, but in a more friendly and familiar tone. 'You see, I am so interested in you.'

'Thank you, ma'am,' the stranger said. 'You are indeed very kind to me. But I have a very insignificant name, which a lot of people don't like to hear. So please don't bother about it. As to my birthplace, it is not very far from here. It is in the next county.'

'How exciting!' my mother cried. 'Is it the county where the first what-d'you-call-it – president or emperor – of our Republican dynasty was born?'

'President,' the stranger corrected her. 'His village is not far from mine.'

'Say! You're an extraordinary person then!' Uncle Pan put in a remark and poured him another cup of wine to show his admiration for him.

'Are you related to him?' my mother asked.

'Not particularly. But my grandfather went to the same village school as his father, so I was told.'

'Then you're an important man, my young guest,' my mother said, her eyes dilated with wonder and admiration. 'You have such good connections.'

'No, I'm only the son of a simple farmer like this comrade.' He pointed to Uncle Pan, who was now completely dumbfounded by the story. 'It's true, my father was a classical scholar, but as the Imperial Examination was abolished in the republic he took to farming. My elder brother is now a regular farmhand. I used to help him plant rice and glean corn left on the field until I was fifteen. Then my Uncle, who was a clerk at a foreign factory in 'The Big City' down the river, took me to the provincial capital and sent me to a modern school there.'

'So you *are* a student?'

'I *have been*, yes.'

'It must be very expensive to be a student in such a big town as our provincial capital. It is just on the opposite side of 'The Big City' across the river, isn't it? Things must be very dear there, too. Of course, now that the Imperial Examination has been abolished, one has to get degrees from modern schools in order to become a government official. Are you going to be a magistrate or a member of the provincial government?'

'No, I'm not going to be either. I know my family saved up their money to send me to the school, hoping that I would be an official some day. But now I don't want to be one.'

'It sounds very strange, indeed,' Uncle Pan said. 'It's nice even to be a village head.'

'Not at all. You see, I found out later on that they wanted me to be an official in order to set them free from poverty and toiling day and night on the overworked land. They expected me to scrape as much money from the people as other government officials could, so that we could buy more land and become landlords, forever free from fear and want.'

'That is the most natural thing to do,' my mother commented. 'I wish I could find enough means to send my sons to modern schools.'

'But I don't want to improve the conditions of my *own* family by becoming a government official.'

'Then what did you go to the school for?'

'I wanted to learn to be an engineer.'

'Engineer? What is an engineer?' Uncle Pan asked with surprise and curiosity.

'An engineer is a man whose job is to plan and supervise building roads, railways, factories and machines.'

'But that is not a scholar's job!' my mother remarked in astonishment. 'It's manual labourers' work. A scholar's occupation is to rule as a magistrate or a minister. People never go to school to learn about manual labour. Never!'

'But I did! And many people of my age still do,' the young stranger said proudly, as though he were the forerunner of a new thought. 'Our country is an old, backward country. We are far behind other countries in science and industry, and for this reason we have been the object of foreign invasion and exploitation. We must become a modern state like any other Western country, so we must have good engineers.'

'What do you mean, Mr Guest? I don't quite understand you.' My mother was puzzled. 'Is our country no good? How can we imitate the foreign barbarians! They don't believe in ancestors, in the Gods of the Kitchen and Household, in the God of Earth, let alone such beautiful manners as we have in our daily conduct. How can we possibly be like the barbarians!'

The stranger seemed to want to laugh, but his face was too serious to permit any light-hearted expression. And in a vague way he seemed even to take pity on my mother for her ignorance, for he said, 'Ma'am, you don't know the real situation. You've lived in this mountain village for too long, just like my parents. The foreigners are no barbarians. Their little men are as good as any of us. Only their armament merchants are terrible. They collaborate with our warlords and corrupt officials to squeeze us dry.'

Now my mother was really flabbergasted. Uncle Pan started scratching his bald head, wondering at the reliability of the statement. We had never heard such things before. It really sounded like fiction. How could foreign merchants exploit us? We had not even seen a single one. 'I think you're mistaken, Mr Guest,' my mother said, with a serious face. 'They are barbarians, all right, because they don't believe in our gods. But it is Landlord Chumin who makes the peasants miserable by increasing land rent steadily every year.'

'Yes, it is Landlord Chumin,' Uncle Pan echoed. 'Do you know Landlord Chumin, by the way? He is a man with a huge odious beard. But please don't repeat my words to other people, I beg you.'

The stranger nodded to himself, saying 'Yes, certainly I've heard of him. He is a most ruthless tiger!'

'You're right!' Uncle Pan agreed, encouraged by the visitor's sympathetic comment. 'And he bites people right into the bones. He is even fond of such old bones as our schoolmaster Uncle Peifu's!'

'Uncle Pan!' my mother shouted, winking at Uncle Pan.

'Don't be afraid, ma'am,' the stranger said, watching my mother warn Uncle Pan with her winks. 'I'm not going to denounce you to the old tiger, because I am not his "running dog". Uncle Pan is absolutely right. He is a real proletarian, with an instinctive hatred for the exploiting class. But people like Landlord Chumin are only a part of the game, mere cogs in the whole machine. There are, as I've said, warlords and rotten officials and foreign armament merchants, who co-operate with one another to suck our blood dry.'

As he went on talking his voice grew fiercer and fiercer as though all these people he mentioned had been his mortal enemies. His face turned red, blue veins stood out on his temples, and his hands clenched. 'That's why I have even given up engineering,' he said. 'We can't build up railways and factories while these rotten people are still in power and the masses in poverty. We must have a new, efficient administration before we can talk of any national reconstruction!'

He broke almost into slogan-shouting with his loud voice, which frightened us all. Besides, we did not understand what he was talking about. So my mother diverted the conversation by asking:

'Mr Guest, you said that you knew my elder son. How did you get to know him? He was not a student. Certainly he did not go to your school.'

'Certainly he did not,' the stranger said in a matter-of-fact voice. 'But we are great friends, no, great comrades! I know everything about him. He was betrothed to a poor girl when he was little, wasn't he? But . . .' Suddenly he paused, conscious of the presence of O Ran, who had been listening to him with great interest. He looked at her uneasily. Meeting his gaze, O Ran unhappily bent her head with great embarrassment. My mother also glanced at her uncomfortably. There was a queer silence. The only sound was made by Uncle Pan, who was nervously knocking the ashes from the bowl of his long pipe against the leg of the stool he was sitting on. Finally, O Ran got up, and having cleared the bowls and chopsticks off the table, she vanished into the kitchen.

'Is she *the* girl, ma'am?' the stranger asked after O Ran had disappeared. 'I am so sorry! She looks a real proletarian! But like every girl from the poor classes her face is so hopelessly damaged by poverty . . .'

'Oh, don't talk about that, please,' my mother implored the visitor. 'She has had a hard fate. But do tell me how you came to know my son so well. It is so interesting. You seem to know so much about him!'

'Ma'am, I do know a lot about him – that is why I stopped at this village this evening. He gave me the address. I met him in an evening class which was operated by his trade union and where I taught the history of Chinese Social Evolution. I saw him almost every day. Ma'am, during the past four years I've devoted myself entirely to the education of the working people. They haven't got as much chance to improve themselves as I do. So I went to the class every evening and helped them with all that I could. Your son was very intelligent and worked hard too. We used to have private discussions after the class. He proved a genuine intellectual of the working class. His interpretation of our modern history, of the strategy of the revolution in an old-fashioned country like ours, seems to me even much more correct than Mintun's. Of course, Mintun's background is different, he being an out-and-out proletarian.'

We all stared at him, agape. He was so voluble in his speech, yet we could not understand a single word he said. His phraseology was so new to us that it sounded like quotations from some foreign Bible. But Mintun's name aroused our interest. We had not heard about him for years. People even thought that he might be dead.

So Uncle Pan asked, half in doubt, half in surprise, 'Do you really know Mintun?'

'Of course I do, very well indeed,' the stranger said.

'Does he go to the evening class too?' my mother inquired.

'No. He has long passed that stage. He doesn't have to, anyway. He has been the nucleus of the movement.'

'What do you mean? A nucleus? What is a nucleus?' Uncle Pan was confused.

'Oh, I am sorry!' the ex-student said, with a flicker of nervousness in his eye. 'I shouldn't tell you such things. But you're a born comrade, Uncle Pan, I believe. I trust you won't repeat my words to anybody. I tell you everything because I cannot resist the temptation of the frankness and honesty of a proletarian like you. Anyway, he is no longer in China. He has gone abroad.'

'What do you mean?' my mother, who had been absorbed in the unexpected, revealing dialogue, suddenly started. 'Was he kidnapped by foreign devils and smuggled to their country in potato bags as a coolie to build railways and factories? Poor Mintun! He shouldn't have left the village. No gold on earth is easy to find.'

'No, ma'am!' the stranger corrected hastily. 'There was no such smuggling business. They want no Chinese. The place Mintun went to was the fatherland of the working masses of the world. He is now doing research in a university there.'

'What? Has he become a learned man?'

'Yes. He is a learned man, a scholar of the poor people.'

'What do you mean?' Uncle Pan asked with surprise. 'I don't understand you, Mr Guest. How can poor people be scholars? They have no time, no money. They have to work all day long.'

'But poor people can become scholars now, with the help of the poor people's fatherland,' the stranger explained. 'And only poor people make good scholars. I know Mintun had a dreadful time: he earned his living in the big city first as a rickshaw-

97

puller, then as a newspaper vendor, and finally as a railway workman. But thanks to these hardships he at last became class-conscious and made an excellent proletarian fighter. That is how he got elected by his trade union as a candidate for the advanced study of proletarian theories at the capital of the poor people's fatherland.'

Uncle Pan's eyes, as well as his mouth, opened wider and wider, thrilled by the stranger's incredible story. After the young man had finished his speech, Uncle Pan suddenly blurted out: 'What do you mean by fatherland, Mr Guest, by the way? I have never heard of such a place. Is it a remote province of our republic dynasty, or a big village? Mintun's fatherland should be this village, where he was *born* and got *married*.'

The visitor's lips nearly ripped into laughter, but he restrained himself. Quietly he explained: 'The poor people's fatherland is a big country, much bigger than even America. He is our great neighbour, having a long frontier in common with us. The poor people there have built up a new dynasty, the proletarian dynasty, which works for the good of the miserable folk. They have set up a university for the working people of our country. It is called Dr Sun Yat-sen's University, in honour of the founder of our republic.'

'I see,' my mother said, becoming thoughtful. 'We village people never dreamed such strange things happened in the outside world. But tell me how long he'll have to remain there.'

'Probably he will be back very soon. He can't possibly stay there too long. We have so much to do at home.'

'How exciting!' Uncle Pan broke out enthusiastically. 'He will be back in the village an entirely different man then. I must tell Aunt Chrysanthemum! Poor woman, she has dreamed of him as a great man, and now her dream has come true. I must tell her!'

And he stood up, knocked the ashes out of his pipe, and made for the door, murmuring to himself, 'I hope she won't be annoyed with me for intruding so late in the evening. Such good news!'

'Who is Aunt Chrysanthemum?' the stranger asked surprised, and got up, too.

'She is Mintun's wife,' my mother replied. 'She has been waiting for him for years. Poor woman, she has practically wasted her youth in waiting.'

'No!' the stranger shouted to Uncle Pan, who had already lifted the bolt of the door. 'You mustn't tell her. I trust you're a genuine friend. You mustn't spread the news about our comrades, because our enemies are lurking everywhere in the district, seeking for the chance to destroy our movement.'

Uncle Pan stared back at the young visitor, puzzled by the words, which none of us could understand. 'What did you say?' he asked incredulously. 'I mustn't tell the news to his own wife, who has been so faithful to him?'

'Wife or no wife, it is not my concern,' the young man said, his face set and his eyebrows knitted into a frown. 'But you must not tell anybody what I have said.'

'Why? I don't quite understand you, Mr Guest.' Uncle Pan widely opened his eyes, stupefied like a fool, standing against the door. 'Don't you bother about your own wife, who has waited for you faithfully through many a cold winter night?'

'No! That is only a personal matter. We have no time and energy to bother about it nowadays. We have a much more urgent task to accomplish.'

'Strange! The modern young people! They are strange!' Uncle Pan muttered to himself, scratching his old head with his stumpy fingers. 'I don't understand them. The world has really changed.'

'You will understand if you join the struggle yourself, old Uncle,' the visitor said, his voice quieter now, 'because you're basically a proletarian. But please do me a favour, don't tell anybody what I have said.'

Uncle Pan rolled his puzzled eyes at the young man, still doubtful about what he was saying. 'Well, well, I will not tell her,' he stammered, his throat gurgling as though obstructed with something heavy. 'I will not tell her,' he said slowly, with a heavy voice. 'I'll not tell her.' And he bolted the door again and moved unsteadily towards the bench he had been sitting on, looking blankly at the oil lamp.

To cheer him up, my mother said, 'Uncle Pan, perhaps we can *suggest* to Aunt Chrysanthemum later on that Mintun has been getting on very well in the outside world, and may come back to her soon.'

'But don't say a word about his going abroad!' the stranger warned, 'because the reactionaries . . .' Suddenly he dropped his voice, jumped up from his chair and raised his right hand to shade his ear to listen to a sudden violent surge of barks rising outside.

The renewed yelps aroused our suspicion. It was generally at this time of the night, when all our villagers would have fallen asleep, that burglary was committed. We looked curiously at our visitor, who was now all attention and whose eyes were staring searchingly and inquisitively like two lanterns. Presently we heard footsteps and a confused din of voices that sounded fierce and threatening, and the dogs began to whine and occasionally uttered cries of pain. They were being beaten up, apparently. It was not burglars or late vagrants, because people like them generally dared not beat dogs. Our strange visitor lowered his hand, and turned deadly pale.

'Ma'am, have you got a place to hide me? They are coming to search for me!' he said in a desperate voice. 'Help me, ma'am! Quick!'

My mother was absolutely taken aback by the sudden change in the situation. The visitor had lost all his composure and appeared childishly helpless like an orphan. Nobody could believe that he was the same person who had expounded theories so profound that none of us could understand them. 'Help me, ma'am! Help me, ma'am!' he urged, his voice faltering. 'They have been chasing me all over the place these days. They want to kill me!' The stranger was now only a child, talking as though in a nightmare, his lips quivering fitfully. His legs were shaking so violently that he might, it seemed, slump on the floor at any moment.

Amidst all this confusion Uncle Pan, however, was moved by the sight. He walked to the visitor, steadied him by embracing him with both his arms and said, 'Don't be afraid, my child. I am standing by you!' Meanwhile, the steps outside drew nearer and nearer and the yelps of our watchdogs rose higher and higher.

'Find me a place to hide, comrade! Find me a place to hide, comrade! I'm working for the poor people. I am not your enemy!' The stranger clung tightly to Uncle Pan as though the old farmhand were his father. 'I am your friend! You mustn't betray me!'

'What are you saying, my child?' Uncle Pan said confusedly, staring at the young man with a paternal look, meanwhile hugging him more closely. 'I don't understand you, my child.'

'Don't ask me, Uncle! Get me a place to hide!'

And the steps outside stopped at our neighbour's door and we could hear repeated and furious knocks. And there was shouting: 'Open the door, please! Open the door, please! This is the gendarme from the county government!'

'Uncle!' the young man uttered a subdued scream. 'There they are! There they are! They will kill me! They have killed dozens of young people like me!'

'Come along, my child!' Uncle Pan loosened the stranger's hold, his face livid; and he made for the back yard through the kitchen. 'Come along! I'll find you a place to hide.'

The young man followed Uncle Pan and disappeared into the darkness. We heard our neighbour's door open and a hubbub of steps walking in and then intimidating commands and shoutings. My mother put out the light and told O Ran and me to go to our bedrooms. O Ran was shivering all over, unwilling to go alone, so my mother instructed me to go to O Ran's room instead, to keep her company. 'Oh, how dreadful!' O Ran said to me as we walked into her room. 'Do you think they are bandits?'

'I don't know,' I said, and in order to appease her fear, added,

'But you don't have to be afraid, O Ran. They wouldn't harm you even if they were bandits.'

'Why not?' she retorted, her fear suddenly replaced by curiosity and displeasure. 'Has my face become so ugly as to attract no attention from them?' She was thinking of her pock-marks: she was always nervous about this aftermath of her smallpox. I could not make an answer.

We remained quiet in the room. We heard Uncle Pan's footsteps coming out of the kitchen.

'Where have you put him?' was my mother's voice.

'In the straw in the store-room attic,' was Uncle Pan's answer.

'Then he will be suffocated to death, the pile is so heavy and thick.'

'No. I placed him by the wall near the window. He could even spy things outside. The straw just covers him from view.'

'Fantastic young man, he nearly frightened me out of my senses . . .'

My mother was interrupted by steady rapping on our door outside. 'Let us in! We have an inquiry to make!' The shout sounded like thunder, hasty and threatening. O Ran shut her ears with both hands and stood against the walls in a corner. I put out the light and pressed my eyes against a crack in the door so that I could see what happened in the sitting-room. I was worried about my mother and Uncle Pan.

Uncle Pan opened the door. Five gendarmes burst in. They were armed with shining pistols, red tassels hanging from the holsters like flowers. Each had a storm lamp in his hand, which cast weird shadows on the floor. One of them walked up to my mother, who was now standing by our dinner-table, shivering, and he asked her:

'Have you seen a young fugitive this evening?'

'No, sir,' my mother answered in a trembling voice. 'I haven't been out since the sun set. I haven't seen anybody, not even a beggar.'

'But that fellow disappeared in this direction – many people who have seen him told us so,' the man explained. 'He can't possibly have gone any further, since it is so dark.'

'I haven't seen anybody, sir,' my mother said. 'It is so cold. We shut our door before it gets dark.'

'Are you sure?'

'Sure, sir. I haven't seen anybody.'

'Very strange, indeed,' the questioner murmured to himself, lowering his head in profound thought. 'He is really a fox, the young bandit. We've been on his track for three days and yet cannot catch him.' Then he turned to Uncle Pan and measured him for a few seconds and said, 'Have you been out this evening, old man?'

'Yes . . . no,' Uncle Pan answered in a babble, his lips twitching convulsively.

'What do you mean?' the inquirer asked suspiciously, moving a step nearer to him.

'I never go out in the evening, because our story-teller, Lao Liu, is now having a holiday. But tonight, after supper, I walked out to the corner of the cottage and passed a bladderful of water. It took me ten minutes. Exactly ten minutes. I didn't mean to be so long. But it is so cold, you see?'

'Did you see a young fugitive then?'

'No, sir. Not a single human shadow. But our watchdog came to me. He sniffed first at my feet, and then at the steaming water I passed out.'

'He is a hopeless idiot,' another gendarme came up to the questioner and said, pointing to Uncle Pan; 'Don't waste time on him.'

Then the questioner turned to my mother again.

'Ma'am, do tell me honestly if you have seen any stranger in the village this evening,' he said. 'He is a leader of bandits. If we let him loose, he will never give people any peace. He hasn't been at his activities for long in the western district of the country yet, but he has given us enough headaches already. Soon he will foment trouble in this place, I am sure. So it is to your own advantage to give us any information about him you can.'

My mother looked wonderingly at the questioner with her staring eyes, trying to make out what he meant. There was a threatening silence for a moment. Suddenly she pronounced in a decisive voice: 'Sir, I haven't seen any bandit. I assure you, sir, I haven't seen any *bandit.*'

'We are poor villagers, sir,' Uncle Pan joined in. 'Bandits would not visit us. Only burglars come occasionally, but they never let themselves be seen.'

'So that rascal has escaped again!' the interrogator said to one of his men. 'He hasn't come to this village. He is a real fox!'

And they turned round and disappointedly walked out of our house, leaving the door open, without saying goodbye. Both Uncle Pan and my mother stood speechless, blank, staring at the darkness outside, into which the gendarmes disappeared like a nightmare. A draught swept in, waking Uncle Pan up from his day-dreaming. He slammed the door and then sat on a bench and lit his long pipe. O Ran and I came into the room, she still shivering with fear. We stared at one another, and had nothing to say. Nor did we want to go to sleep. We just sat, watching the flame on the oil lamp grow weaker and weaker and listening to the occasional squeaking of mice in the rafters. Suddenly the cock started crowing, its cock-a-doodle-doo vibrating and trailing in the quiet air like the last note of a soprano singer at the end of a performance.

Uncle Pan stood up, knocked the ashes from his pipe and walked into the store-room. In a minute he came back with the strange visitor. The young man looked like a scarecrow now, so many straws were attached to his hair and clothes. But he appeared quite happy. He had a childish smile on his lips. Uncle Pan said to him repeatedly, like an old father, 'My young guest, don't be afraid. They are gone, gone a long time ago.'

'I know, Uncle, I've heard everything. And I saw them from the window marching away on the highway. Thank you, Uncle, you're a born proletarian.' Then he turned to my mother and continued, 'Ma'am, I thank you. I heard what you said to the gendarmes. You're really kind. You're like my own mother. I'll remember you forever. I must go now.'

'No!' my mother said. 'It's so cold and dark. You must have something to eat.' And she glanced at O Ran and went on in a low voice, 'My child, be so good as to make the guest another cup of tea.' O Ran went to the kitchen without a word.

'It is awfully sweet of you,' the stranger said to my mother, sitting down. 'I have given you too much trouble already. I am sorry.'

'But tell me,' my mother said anxiously, 'are you really a bandit?'

'Do I look like a bandit?' the young man retorted.

'No, cerainly not!'

'Then I am not a bandit.'

'Then what are you?'

'I've told you, ma'am. I have been a student, but am a patriot, because I'm now grown up. I want to make our Republic a new and happy country. It is too old, too old, and too weak, pitiably weak . . .'

'Then why do they call you a leader of bandits?'

'Because I organize the poor peasants to fight against the old corrupt regime and its adminstration. The warlords and their defeated troops that passed through the district have squeezed every ounce of oil out of the poor people, and the landlords and merchants bled them literally white. I taught them how to overthrow these real bandits and seize the power for themselves. So the landlords and their running dogs want to kill me and destroy the movement. But it is too late. It has spread out like wildfire and is active right under the nose of the authorities of the county city. They are afraid of the poor people, who are so many, ma'am. Poor people are always the majority.'

'So that is what you are doing!' my mother said in surprise, her eyes downcast. After a moment she lifted her head again, and scanned the young man, and asked, 'Is this also what my son and Mintun have learned to do?'

105

'Well,' the young man hesitated. Nervously he looked at my mother, whose face now appeared panic-stricken. 'Ma'am, I don't know. All I know of them is that they are very patriotic.'

'Patriotic!' my mother murmured incredulously to herself, lowering her head and lost in thought.

O Ran came out of the kitchen, with a tray of tea and cakes. The visitor sat down at the table and helped himself to the food and drink. He ate in great haste, for the cock had crowed for the second time. After he had finished his tea he stood up, said he must go, and warned us not to tell anybody about him as the enemy would punish even those who had sheltered him. Uncle Pan picked off the straws that stuck on his hair and clothes, and my mother wrapped a small parcel of cakes for him in case he felt hungry. Then quietly they crept to the door and pulled it open carefully without making any noise. Our watchdog Laipao sneaked in and sniffed at the stranger. But Uncle Pan muzzled its mouth with one hand and caressed his back with the other, so it became very quiet. The stranger slipped out of the door and disappeared into the dawn.

'What a queer young man!' Uncle Pan commented on the departed visitor. 'He sounds like a second Mintun. By the way, ma'am, shall I tell Aunt Chrysanthemum all that I have heard about her husband?'

'No! Not a word!' my mother said. 'We must forget about the incident altogether, because somehow it makes me very unhappy.' She paused thoughtfully for a second. Then she went on in a monologue, 'The world has become so strange now. Yes, it is a strange world.'

The wick on the lamp began to gutter as though echoing my mother's words, and its feeble light started flickering unsteadily. The oil was exhausted. But no one seemed to be in the mood to pour in more, all being paralysed by the heavy atmosphere that was around us. We watched the wick complain drily and the light on it die and the darkness close in. Finally the threatening quietness was resumed. And in the silence a small, pitiable snore piped up rhythmically, in defiance of the stupendous

tranquillity. It was from our hard-working O Ran, who had
dozed off from sheer fatigue.

CHAPTER 7

The miserable winter had at last gone, together with the two unpleasant memories that had haunted the dreams of our villagers many a night: the land agreement which was renewed at the New Year with Chumin, and by which the land rent was unprecedentedly increased by twenty per cent; and the poor presents which we had offered to our God of the Kitchen on the eve on his departure for heaven. The sun was now very bright, and its fresh warmth dispelled all our apprehensions and even brought us new hopes.

It was now the season of sowing. And whenever it was a matter of sowing, we not only got busy, but also became incredibly cheerful. We carried out the little sacks of seed rice from our lofts, and unpacked them and poured out the contents on the drying mats and exposed them to the smiling sun. Then we packed the seed up again into small bundles, the size of water buckets, and tied them on to long ropes and lowered them into the pond below the village square.

Three days later we pulled the bundles out of the pond by the ropes. Water trickled out, making small pools on the ground; and small fish and shrimps jumped out of the straw and swam in the puddles, believing that they were still in the pond. Hens and cocks gathered about with watchful eyes, waiting for the water to be soaked up by the earth, and then they pecked up the aquatic creatures one by one like grains of corn. Our villagers watched the deeds of aggression and brutality with perplexity and amusement. After the water had been drained from the straw bundles they were taken to the threshing floor, already warmed by the sun. We undid the packs. The rice had already sent out tiny, whitish sprouts. The weather had been exceptionally warm for the season.

There was a smile on the face of every villager. Even Benchin our Taoist priest smiled whole-heartedly, although he farmed no land. But the most cheerful of all was Mao Mao. He had farmed more land from Chumin this year than ever before. He knew this would be a hard business as the terms were very harsh, but there was no alternative. As his wife had a good appetite and a spacious stomach, he must produce more food; or else she would desert him as she had announced in public many times. And Mao Mao was a tender-hearted man. This step, extremely intelligent on her part, would tear his heart to pieces. But now what a promising spring! It might be a bumper year. And how lucky he was that, thanks to his wife, he had signed the contract for more land.

Like all the farmers in our village, Mao Mao carefully sowed the fine seed in one of his best rice fields. Again like everybody else he sang a song while sowing. He had seldom sung songs since his marriage. Sometimes when he did sing, his notes sounded sad. But now he had a cheerful tone. The vernal breezes seemed to help in lifting the sprouts of the rice. Soon the surface of the water field turned from opaqueness to yellowish-green, and then from yellowish-green to blue. The rice had grown three inches high.

What our villagers hoped for above all was rain, a good downpour. And one evening, before supper, clouds suddenly gathered over our heads, hanging low on the tops of the tall maple and oak trees about the village; and before we went to bed, there was the first rumble of thunder in the distance, and then a crash, followed by a heavy shower. It lasted for two hours, but the eaves kept on dripping till next morning.

Now every field was filled with water, fresh water from the sky, even the terraces on the hillsides were glittering with the life-giving nectar. There was nothing more to wait for. The rice had grown up and had to be planted. So everybody went out to the fields. Mao Mao had more fields to work on, so his wife, She-crow, had to help him. She was really marvellous as a rice planter. She took off her shoes and socks and rolled up the ends of her trousers knee high. Her feet were gigantic and her legs thick. She dipped them into the water at first gracefully like a grand lady, but soon she became her old self when Mao Mao handed her a bunch of the young rice. She bent her back and planted it as fast and dexterously as any skilled farm labourer. Thanks to the many mouths the prolific wine-maker had to feed, She-crow had been trained as a regular farm hand since she was fourteen.

In a week's time all the planting was done in the valley. For the time being, the only thing to do seemed to be the singing of the old silly song. So the air began to vibrate again with the tremor, heavy accentuations, and the trailing refrain:

> Aiyu, aiyu, ai-aiyu, ai-ai-yu, ai-yo-ho-ho . . .
> Aiyu, aiyu, ai-aiyu, ai-ai-yu, ai-yo-ho-ho..
> This yellow earth gave us rice in spring,
> And in autumn, soya beans and sweet potato . . .

While humming the age-old air, our villagers waited confidently for the rice to grow and for the rain to nourish it to maturity. Their expectations were always fulfilled, because there were always regular rains in the spring. One could even tell by the calendar when a shower would come and how long a drizzle would last. But this spring, so far, there had been only one downpour. The days were getting hotter and hotter as the sun increased its heat. And the heat evaporated the water in the fields.

There was no more rain to counteract the evaporation.

The sky smiled all the time, without a trace of cloud or frown. This made us nervous and suspicious of the intentions of the god in heaven. Did he want to send a drought to the poor farm hands in the valley? Yes, sometimes he did. Generally once in ten or fifteen years there was a rainless spring, which killed all the planted rice. Who could tell that this year might not be one of those drought cycles? Our villagers began to get cautious and packed up the light-hearted silly song. The valley became quiet under the smiling sun.

There was no frown in the sky, but there was one on everybody's brow. A heavy load began to weigh on our heart, intensifying its gravity every minute. It had less to do with drought itself than with the God of the Kitchen and Household. The memory of our impoliteness towards this Old Man was revived: it had been revealed that we were not the only family who had treated this kind god to the sticky barley sugar, as many others had done more or less the same thing. Whenever we thought of this incident we turned pale. Was the drought a form of punishment meted out to us by the Supreme God, who had heard of our wickedness and meanness? Mao Mao firmly believed that this was the case, based on the following fact which he himself confessed: he had managed to scrape enough money to buy a box of cakes as the New Year present for his God of the Kitchen, but She-crow was so fond of eating that she could not resist the temptation and consumed the delicacies before they were offered to the god.

Such contempt and neglect of the Household God as manifested by She-crow, the housewife, had certainly infuriated the Old Man, no matter how kind He might be. All our villagers, having heard the story, unanimously concluded that Mao Mao's God of the Kitchen must have acted as a ring-leader and agitated all the Household Gods of the whole village to send a joint unfavourable report to the Supreme God so that the latter withheld the rain from us mortals.

'But what has been done cannot be undone,' said Benchin our Taoist priest on the village square. He had been neglected just like the God of the Kitchen and Household and was on the verge of starvation.

'What shall we do then?' Mao Mao asked anxiously, his brows knitted tightly together.

'Give your wife a heavy spank on her fat bottom!' was the priest's reply.

Mao Mao had no more comment to make, his head dejectedly hanging. He could not possibly do that because he was a chicken-hearted husband. Besides, he was rather afraid lest Benchin really meant it. He had always regarded this lanky man as his dead rival before he got married. This frustrated old bachelor might take the present opportunity to mean something else.

Uncle Pan, who was also on the square, chuckled at the priest's suggestion. But glancing at the sad face of Mao Mao, his heart grew soft. He tried to reconcile them, saying,

'Benchin, let's be serious. You're a holy man. You ought to reveal to us what's wrong with the God in Heaven. You ought to tell us what we should do to remedy the situation. Mao Mao was perfectly sincere in asking you the question, you see.'

Benchin was flattered by being qualified as holy. He rolled his short-sighted eyes several times and then put on a mysterious air by composing his face and puckering up his lips. Finally, giving a disdainful glance at Mao Mao, who still held his head low, he said:

'What shall we do? Well,' he paused as soon as he had begun, giving another contemptuous glance at Mao Mao. 'Well, we ought to repent our sins. We should, from now on, try to make a good impression upon the Supreme God so that he may change his mind. We have been too greedy and brutal. We kill pigs to eat, for instance, She-crow went so far in her greediness as even to eat up the present to the God of the Kitchen. We must prove to the Supreme God that we won't do the same thing again, that we won't kill any pigs for food, that we will regard all animals, especially pigs, as equally his creation. Only this can move the heart of the Old Man. Of course, you have henceforth to pay due respect to the Taoist priest, too.'

'Yes, *sir*,' said Mao Mao bashfully, nodding his head in assent. It was the first time he had addressed his old 'rival' as 'sir'.

Mao Mao was now willing to do anything, to call the Taoist

112

by any title, or even kneel in front of him, if only he could save the rice. He had planted too many fields. The failure would ruin him completely. It would mean that he might not only have to mortgage his only property, the cottage, to Chumin in order to pay for the promised rent, but also lose his darling wife, for she certainly would run away if she had not enough to fill the 'bottomless pit' – her stomach. It seemed, however, the failure was certain. The water in the field had been dried up by the hot sun and the blades of rice were withering.

Mao Mao was driven mad by the prospect. It seemed to him that the cynically smiling sun was going to fall, burning up everything with its fire, everything, including himself. He began to get fidgety, like an ant on the rim of a hot frying pan. At last, however, an ingenious idea struck him – he was always a master of innovations. He jumped up from his chair, in which he had been sitting opposite his growling wife, dashed to the pig sty, tied the three-month-old hog up with strong ropes, dressed it in his New Year gown and put it in an armchair. He carried the chair on his shoulder as if for a parade, marching about the village officiously, and shouting to anybody who happened to be in his way: 'Aside, please! His Excellency the Pig is passing!'

'You are absurd, Mao Mao,' said Lao Liu our story-teller, who saw him carrying the animal like a grand seigneur while the ungrateful creature kept on grunting desperately in the rather tight New Year gown.

'Why? You're an intelligent person, aren't you?' Mao Mao retorted righteously. 'I'm now treating the pig not only as an equal creation of God, but even as a lord. This ought to move the heart of the Old Man.'

'Ridiculous! Absolutely ridiculous!' our story-teller refuted the statement. 'You eat pork whenever there is some, even stale and rotten stuff. And now you want to change the judgement of the Supreme God and his punishment on you at the last minute by this childish gesture. I think he is not so foolish as you suppose him to be.'

'But I'm sincere, Lao Liu. I'm perfectly sincere,' Mao Mao

explained. 'To tell you the truth, I haven't tasted any meat since last winter.'

'Nonsense! Who could have after the town was ransacked? I have not even tasted a drop of meat soup.'

'I've not even tasted a drop of bean-curd soup, let alone the delicious meat soup.'

'Didn't you get some soya bean to make a little curd for the New Year?'

'Yes, but my wife, you know . . .' Mao Mao became bashful, lowering his head.

'Know what?' Lao Liu pressed Mao Mao. He was always interested in things concerned with She-crow.

'Well . . .' Mao Mao's face reddened and could not go on.

'Well what?' our story-teller pressed again.

'Well . . .' Mao Mao's head was now downcast, shy and uneasy like a three-year-old. 'Well, she consumed it before it got condensed into curd.'

'Really? How exciting! Tell me a little more about it, please. She is a wonderful character, indeed!'

While they were chatting away, standing face to face, like two philosophers, the pig in the chair began to get impatient and struggled against the gown and the ropes with which it was bound. As the conversation reached the most interesting point and called forth all their attention, the pig suddenly had its own way and manged to loosen itself from the bonds, slipped out of the chair, and fell on the ground headlong. Its nose hit an angular stone and began to bleed very hard, and one of its legs was seriously twisted. The sharp scream the wounded animal sent out sounded like the funeral bugle.

'This is how you treat a pig like a lord!' Lao Liu said, pointing to the disfigured creature, now wallowing in dust.

As there was no point in going on debating, Lao Liu turned round and went away. But Mao Mao remained standing there, staring at the poor pig like an idiot. The unexpected fall not only annulled entirely his attempt to please the Supreme God and the respect he had tried to show to the animal, but also tore his only presentable garment into pieces.

Indeed, the whole thing proved a complete failure. The sun went on blazing and the field cracked and the rice finally died to the root.

It was really too bad. The drought killed not only rice, but also all the vegetables. Nobody in the village had any reserves of food. As the famine covered a great area, there was practically no place where people could go and make a living. Some districts were even worse because people had been starving there ever since the previous winter as a result of large-scale looting by the passing vanquished troops. They even tried to come to our district in quest of relief. Already we saw on the highway refugees from other places, with crying children on their backs and emaciated watchdogs behind them.

Mao Mao was depressed all the time. In the morning he would sit on the top of a hill that overlooked the valley, and stare stupidly at the cracked fields and the dead blades of rice, now reduced almost to ashes by the sun. In the afternoon he would perch on the low wall of his pigsty, which was now empty because the poor hog had died after the fatal fall from the armchair. His mind was now again haunted by two things: the rent which he must pay to Chumin if he wanted to continue farming the latter's land next year, drought or no drought; and his wife, who was complaining all the time that she was terribly hungry. But she did not desert him, strangely enough. She stuck to him like glue.

As everybody expected, Chumin sent his steward to the village one day early in July. He was a fearful fellow, with a huge bushy moustache, a pair of thick dark brows like two broomsticks and a voice as loud as a broken gong. His words had always to be carried out and his appetite satisfied. He was worse than the God of the Kitchen and Household, because his mouth could never be sealed by barley sugar. And he did not make reports about the farm-hands to his master only once a year, but any time he felt like doing so. So his shadow was like an enormous bank of cloud that darkened the whole village.

Mao Mao was shivering with fear when this gentleman stepped into his cottage. But to Mao Mao's astonishment, this time he did not shout like a broken gong, nor did he demand a bowl of hot meat soup before he started his business. He said quietly,

'Mao Mao, I know you are very hard up this year, as every farm-hand is, in the district. According to the contract you ought to pay the full rent in kind, right after the season. But Chumin is a kind-hearted man as you know. He doesn't want to drive you into a corner as many other landlords would do so as to make their farm labourers turn into rebels at the risk of their poor lives. Chumin is not that sort of person. He gave me authority to promise you that you may pay the rent after the next planting season. But you must guarantee that you will be good and obedient to his orders.'

'Yes, sir, I guarantee that I will take whatever orders he gives me,' said Mao Mao with a bow.

'Good. Now then, I want you to mortgage your cottage against the pay next year. You can still occupy it and will forever occupy it when you clear up the rent. Look here, this is the agreement.'

Mao Mao signed the new agreement to mortgage his cottage without a word. And the steward went away to do the same thing with other villagers who farmed his master's land. During the last famine Chumin had got hold of all the land in the district and, during this one, all the cottages. But the transaction did not seem to trouble Mao Mao much; on the contrary, it helped to relieve him of a great crisis. He had now only one worry: the feeding of his dear She-crow. And this was not so terrible to him as the loss of his land.

But people other than manual labourers, people like Lao Liu, Benchin, and Aunt Chrysanthemum, were really hard put to it. Aunt Chrysanthemum especially. Spinning had become a hopelessly obsolete trade. As there was little market for food,

116

there was still less market for yarn. Her spinning-wheel had to stand still. And she was such a delicate person that she could not possibly do other, heavier work. She had, therefore, to feed on diluted gruel and to give up the beautiful habit of powdering her small freckled nose. Thus she looked paler and paler, fragile and weak like a heroine in one of Lao Liu's tragedies, pining away in poverty with the thought of her adored man.

The sight grieved Lao Liu intensely, who had been closely watching for her eventual change of mood under the new circumstances. One afternoon when she went to the river to draw water for supper, she collapsed on the sand, her tender hand with fine fingers still holding the handle of the bucket, but her eyes pathetically closed. She looked at that moment like Kwang Yin, the Goddess of Mercy, in her gracefulness, but a starved refugee with her pallor. Lao Liu, carried away by sympathy and love, lost no time in giving her help. He lifted her up in his arms and carried her home like a sweetheart of her dreams, her slender arms dangling helplessly in the air.

It was when she was placed in an armchair in her house that she came back to consciousness and opened her eyes. She gazed confusedly at Lao Liu, who was attending her, standing by like the page of some legendary lady. This vacant wondering stare of hers enchanted the heart of our story-teller. He had never seen her in such a state, childish and pathetic, yet extremely sweet.

'How did you get here, Lao Liu? Am I dreaming?' she asked with an innocent blink.

'No, you're not dreaming, *my dove*,' Lao Liu replied in a soft voice, addressing her with the sweetest title he could think of. 'You collapsed on the sand and I carried you home. Oh, my poor Chrysanthemum! You weighed on my arms as light as a feather. You're withering away like a rose in the malicious sun. My heart bleeds for you!' Lao Liu now talked like a lover, with exclamations and stresses as well as smiles and gestures.

'What did you say?' Aunt Chrysanthemum questioned,

117

opening her eyes wide. 'Lao Liu, your choice of words is inappropriate!'

'I did choose the most appropriate words, my sweetie,' our story-teller explained, his eyes drinking in the astonished stare of her brilliant, dark pupils. 'I adore thee. I have been dreaming of thee like a princess, like a flower, like a butterfly amidst a cluster of peonies. I have coined many a story about thee, although thou didst not know that. Thou hast been my inspiration, my Goddess of Arts . . .'

'Are you telling a story?' Aunt Chrysanthemum interrupted him.

'No, I'm pouring out my heart at thy feet.'

'Then go away, please!' Aunt Chrysanthemum said in a serious tone, showing him the door. 'I have in my thoughts only one man, a *manly man*, you see?'

'I know what you mean, Chrysanthemum,' our story-teller babbled, his face already blushing. 'But Mintun may not be a *hero*, or else he would have written to you.'

'I'll wait for him for ten years, twenty years, even thirty or forty years, whether he writes me or not!'

'Really?'

'Leave me alone, Lao Liu, please!' Aunt Chrysanthemum urged him in an imploring voice.

Lao Liu's face went from crimson to a dead pallor. His lips trembled fitfully. 'O, you're a heroine! A real heroine!' was all he could say, but his voice was hardly audible. Dejectedly he dragged his heavy feet across the doorstep and turned in the direction of his cottage. On the way, he kept on saying to himself: 'She is a living legendary heroine. She is a living legendary heroine. She is exactly the type of person I have created for my stories. But ah, what a mistake I have made! I have made the beautiful females worship heroes, and yet I am not one . . . No, I can't possibly be a hero!'

For the first time Lao Liu began to feel sad about his much-admired profession. As he approached his door, he exclaimed, like a madman, in a loud voice, so loud that practically all our villagers could hear it: 'It gets me nowhere, this business of story-telling. It can't win me the heart of the woman I adore. What am I going to do? What am I going to do? I can't go on coining legendary tales now. Aunt Chrysanthemum has withdrawn the inspiration from me . . .'

But the greatest disillusionment he received was when Aunt Chrysanthemum had to leave our village for the town where she was to earn her living by a new profession.

During the rainless summer she had exhausted all her resources. And she was too respectable and shy to ask for help from anybody. My mother occasionally gave her a bowl or two of rice. She accepted it at first as a token of friendship, but later on she declined, realizing that it was a kind of charity. 'If Mintun knew that I was living on charity, what kind of woman would he think me?' she explained to my mother when pressed hard to accept the gift one day. 'I must keep up his name. You see, he is a man of strong character, he doesn't like such things.' She was talking as though she had seen Mintun the night before. 'Some day he may come back a warrior with medals or a repectable gentleman. How awkward it would be for him to find that I've lived like a beggar!' she added.

Thus she was languishing away all by herself. But her reputation spread abroad as that of the most virtuous woman in the district, a woman who supported the ancient morals in the storm of dearth like a bulwark against an evil wind, a woman who stood as a pillar for the traditional social order.

One day she was visited by a guest, an important man – the landlord Chumin's steward. It was indeed a grand occasion when this gentleman came specially for the purpose of talking to her. He was all smiles and had reduced his voice, usually like a broken gong, to a pleasant chirp. He said:

'Chumin has heard much about you, Aunt Chrysanthemum. You are the finest member of this society, the exemplar of our ancient civilization, while all the others, unable to bear the hardship, are becoming either thieves or rebels, you stand alone as the most law-abiding citizen in defiance of evil influences. He wants to help you.'

'I don't want any help, sir,' Aunt Chrysanthemum replied.

'No, excuse me, I was awkward in my wording,' the steward apologized, smiling like a sunflower. 'He wants your help.'

'What do you mean? How can a poor woman like me help such a grand personage?' Aunt Chrysanthemum asked in great astonishment.

'You can, Aunt Chrysanthemum, and no one else.'

'How? I don't understand you.' Aunt Chrysanthemum stared at the visitor, stupefied.

'You see . . .' the steward lowered his voice, smiling bashfully this time. 'Landlord Chumin has bought, well . . .' he paused for a moment, 'out of charity, of course, a starving girl of fifteen for a concubine. You see, Chumin is a kind-hearted man, he does not want to treat her just as a third wife, but as a daughter. He wants to have a virtuous chaperon to keep her company and educate her in all womanly good qualities. You are the ideal person to do this. He has a great admiration for you.'

Aunt Chrysanthemum blushed a little, but was flattered. 'Well . . .' she murmured indecisively.

'Don't hesitate, Aunt Chrysanthemum,' the steward urged her. 'Mintun would be pleased if he knew that you were to inculcate a young girl with your virtues and that you were going to establish such good connections for him as those with Landlord Chumin.'

'But he did not like people of Chumin's society,' Aunt Chrysanthemum said hesitatingly.

'That is only because he was hard up then,' the steward explained. 'When he becomes an *important man* himself – I'm sure he will – only people of Chumin's status deserve to be his friends. Please think it over, Aunt Chrysanthemum. I'm trying to help you.'

'Perhaps you are right,' Aunt Chrysanthemum said, and became thoughtful, lowering her head. 'But . . .'

'Don't but . . . Aunt Chrysanthemum. Hesitating doesn't

help. You are paving a highway for Mintun by your connection with Chumin.'

Aunt Chrysanthemum raised her head and said, 'All right then, if it be so, I'll try. But I don't want to accept charity. I mean I don't want to receive a higher wage than I deserve.'

The steward beamed up with fresh smiles, his small eyes squeezed into threads. 'That can be done very easily. I can assure you that you will receive *no charity*, that you will *get no more* than a chaperon does. I can absolutely assure you of that by my word of honour.'

So the whole thing was settled.

Two days later Aunt Chrysanthemum went to town as chaperon to Chumin's concubine.

This unexpected development shocked Lao Liu. He was sad as well as curious. He followed her steps to the town and, using all his good connections with the townsfolk, managed to discover that the so-called concubine was but an ignorant village lass, whose father was one of Chumin's poor peasants. This wretched farm-hand had no cottage to mortgage to his master and therefore had to sell his daughter to him, simply as a hot-water bottle to warm up the old fellow's bed in the approaching winter nights. 'Chaperon! What a defiling title for such an elegant woman as Aunt Chrysanthemum!' Lao Liu said angrily as soon as he heard the story.

Ruminating over this development, day and night, however, Lao Liu gradually became disappointed with Aunt Chrysanthemum as a legendary heroine of beauty and virtue, of gracefulness and elegance. This disappointment upset him so much that he nearly went mad. Often we saw him pace up and down on the village square, his head hanging, his eyes downcast, murmuring all the time like a Taoist priest chanting a sutra: 'How vulgar! To look after the hot-water bottle of an old skunk, who has nothing cultured or beautiful but dirty money squeezed out of the poor peasants. And yet this adored woman of mine has bowed to this dirty money and flatly rejected my admiration and love. I don't have to be a hero then! O, how stupid I have

121

been. I simply have to be a landlord – that's all. What's the use of beautiful stories? What's the use of poetry, of refined language, of a golden voice? O, what a fool I have been! I've wasted my youth on an empty dream . . .'

No one in our village could understand him. All we could understand of what he said was the title 'old skunk', which sent chills down our backs. People began to avoid him as he paced up and down the square, murmuring like a complaining brook. And he became lonely, and also restless. He began to wander about in the neighbourhood, all by himself, like a vagrant minstrel. He began to make friends with the refugees, who were found everywhere, in the valleys and on the highways.

He suddenly came to us one evening and asked Uncle Pan a question: 'Uncle Pan, is it difficult to be a fighting man?'

'What are you talking about, Lao Liu?' Uncle Pan asked, rather astonished.

'I mean, is it difficult to be a fighter?' Lao Liu said seriously.

'Well, I don't know.' Uncle Pan scratched his head.

'But you came from the North, my old uncle, where every young man would go to the army when he had nothing to eat.'

'Ah, that I can't tell you, but I don't like soldiering. I don't like the fighting business at all. I'm a farm-hand, you see. That's why I never return to the North.'

'I see.' Our story-teller fell into a dilemma, his face sullen.

'But my dear fellow, what makes you ask such a question? You have been such a mild, poetic person.'

'I want to destroy land and landlords. I want to do away with all the ugly things.'

'Ah!' Uncle Pan started and uttered a cry of surprise. 'That is rebellion. Where do you get such ideas? They are dangerous.'

'Many people are now talking like that. I have heard many refugees talking that way. I think they are right. The landlords have robbed them of everything, their inherited land, their cottages and even their daughters. Yes, even Aunt Chrysanthemum, who doesn't farm land at all.'

'What are you saying, Lao Liu!' Uncle Pan exclaimed with

alarm, putting his fingers on his mouth. 'I really don't believe my ears. But be so kind as not to talk too loudly. If landlords should hear it they would withdraw all the land from the peasants. You don't have to be afraid, I know, because you live by your mouth. But think of the poor farm-hands! If they lose the land, perhaps you won't be able to go on telling stories either.'

'I don't want to tell stories any more, in any case.'

'Ah, don't say it too soon.'

'I will not!' Lao Liu said angrily. But instantly he lowered his head unhappily, and his voice grew feeble and thin like a murmur: 'Oh, I've no longer any story to tell. My inspiration is gone, forever gone!'

And he stared blankly at the ground like an idiot, hypnotized by a vacant day-dream. Our watchdog Laipao sneaked in, sniffed at his feet, and whined at him hostilely for a moment. But he did not stir. Uncle Pan lit his pipe, and the flame of the light shrank each time he sucked – a phenomenon which always attracted my attention. But Lao Liu did not seem to have seen it, although his eyes were wide open. He remained speechless until at last Laipao pulled playfully at the edge of his long gown. Then he woke up. Without saying goodbye he walked out with dejected steps.

'Lao Liu!' Uncle Pan called from behind in a warning voice, 'don't talk of dreadful things about land-owners in public, or they might hear you!'

Lao Liu did not answer.

But Uncle Pan's warning proved futile. Lao Liu was not the only person who talked of landlords in this impulsive way. Many other people, including some in the town itself, started talking of the same thing. The landlords certainly had heard of what was in the wind, for one day Chumin's steward again appeared in the village. He had now nothing to do with land. He wanted to make a speech in the village square and wanted all the able-bodied farm-hands to come to hear him.

He said, 'My dear friends, Landlord Chumin has been worried about you all the time. He knows that you have not got enough to eat, and he is very sad about it. However, we can't possibly have another famine next year. It has never happened in the past. So let's bear the hardship with good humour. What makes him most anxious is rather your safety. He has heard of many bad peasants who, under the agitation of seditious young people from big towns, have turned into bandits and tried to share others' property by illegal means and even force good farm-hands to join them. In a word, they want to ruin our traditional, peaceful life. I am sure that you don't want that. So Landlord Chumin and may other councillors of the Chamber of Commerce, for the general safety of our community, have planned to organize an Order Preservation Corps, to keep down those evil elements. I am glad to tell you that Wang the Lion has promised to undertake the job. But his men are not enough in number. We want more . . .'

He paused to give us time to think over the proposal.

Wang the Lion was the leader of a secret society, which had its headquaters in the mountains. His followers were chiefly thieves, burglars and pickpockets, famous for boxing, acrobatic feats and for superhuman endurance of hardships and physical strain. They used to roam about in the countryside and market places and rob travellers on the highway in the dark, but never harassed landlords and local 'celebrities' who connived at their activities.

'What do you think about it?' the steward asked. 'I hope some of you can join the Corps.'

There was no response. We looked at one another inquisitively, but without a word.

'I may further explain to you,' the steward went on, 'the joining-up won't harm your farm work, because by next spring, if there is good rain, we won't have to keep the Corps and you can all go back home to work on your land.'

A buzz began to rise in the crowd. Some muttered. 'No, we are not interested in soldiering. Only bad people become members of an armed force.' Others babbled, 'We are so poor.

We have nothing to be stolen or shared. We don't have to have protection.'

The steward's face gradually turned pale in spite of the hot sun. His lips were livid and shook in violent convulsion. But his hands were clenched. The sudden change of his expression imposed a dead hush among our stuttering peasants. Everybody was expecting a thundering voice, which was so characteristic of the steward. But, to our surprise, the sound that broke out from between his angry lips was quite mild:

'It is a wrong way of thinking, my friends, that you have nothing to lose. Suppose the bandits take away your ploughing cows, what would you do then when the spring comes? Don't misunderstand! Landlord Chumin's original idea is not exactly to put you in uniform. He has a charitable point of view. He wants to give you some job to do in order to pass the severe winter, because you will receive pay if you join the Corps. And it will be good pay.'

Still there was no reaction. Only cynical eyes greeted the speaker. Landlord Chumin always made promises, but never was in the mood to carry them out.

'What will you pay with? Rice or money?' A brave voice broke the silence. It was She-crow, Mao Mao's wife, who was standing by her husband in the crowd.

'Both!' the steward answered in a firm tone.

'Good!' she said cheerfully and clapped her hands with excitement. Then she turned to Mao Mao, and said in great earnest: 'Mao Mao, you must join the Corps! You must join the Corps! Oh, I can't bear the watery gruel any more. Mao Mao, if you really love me as you vowed to me the other evening, you must join the Corps.'

The cynical audience was amused by She-crow's candid confession about the watery gruel, and burst out into a fit of laughter, although the note was rather sad. But the steward was very serious. He waved his hands like two wings to quieten down the roar. After that he said, like a magistrate, 'She-crow is a sensible woman. I admire her for her clear judgement. I wish all the wives here were like her. Mao Mao, you must take her advice. I envy you for having such a good wife. I wish my wife were as clever!'

Mao Mao was confused by both the laughter of his fellow villagers and the enlightening lecture of the steward. She-crow, however, did not mind the uproar in the least, but kept on nudging him, saying, 'Join it! Join it! Mao Mao, I want you to join it.'

'Yes, sir,' Mao Mao said to the steward at last. 'I'll join the Corps.'

Mao Mao thus became a member of the Order Preservation Corps, and was the only member from our village. He went down to the town the next day, where the Corps had its headquarters.

We refrained from commenting on the event, because we felt a little sad about it. There never had been a farm-hand in our village who had gone away to earn a living by soldiering, and with such a disreputable band as Wang the Lion's. Benchin, our 'old bachelor', kept on saying to anyone he met, 'Thank my Lord Lao Tzu that I haven't married the greedy She-crow! Otherwise I would have to be at the beck and call of such an ignorant boor as Wang the Lion.'

'I sympathize with you,' Lao Liu would echo him. 'But I consider it more disgraceful to receive dirty pay from Landlord Chumin.'

CHAPTER 8

The hot summer passed away together with the drought, leaving behind dusty earth and cracked fields. And the sun grew paler and paler. The sky hung low and looked grey and dull. Sometimes a few patches of cloud appeared, sailing westward. As they moved on they caused gusty puffs, and there was a kind of chill in the air. Later on, the puffs developed into wind, which stripped the trees bare. The leaves danced frantically in the air like bees without a queen. We began to feel cold, to put on more clothes and to desire more food. And all of a sudden we discovered many wanderers in the neighbourhood, without enough clothes and without enough food.

Never before had we seen so many vagabonds in the district. We did not know where they came from. The highway was dotted with their haggard forms: women with babies on their backs, men with bundles of rags on their shoulders, and old grandfathers followed by watchdogs hanging out their tongues. They all headed for the town as though the place were a sort of Mecca – and then they fell back and scattered about in the valleys and hills like locusts. When we asked them why they did not go to the temple in the town for shelter, since it was now so cold, they all replied that the Order Preservation Corps repulsed them each time they tried. Then we asked them why they did not go back home and they said unanimously that it was not worth doing because the whole region was devastated by the severe drought, together with the heavy looting by the passing vanquished troops. They talked with a coarse accent and we knew that they came from the district near the county city up in the big mountains. We sighed in sympathy with them, but could not help them in any way. They did not bother to visit our village, either, because we had no food.

One day, however, one of the vagabonds turned up in our village, a woman. She looked quite shabby, but not like a beggar, for her face was not so pale and thin as that of most of the destitute people. She wore a shabby jacket and a pair of faded pink trousers, which were so long that one could hardly see her feet. She wandered about, peering this way and that like a thief. Our watchdogs gathered about her and yelped at her like wolves. She waved a long bamboo stick against them. But each time she raised the weapon, the dogs jumped at her. Laipao even tore the hem off her skirt, and threatened her with another attack, baring his fangs. She uttered a cry of alarm, as dry and coarse as a man's voice.

She backed off as the dogs continued pressing in on her, goggling at her with their blood-shot eyes. At last she approached our house. Uncle Pan was then brushing the young cow – she was now grown up and looked sleek and graceful like a lady, but still as bashful as a girl of sixteen. Seeing the woman approaching amidst the dogs, he put away the brush and shouted at Laipao: 'Get away! You shouldn't attack a stranger close to our own house.' Laipao seemed to understand the words for he remained standing and only whined quietly instead of barking. The stranger slumped on to a bench in the porch and heaved a sigh of relief. Then she said, laying aside her bamboo stick, and staring at Uncle Pan,

'Thank you very much, Uncle! Had it not been for your interference the dogs would have torn me to pieces.'

Uncle Pan scanned her sceptically and asked, 'Are you a beggar?'

'I'm a refugee, Uncle,' the stranger replied and took off her kerchief, revealing a head of short hair. 'But if you want to give me something to eat I won't refuse.'

At that moment my mother came out, with a pair of socks

she was mending in her hand. She stopped at the doorstep, taken aback by the sight of the stranger.

'Don't be afraid, ma'am,' the woman said and stared back at her. 'I am only a refugee. I have travelled three days and three nights and had only four meals. So I am very tired. I just want to have something to drink and a little rest. That is why I came into the village.'

'Oh, I see,' my mother said slowly, still wondering suspiciously about her. 'Are you going to some monastery to be a nun?'

The stranger started and her eyes stood out like two balls. 'What makes you ask that question, ma'am? Why should I be a nun?'

'I was just wondering why you cut your hair so short like a man's. All nuns crop their hair, don't they?'

'Oh, yes!' the visitor agreed, with a sigh of reassurance. 'But I don't want to be a nun – I am not as hard up as that yet. I have cut my hair short simply because I found doing it up every day a nuisance. This is a year of famine, isn't it? I'm not in the mood to care about my looks. Well, ma'am, could you give me something to drink?'

'Yes, wait,' my mother said. Then she shouted to O Ran, who answered immediately from the kitchen, and told her to prepare a cup of tea and some cakes for the stranger. In a few minutes O Ran came out with a tray. She said there was no cake in the kitchen but that instead she had warmed a piece of barley bread. The stranger sipped at the tea, which was very hot, making a terrific sucking noise. Then she munched the hard barley bread like a cow, her protruding eyes searching furtively in every direction.

'Ma'am, this village seems very quiet,' she mumbled, as her mouth was stuffed with the food.

'Yes, it is a quiet village,' my mother replied, and started mending the socks. 'People don't have much to work on now.'

'Then how do they make a living? Do they all join the Order Preservation Corps?'

129

'No, not many. We have only one person in the village who has become a member of the Corps.'

'Really?' the stranger exclaimed in a surprised tone. 'Don't you like it?'

'No!' Uncle Pan put in a remark, 'we are simple farm-hands. We don't like fighting business.'

'You're right, Uncle,' the stranger nodded. 'But don't you want protection for your property? There are so many of us refugees about. Aren't you afraid?'

'Why should we be afraid?' Uncle Pan retorted. 'Our conditions are almost as bad as yours.'

'Well said, Uncle. I agree with you.' The woman winked. 'To be quite frank, I think the Order Preservation Corps is only good for the townsfolk. They don't let us come into the town even though we promise not to demand charity in rice. They certainly need protection, because they are afraid of us.'

'Why should they be afraid of you?' Uncle Pan asked.

'Because we are poor and numerous. They are afraid that we may storm the town and take their stock of rice.'

'That is certainly illegal, if not robbery.'

'You're mistaken, old Uncle, if I may say so.' The strange woman made a grimace with a forced smile. 'Is it legal for the landowners to increase the land rent by twenty per cent in a year of famine? What do you say to that?'

Uncle Pan scratched his head irresolutely. He could not answer the question.

'I come from the district of the county city,' the woman went on. 'We had a much worse drought there. Even the bark was scorched off the trees by the sun. Still, the landlords insisted on raising the land rent. When my poor husband protested against the increase, they called him a bandit and beat him to death . . .'

'Had you a husband?' my mother suddenly interrupted her, and ceased mending the socks. 'How sad, if that is the case.'

'What do you mean, ma'am?' the stranger protested in a loud, furious voice, which had now an entirely masculine tone. 'Can't I have a husband? Do I look so hopelessly ugly?'

'Oh, no!' my mother said apologetically, but she could not stop wondering at her hair, which was grotesquely short. 'I beg your pardon. You look extremely nice.'

The stranger became quiet, trying to smile in answer to my mother's compliment. Then, resuming the artificially high-pitched voice, she turned to Uncle Pan and said, 'What do you say to that, old Uncle, that rich people should increase the land rent in spite of the famine?'

'I think they are wicked,' Uncle Pan answered. 'Their conscience is wicked.'

'Now you've seen the point, Uncle,' the woman gave him a smiling squint. 'So, you see, it is absurd for *us* poor people to serve in the Corps for the rich! By the way, what is the name of the person in the village who is a member of the Corps?'

'He is called Mao Mao, She-crow's husband. Do you know She-crow, the first of the wine-maker's nine daughters?' Suddenly Uncle Pan paused and his nervous eyes stared at her with suspicion. 'Why do you ask for his name? Did you ever know him?'

'No. I am only interested in people's names,' the stranger explained, trying to laugh. 'You see, I am a fortune-teller by profession. Perhaps I can earn a cup of tea by telling his fortune so that he may know how to take care of himself. It is a dangerous job to be a member of an armed corps, you see?'

'Yes, I quite agree with you.' Uncle Pan was moved by the words. 'That is why I stick to farming, which is a peaceful and honest profession.'

'Yes, you are right, but tell me, is Mao Mao a rich peasant or a poor one?'

'Oh, a poor devil! And he has become poorer and poorer since he married that greedy wife!'

'Then why should he join the Corps which works against the poor people? He must be a traitor to the poor, a dirty watchdog of the rich!'

'Why, guest!' my mother suddenly exclaimed, putting away

the socks, her face pale and her eyes wild, 'you talk like that fugitive who visited us one night!'

'Fugitive!' the woman shouted with fright. 'Fugitive? Whom do you mean? Who is he? Has he been to this village? I don't know him. No, no, no! Oh, no! I have never heard of any fugitive,' she said repeatedly and nervously to refute any knowledge of the person my mother carelessly mentioned. But her face grew perceptibly white and looked scared. Her eyes searched surreptitiously around, and she fidgeted.

My mother put her hand to her mouth, alarmed by the warning and nervous stare Uncle Pan was giving her. We were reminded of the persecution by the gendarmes of the student who sought shelter in our house. And the thought sent tremors through my body. My mother also shivered. Her lips quivered like two pieces of tinfoil. Finally she stuttered:

'O, guest, I was talking of something past, long past. It has nothing to do with the present.'

'I see, I see,' the woman jabbered like a idiot, still staring at my mother unbelievingly. Then she went on in an absent-minded manner, 'I thank you very much, ma'am, for the good tea. You're the kindest woman I've ever met. I was so tired that I could not move my feet. Now I feel fine.'

Neither my mother nor Uncle Pan could carry on the conversation. They glanced at each other knowingly in a secretive way. The woman was confused by this. She took a comb from her pocket to smooth her hair, in order to pretend unconcern. But the comb did not help, because her hair was short and straight. The more she combed, the more she became embarrassed. Then she tried to dust her long, red trousers with a handkerchief. As she beat them hard, her feet were revealed – a pair of enormous feet. She started hysterically at the sight herself, and got up.

'Thank you, ma'am, for your hospitality,' she said, Then turning to Uncle Pan she went on, 'Thank you, too, Uncle, for your kindness. I must go. I've an engagement with a group of refugees to tell their fortune in the evening. They want me to explain to them when they can go back home in the big mountains.'

And she went away. Uncle Pan accompanied her to the end of the village, guarding her from the watchdogs. My mother remained in the porch, looking stupidly at the bench the woman had been sitting on a moment ago. She was unable to mend the socks any more. Something was weighing heavily on her mind. The woman talked so much like the student who had taken refuge in our house one night. Could they be of the same crowd and for that matter could she also know my elder son?

The sun was touching the peak of the western mountains. The sky seemed to be falling lower and lower. Many patches of cloud began to gather into a gigantic lump hanging oppressively overhead, and threatening to break into pieces and to fall on our roofs. The air was now heavy and saturated. Sparrows looked out furtively from the eaves and chirped nervously. A storm was brewing. It was always like that after a long drought; a heavy shower that kept the dry earth busy sucking the liquid of life for hours and hours.

We went to bed very early that night, knowing that it would be cold. When it was barely ten we began to hear pattering drops on the roof and violent cat calls. Then a gust of wind swept over, making the tiles clatter, and drowning all the other noises. The rain was pouring down. The gutters let loose a cascade that beat the pavement furiously.

That evening I moved to my mother's room, for she was afraid of these queer sounds. For a long while we could not fall asleep, listening to the rain and the gusty wind. My mother kept murmuring: 'Poor refugees, I hope they have found decent shelter for the night.' And I had the vision of them hurrying to the town and being pushed back by the bayonets of the Order Preservation Corps. Then I thought of Mao Mao, who might now be standing on the city wall on night duty. I also thought of the fortune-telling woman. Where had she gone? She was a strange female.

The rain kept on falling, but the wind gradually subsided. Now only a monotonous music reigned over the night: the pattering on the roofs. It soothed our nerves, though. I heard my mother turn on her other side, and then pipe up a little snore. And the picture of refugees, of Mao Mao, and of the strange fortune-telling wife, grew dim in my mind. A wave of somnolence overcame me and I fell into a slumber.

I did not know whether it was in a dream or in drowsiness that I heard a squeak. It was very sharp at first and then dull, and a draught stole into the room. I opened my eyes with a start. I discovered that the door of the room was ajar. My mother perhaps had not perceived this, because her bed was farther away. I did not want to disturb her, so I remained in bed and did not bother to get up to close it. I thought it might be a stray wind that blew the door half-open. I closed my eyes and tried to recapture my sleep.

Just as I was about to fall back into my dream again, I faintly smelled a sharp scent, which irritated my nose. I turned on my back and lay wide awake, for the smell was so caustic that I nearly choked. To my great surprise I saw a cluster of scintillating sparks moving along in the air from the door into the room. It zigzagged like a flying snake; and as it wriggled its way, the smell became more and more pungent. I nearly coughed but was restrained by the nameless fear that seized me. I thought my mother must have been roused from sleep too, for there was a queer silence in the room, her feeble snore having come to an end.

In the strange stillness I watched the bunch of sparks crawling its way into the middle of the room and then change its course towards the wardrobe which stood by the wall. The snake suddenly coiled up in the air there. I heard the door of the wardrobe shake. Somebody was pulling it open. And another bunch of sparks moved in from outside. I began to discern a light sound of tripping steps. The air, pervaded with the scent, was getting tense with human breathing, which I could now perceive.

'Help! Help! Burglars have stolen in! Help!' was the abrupt wild cry from my mother. She must have been watching the movement of the sparks all the time. Her scream rent the air.

At my mother's shout the two collections of scintillating sparks dropped to the ground with a thump, like two falling comets, and heavy steps hastened out of the room. My mother had already jumped out of bed and lit the oil lamp with a match. We dashed out into the corridor, shouting at the top of our voices: 'Burglars! Burglars!' When we reached the hall, the burglars were standing there in the middle, two of them. They both wore black masks with horrible crooked noses, standing there motionless and staring at us threateningly through the two holes, in which their eyes were glittering with weird fire. They were not afraid. They knew my mother and I could not engage them in a fight. She shrieked and I stared at the masked men, my legs shaking violently.

'Don't screech and don't be afraid,' one of the intruders said. 'We won't hurt you! We come here only to borrow something. We are hard up, you know. Were it not for the famine, we would not come here to disturb you.'

The voice was so plain and even that we felt a chill creeping up our backs. My mother gaped at them with subdued horror, her hands raised in the air as though she were a soldier ready to be disarmed by the conquerors. The two men, however, kept a formidable silence, standing still, their bulky forms casting two ghostly shadows in the dim light. 'Ai–' my mother shrieked again and backed away unsteadily in the direction of the kitchen.

'I've told you not to shout,' one of the men said angrily. 'Otherwise we'll stifle you to death! We are not burglars, understand? If your town had been kind enough to give us a little food – which we know they have plenty of – we would not have come here to trouble you in the dead of night. We have much better hearts than your people in the Order Preservation Corps.'

The intonation of the voice was so clear that I could now

discern the accent. It was coarse and abrupt. They must have come from the crowd of refugees.

'Keep quiet!' the other of the masked men shouted. 'When things get better, we'll return to you what we have taken from this house.'

And quietly they retreated backwards and vanished into the darkness outside. My mother remained standing by the wall, her hands still up in the air. She seemed to be hypnotized by something. It was only when a strong blast of cold air poured in, that she came to, rousing herself from stupor and fear. She took up the lamp and we began to examine the room. By the door a big hole about three feet high and two feet wide had been made in the wall. It presented a ghastly sight indeed, because it deprived us of all sense of security. The cottage was now defenceless, with the door wide open.

We went to Uncle Pan's room, next to our cowshed. It was a shabby place, but he liked it because he could hear the breath of our cows there and smell the odour of their sleek skin. He used to say that he could not sleep anywhere more comfortably than in this place. Indeed, he was now deep in his slumber as though nothing had happened in the house. Even when we bent over him by his bed, he did not stir. He was having a very sweet rest. But he did not snore as he usually did. He breathed very feebly. His eyelids were fluttering in agitation. Was he having a nightmare then, I asked myself?

'Uncle Pan! Wake up! We have just been burgled!' my mother shouted at his ear.

He did not seem to hear anything, although his eyelids kept on moving.

'Uncle Pan! How can you sleep like that at this moment?'

Uncle Pan had absolutely no sense of hearing. His lips moved and the tip of his tongue crawled out to lick the lips as though he had just had a good meal. But he did not open his eyes, nor make an answer.

At her wit's end my mother began to shake him violently with both hands. He did not offer any resistance. He let his head be

136

pushed this way and that like a pumpkin. However, his neck grew stiff at last. Slowly his eyelids parted, showing a pair of idiotic, dull pupils. The light from our two lamps dazzled them. He began to perceive our presence. He sat bolt upright and began to scratch his head as if trying to recall something from his memory.

'What's the matter with you? You did not seem to hear anything,' my mother said.

'I was having a dream, ma'am, a beautiful dream,' he babbled, still scratching his head. 'I dreamed that I had returned to my village up in the North. They have no more civil wars there now. And my nephews are grown up and married and have children. They gave a splendid home-coming dinner party in my honour. Ma'am, it was delicious, heavenly delicious! And the wine was fifty years old. It had been buried in the cellar by my father and was only recently discovered and unearthed. Heavenly taste, ma'am!'

'What are you talking about!' my mother shouted angrily. 'We have just had a burglary. A huge hole was made in our wall. What are you talking about?'

'What? Burglary?' Uncle Pan shook with alarm. 'What have they stolen? Are our cows all right?'

And, without waiting for the answer, he jumped out of his bed in his pyjamas and dashed off to the cowshed with bare feet. But he suddenly stopped in the middle of the room and uttered a cry of pain. He had stepped on something burning. When I brought the lamp to the spot, we discovered a pool of burning incense. It was sending forth a mist of intoxicating smoke. Immediately, we understood what the clusters of sparks that had been crawling in the air in my mother's room were. They had served as torches, but at the same time as an inebriating agent.

'Fortunately we were awake, then,' my mother remarked with both surpise and fear, 'otherwise the whole family would have been intoxicated by the smell and the burglars could have carried off the whole house.'

'I see –' Uncle Pan murmured thoughtfully to himself. 'That's how I had such a queer dream. I was intoxicated. Oh, what a blockhead!' And he beat his head heavily with a fist. But he lost no time in getting into the cowshed.

The door of the shed that led to the outside as a separate entrance was wide open. There was now nothing there except for the draughts that kept on pouring in through the door and whirled round by the wall. The mother cow and the daughter had disappeared. The rack, filled with hay, looked very odd in the middle of the stable without the two familiar animals pulling at it. Apparently more than two burglars had stolen into our house. The two cows might have been led away long before the thieves got into my mother's room.

Uncle Pan stamped on the ground, wringing his hands and shouting at the top of his voice: 'The heartless burglars! They dare even to steal my cows! I have nothing in this world but two cows! That they could be so ruthless!' But he did not seem to believe his eyes. He overturned the rack as though the animals might be hiding under it. Then he kicked it along as it it had been a ball. As it rolled along the hay spread out all over the room, making a ghastly mess. Finally, it reached the end of the room and was stopped by the wall. Uncle Pan remained standing there, facing the wall, as mute as a dumb person. For a long time he did not stir. Then he turned round with a jerk of his whole body and scampered off to the darkness outside, shouting: 'Where is Laipao? He has betrayed me. He didn't even utter a bark!'

My mother lit a lantern and we followed Uncle Pan to the threshold. Laipao was there, lying pitiably against the wall, drenched with rain like a drowned rat. He was breathing weakly, his stomach faintly heaving up and down. My mother shook his head. Idiotically he parted his eyelids, gave us a wooden stare and then closed them again.

'He is poisoned too!' my mother said, looking round for help. Uncle Pan went on cursing the burglars all by himself and did not care about Laipao. 'O Ran! O Ran!' my mother shouted. 'Bring some tung oil! He needs a strong laxative!'

Meanwhile Uncle Pan shifted the target for his foul abuse from Laipao to the Order Preservation Corps. 'What is the Order Preservation Corps doing? They keep peace in the town but force burglars to the village to steal my cows!' Then his fury was diverted from the Corps to Mao Mao. He shouted as though Mao Mao had been on the spot: 'Mao Mao! What good are you? The thieves stole my cows right under your nose. You good-for-nothing, what are you doing? Tell me what are you doing?' And he rushed to Mao Mao's cottage. Mao Mao happened to be home on leave that night.

O Ran came out with a bowl of tung oil. I opened Laipao's mouth, and my mother poured the oil in. He began to gasp and choke. I held his jaws apart and O Ran fed him with a bowl of water. Then we carried him in by his legs and left him by the fire to get warm.

Uncle Pan was away all the time. We heard him quarrelling with Mao Mao in the village square. Mao Mao kept on saying, 'Yes, Uncle Pan, I'll try to find them. Don't beat me! I'll try to find them. I think the burglars must have something to do with the woman fortune-teller, who came yesterday afternoon. I saw her on my way back home. She looked very much a suspicious character.'

'I don't care about any woman. I hate such creatures. I only want my cows,' Uncle Pan blared.

'I know, I know. I know you don't like females because you haven't got one,' Mao Mao said, not without a touch of pride in his voice.

Uncle Pan stared hard at Mao Mao, yelling at the top of his voice: 'What did you say? Are you trying to show off about your greedy She-crow at such a moment?'

Mao Mao inmmediately went pale. He babbled as fast as he could manage: 'Please be quiet, Uncle Pan. Listen, you had better go right away to trace the cows. I'll try to catch the woman so that we can find clues as to the burglars. I'm sorry to say we Order Preservation Corps bother only about bad characters. That's the instruction Wang the Lion gave me. I can't help it.'

'Get away with your instructions! I only want you to find me my cows!' Uncle Pan insisted.

'But I must take the orders issued by my commander,' Mao Mao said in a louder voice, stiffening his attitude a little, 'because he pays me!'

'Get away with your commander!' Uncle Pan became furious.

Thus the controversy went on for half an hour without result, until their voices grew hoarse and their strength exhausted. Then they went off, one to search for the cows, the other to arrest the woman fortune-teller. The day began to break. Laipao, now warmed up by the fire, began to tremble spasmodically and vomit. He poured out a pool of black liquid, which gave off a very bad smell. But his eyes were now open and even started to shine. His life was saved. And the red sun came out halfway behind the mountains in the east.

At breakfast time Uncle Pan came back with the young cow, to our great surprise and delight. 'Poor baby, she looks as miserable as a motherless child, wandering about in the wet valley,' Uncle Pan said to my mother, wiping his dripping nose with the sleeve of his gown. 'I hope she hasn't caught cold. You see, ma'am, she recognized me. The moment she caught sight of me, she lowed feelingly, wagging her tail this way and that.' And he waved his hand right and left to show how she wagged. 'See? Just like a loyal daughter. When I came near to her, she sniffed my hand and licked it with her tongue. O, it is a very tender tongue. It is as soft as cotton . . .'

'How about the mother?' my mother asked. 'Have you seen the mother?'

'No!' Uncle Pan said, his eyes downcast. 'Ma'am, I put a new tether on her the other day. They must have led her away. Her footprints were not distinguishable when they came to the rocky hills. They went over across the hills into the forests, ma'am.'

'Well . . .' My mother was interrupted as soon as she had begun. A roar was rising outside and approaching our house. It was Mao Mao's voice: 'You dirty bitch! You came to spy out the ways and lanes for the burglars. I'll beat you to a jelly if you don't tell me where they are.' We went out to see what was happening. Mao Mao was dragging a woman in our direction by her collar. We could recognize at the first glimpse, that she was the wandering fortune-teller we had seen the day before. Her gown was smeared with mud, her kerchief gone, and her short, sticking-out hair looked unusually grotesque.

'Ma'am, she was not even afraid when she saw me,' Mao Mao said to my mother, still holding the woman firmly. 'She stood at a crossroads doing some sort of sketching like a geologist, pretending that she was a learned, respectable woman. Look at this nonsense!' He threw out a small sketch-book. It was the geography of the neighbourhood; the river, the highway, the valleys, the hills and the mountains, that she had delineated.

'What are these for?' my mother asked, puzzled by the map.

'What for?' Mao Mao put in his comment, 'for the convenience of her comrades to find roads at night.'

'I've nothing to do with any burglar, I tell you!' the woman protested and tried to snatch the book.

'You dare to wag your tongue?' Mao Mao shouted. 'You know who I am?' Mao Mao tightened his grip on her and glowered at her like a legendary warrior at a victim. He had never been regarded as a person of any consequence in our village. So he now put on airs of importance and added: 'You know who I am?'

'I know you are a running-dog of the rich!' the woman said loudly in her bass voice.

Mao Mao clenched his teeth, but his face was pale. 'You beast! I want you to explain to me what is meant by a running-dog.' And he began to tear her gown and kick her behind. She also started struggling with him. In a minute her dress was torn open, exposing her chest. Two balls made of straw fell on the ground. She had false breasts! She was a man, disguised as a woman! Seeing the two strawballs, she gave up fighting.

'Ahem,' Mao Mao said, imitating the cynical voice of Landlord Chumin's steward, which always had a touch of mockery. 'So you are a man! Come with me to the headquarters of the Order Preservation Corps!' Mao Mao dragged him in the direction of the highway.

The false woman immediately slumped down and refused to move, her face waxen.

'Brother,' she said to Mao Mao in a desperate voice, 'I know you're a poor peasant. I'm no enemy of yours, because I work for the poor people. Why should you take me to the headquarters of your Corps? They'll certainly kill me. Would you like to have your friend killed by the running-dogs of your landlord?'

The very expression 'running-dogs' made Mao Mao furious. 'To hell with you!' Mao Mao said. Then he lifted the false woman up with all his might and dragged him away like a reluctant pig.

We felt as if we had been turned to stone, looking at them struggling and then disappearing in the direction of the town.

'Uncle Pan,' my mother murmured at last, as Mao Mao and the disguised woman vanished into the city wall, 'the false fortune-teller talked very much like the young fugitive, and reminds me of the persecution that night. I can't bear to think that he is to be tortured by Wang the Lion. Go to Uncle Peifu and ask him to use his influence with Chumin to secure his release. We don't want to go deep into the burglary case. After all, it is a matter of luck. We did not treat our God of the Kitchen and the Household at the Small New Year properly, so we ought to have had bad luck. Go to the town, Uncle Pan, quick!'

'Yes, ma'am,' Uncle Pan said in panic, also terrified. We all now vaguely felt that this false woman somehow must have connections with the persecuted young fugitive, who was doing some sort of mysterious work among the poor peasants in the district. Perhaps she was doing the same kind of job among the refugees here. If so, Wang the Lion would certainly kill her.

142

Thinking of this, Uncle Pan forgot about the mother cow. Without a second word he went to the town to rescue the captive.

At lunch-time Uncle Pan came back from town, perspiring in spite of the cold weather. He had hurried much of the way.

'Have you found Uncle Peifu?' my mother asked.

'Yes, ma'am,' he said, breathing hard. 'But he is very busy, packing up his books and things. Ma'am, all the shops are half closed. There is very bad news in the wind. It is said there have been many riots of refugees and poor people up in the big mountains. And last night while it was pouring with rain and pitch-dark, the mob managed to break into the county city and disarmed the Order Preservation Corps there and killed the magistrate. The sky is going to fall, ma'am. I don't believe my old ears! I could never have thought that the poor people would dare to kill the head of the county.'

My mother became speechless, staring at Uncle Pan in stupor and fear. 'Ma'am, they killed the magistrate!' Uncle Pan added.

My mother started. 'What did you say?' she asked.

'The poor people have killed the magistrate!'

'How about the false woman then? Is Wang the Lion going to finish his life?'

'I don't know, ma'am. They've put him in chains and are interrogating him. Landlord Chumin himself is doing the questioning, ma'am, and in a secret chamber, too. No one was allowed to hear it. Only Wang the Lion and his armed guards were present.'

'Can't Uncle Peifu do something for him?'

'I don't know, ma'am. He couldn't go into that chamber either. But he promised that he'll try his best to persuade Chumin to set him free. He'll call on us in the afternoon and tell you the result, ma'am.'

We waited for Uncle Peifu to come.

Towards dusk Laipao had entirely recovered from the

poisoning, though he still looked very weak. He tried his first bark at a visitor, who was shouting and growling at him outside. Uncle Pan went out and ushered the guest in. It was Uncle Peifu. This time he came without his cane.

'I'm in a hurry, ma'am,' Uncle Peifu said to my mother. 'I come just to tell you that there is no hope of getting that false woman released. I've used all my influence with Landlord Chumin to help him, but in vain. I even ran such a risk as to say that if the landlord did not order Wang the Lion to give the chap freedom, I would not teach his children – in a joking way, of course. Can you guess what the landlord said? He said "Get away, I can always find a teacher!" These words made my heart beat hard, ma'am. Suppose he really withdraws the children from my school . . .' His old voice broke up. He seemed to want to weep.

'Then what are they going to do with the false woman?' my mother asked anxiously.

'Oh, a dreadful thing, ma'am. They are going to hang him tommorow in public, to make him an example to the lawless people. You see, ma'am, they can't send him to the court in the county city, because it was taken by the mob last night. Ah, a dreadful thing, ma'am!'

'What crime has the false woman committed to deserve hanging? He is but an accomplice of burglars, if not a fortune-teller,' my mother said.

'Oh, no ma'am! They have tortured him in that chamber to confessing that he is a revolutionary agent, whose job is to organize the poor refugees and peasants to fight landlords. He has nothing to do with your burglars, ma'am. It's a mere coincidence that he came to your house the day before. He is one of the mysterious young fugitive's men. Have you heard of the young fugitive, the dangerous revolutionary?'

'Well . . .' my mother stuttered hesitantly. 'Well, no, I haven't heard anything about such a person.'

'He is an extraordinary person, ma'am. It is he who secretly organized the poor people to capture the county city. The false

144

fortune-teller was trying to do the same thing in this district. He has already got in touch with many refugees and poor devils. There might have been a riot here any night had he not been captured. He was not afraid to confess this. So they must hang him tomorrow in order to frighten the mob and quench the fire.'

'Dreadful! Dreadful!' my mother murmured. 'That such things could happen? I don't believe it! I don't believe it!'

'You've got to believe it, Ma'am. It's true, absolutely true. Much more dreadful things are happening in the outside world, ma'am. Has Yunchi written to you about it? I think he hasn't, because he doesn't want to make you worry. You see, the new army - they call it the revolutionary army – from the south has swept over the Yangtse Valley and even a part of the north, and finished off a lot of warlords and the officials of the old regime. The young people, like that fugitive, organized the poor people everywhere beforehand. That is why wherever the army went it won the battle. You see, the new army relies greatly on the assistance and power of the poor people.'

'Why hasn't he written me about all that?' My mother began to understand and was worried. 'Where did you hear about it? It sounds so fantastic. If it were true, then he ought to have come back home, because his master's business would be suspended during the war.'

'It is absolutely true, ma'am. I heard it from Sweet Potato, the town messenger, who has just made a trip to the big city down the river. Yunchi's business was not suspended for a single day, because the revolution came so soon, so unexpectedly, just like the capture of the county city by the mob last night. The poor people had captured the important towns even before the southern army arrived. It's just unbelievable, but true, ma'am. The messenger never tells lies. If he did, people would not allow him to do the job.'

'Could it have happened? Could it have happened?' my mother kept on repeating to herself, stupidly looking outside, where a few sparrows were twittering as monotonously as ever.

'I think our present dynasty is going to change,' Uncle Peifu remarked in a murmuring monologue. 'Everything has been turned upside down: there is drought, there is the murder of a magistrate, and a man pretending to be a woman fortune-teller, and no respect for learning, and the landlord threatening the schoolmaster all the time with starvation . . . Just think what the world is like now. There must be a change. I am sure our dynasty is going to change.'

'What dynasty, then, are we going to change into?' Uncle Pan, who had been sitting quietly, deep in thought all the time, joined in the conservation. 'Are we going to change from the republic to the monarchy again?'

'I don't know,' Uncle Peifu wrinkled up his old forehead. 'A monarch perhaps. The mob and the southern army are now wiping out all the bad people and warlords. I think there will soon be a real god-appointed emperor to appear and wipe out the mob and build up a great unified empire again. You see, things can't go on like this all the time. Parents have no respect for schoolmasters and children have no respect for their parents. Vicious circle, see? Can't go on like that. By the way, did your honourable elder son write to you?' He turned to my mother.

'No, why?' My mother started at the question.

'Well, I think he would have told you about it.'

'What is *that*? Tell me, please!' My mother became alarmed.

'Well,' Uncle Peifu said slowly, heaving a sigh, 'I don't think I ought to tell you. In any case you'll know about it sooner or later. The messenger told me that your son has quit his job and is working in the what's-it-called political bureau of the new army. Incidentally, he is also engaged to a modern girl, whom in their jargon they call "comrade"! Don't be grieved by it, ma'am. It is just the way things are today. I've said that the dynasty is changing. It won't last long. Your son will come to himself in time. I think that is why Yunchi hasn't told you.'

When he had finished his piece, the sound of sobs was heard from the dark corner at the end of the room. It was spasmodic, interspersed with nose blowings. We all turned our gaze to that side and discovered that it was O Ran who was weeping. No one had ever noticed that she had been sitting there on a low bench, listening to the conversation. She was shaking all over with her blubbering, and tears rolled out of her eyes, messing up her face, already disfigured by the deep marks of smallpox. No one dared to approach her. I knew what she was weeping for, but I found no words to console her. She looked, in that corner, particularly lonely, and for the first time seemed to be surperfluous in the house. Indeed, she could never join in our conversation. She was either alone by herself, or working hard like a slave.

'It's destiny! It's destiny that it should be so,' my mother muttered to herself. 'I've brought her up as my successor for the household . . . but . . .' Her voice ceased. Her gaze fixed on the ground before her. But she did not go to O Ran to stop her weeping.

Uncle Peifu could not understand what my mother was saying. He looked around with panic, his lips trembling as though he wanted to say something. O Ran's sobs grew tenser and tenser as we kept silent. 'I'm sorry, I'm sorry,' Uncle Peifu babbled quickly at last. 'I had forgotten about her. I've always forgotten about her, poor O Ran!' And he stood up. He whirled round in the room in search of something, but in vain. 'Ah, my poor head! I even forget that I did not bring the cane with me today. How dreadful! I always feel lost when I miss the cane! I must go now. I must go!'

Uncle Peifu shuffled out of the room irresponsibly, leaving O Ran in sobs.

'How strange the old schoolmaster looks without the cane!' was all that Uncle Pan could say to my mother to break the brooding silence.

CHAPTER 9

The living-room had a sombre look in the evening by the feeble light of the oil lamp. O Ran went on sobbing all by herself, as quietly as a mouse, in a dark corner, and refused to be consoled, and rejected any food. My mother remained religiously silent, now gazing at the guttering wick, now glancing at Uncle Pan, who sat on a three-legged bench by the wall, also mute. I knew there must be something that preoccupied them. Whenever there was something heavy on their hearts, they would become thoughtful and speechless. Uncle Pan would not even smoke his pipe.

The oil lamp began to grow dimmer and dimmer. The silence persisted. But no one wanted to go to sleep. Uncle Pan finally got up, poured a little oil into the lamp and the light immediately rose, much firmer and stronger. Then he seated himself on the bench again and scratched his head. After a while he babbled contritely all of a sudden:

'I wonder what Wang the Lion and his men are doing to the false woman tonight. They may torture him again for more information before they hang him tomorrow. I am worried, ma'am.'

'I am, too, Uncle Pan,' my mother said. There was a tremor in her voice.

'Ma'am, I wonder if it is my fault.' Uncle Pan looked naively at my mother like a child. 'If I had not urged Mao Mao to find me the cows, the false woman might not have been captured. I

148

feel my heart ache, ma'am. I really shouldn't have done such a thing.'

My mother did not reply right away, but stared at O Ran in the dark corner, who, bending low, looked like a shadow. The light on the wick of the oil lamp flickered in the draught that stole in through the cracks in the wall. We had not yet mended the hole made by the burglars the previous night. We had simply stuffed it with straw and some mud, so it let in the night wind.

'The house seems awfully chilly and empty,' my mother began in a murmuring, absent-minded voice, as though speaking to herself. 'I don't think I can sleep tonight.'

'I shan't be able to sleep, either,' Uncle Pan said. 'I feel something wrong with my heart, ma'am. Honestly, something wrong. I think it is getting old, old like myself.'

'Let's pray to God, Uncle Pan,' my mother said, still in her absent-minded voice, turning her gaze away from O Ran. 'We've forgotten to pray for a long time. We can do nothing, Uncle, but pray. Let's pray for the poor young man. Let's pray to God to bless our O Ran, too.'

Hearing her name mentioned, O Ran suddenly burst into tears and shook violently in her obscure, forgotten, dark recess.

'Don't weep, my child, destiny has it so,' my mother murmured.

And she joined hands together, closed her eyes and began to say the prayer. Uncle Pan could not join her, because he could not read much and had never learned to pray. He simply kept a great silence, his childish old eyes wide open. There was a religious intensity in the atmosphere as my mother's murmurings went on evenly and monotonously. Uncle Pan's lips began to fall apart and the gulf between them grew wider and wider, until at last he looked completely like an idiot.

Suddenly a strong wind whistled over the roof and in the gust there was a riotous din that brought my mother's prayer to a pause. Simultaneously with the sound, a wave of furious barks rose in our village and from all the villages around. We all got up, startled and speechless, staring at one another. O

Ran became afraid, stopped sobbing and edged near to my mother in front of the lamp and began to tremble like a young sparrow. Her eyes were swollen and red, which made her pock-marked face look more ghastly. As we all stood in great silence we could perceive the direction of the hubbub. It had not started in the village, and so it had no connection with burglary. It came from afar.

Uncle Pan heaved a sigh of relief. But the din grew more threatening and more tumultuous. And amidst the confused uproar we seemed to hear a sort of whistle swishing through the air. It seemed that a legion of carrier pigeons was passing over our roofs. But it was so dark, no bird could possibly fly.

'What is it?' my mother said, puzzled by the queer noises.

'It sounds very much like bullets flying, ma'am,' Uncle Pan said. 'When I was in the North and when battles were on between hostile warlords, I used to hear bullets whistling in the air that way. Ma'am, it's no music. It is fighting.'

'How can it be! There has never been fighting here!'

'Perhaps it is bandits that come to loot the town in the darkness. Well, let's have a look. I'll not be able to sleep if I am not sure what it is. Come on, ma'am, let's have a look!'

Uncle Pan climbed on to the roof to see what it was. My mother and I followed him. O Ran was too afraid, so she remained in the room. We perched on the top of the house and could hear the hubbub much more distinctly. It came from the town, which now stood in the darkness like an immense invisible sea sending up a gigantic storm that threatened to submerge the neighbourhood. We started shivering, partly from cold, partly from fear. We had never heard such resounding human voices in this quiet countryside. And from this intimidating uproar there emerged hundreds of flaring torches. They danced in a circle about the town like jack-o'-lanterns. Each time the din grew into a rumbling thunder, there was a volley of gunfire. And the report would invariably arouse another roar that shook the earth.

'I cannot understand what it is all about, Uncle Pan,' my

mother said, her teeth chattering with fright. 'I've never seen such things in my life.'

'I don't understand it, either, ma'am,' Uncle Pan said. 'It doesn't seem likely that it is bandits trying to break into the city wall. Bandits are never so many and so daring.'

'Then what is it, Uncle Pan? I'm so afraid.'

'I really don't know, ma'am. I think it may be some kind of rebellion. There have been so many refugees about and the Order Preservation Corps has been so unkind to them. These wandering people may be trying to capture the town to get some food as they have done in the county city up in the big mountains – didn't Uncle Peifu tell us about it?'

'That would be horrible!'

'Hasn't Uncle Peifu also told us that our Republican dynasty is changing? When an old dynasty goes away, ma'am, there are always disturbances to precede it.'

'Change of dynasty! What new system shall we have then? When the old Manchu Dynasty died out, you men had your pigtails cut off. Will you grow pigtails again in the new regime?'

'I don't know, ma'am. Whether we are going to have pigtails again or not, we will remain just the same at heart. We simple farm-hands never change. We like our land and cows and earn our living on the soil . . .'

Another uproar, interspersed with the faint reports of guns, interrupted the dialogue. It swelled up like a sudden onrush of a gigantic billow that drowned everything, but soon subsided, leaving behind an empty space and great quiet. The dancing torches divided into two sections which threaded their way in two lines and disappeared in opposite directions into the darkness like two fire-snakes into sombre caves. But the ancient city radiated above itself a halo of fire that burned the invisible sky.

'The city is captured,' Uncle Pan murmured.

'Are you sure?' was my mother's doubtful question.

There was no reply to this as there was no explanation to the halo in the sky. We groped our way gingerly down the roof and came into the living-room again. 'Well, a new dynasty?' my

151

mother said hesitantly. But her eyes gave out a serious stare, half alarmed and half melancholy. Uncle Pan only rubbed his bald head. After a moment of silence he muttered, 'Anyway I can't grow a pigtail again now. People will have to forget me, in any case.'

'Let's hope that people forget us,' my mother echoed.

And they had no more words to say. The silence became dreary and frightening. We went to bed.

The next day Uncle Pan was the first one to be awakened in the village. There were hasty and heavy knocks at our door and the repeated shout, 'Uncle Pan! Uncle Pan! Open the door!' It seemed that Uncle Pan had become a man of some importance in the village, whom one had to trouble for some urgent affair at such an early hour. I jumped to my feet and tripped out of the room and joined him. He hesitated to open the door, behind which he remained standing, fingering his bald head. He was thinking about pigtails.

I pulled the bolt and the door burst open.

There was a small crowd on the threshold. Uncle Pan was taken aback, his dreamy eyes blinking and his hand still fingering his hairless scalp. The sight was unexpected and astonishing. It was Mao Mao in the uniform of the Order Preservation Corps and bound with ropes like a prisoner, his face badly scratched and still bleeding. A few wild-looking peasants stood by him. They had red badges on their arms inscribed with three awkward characters: *Revolutionary Volunteer Brigade*. They were not local people, because they talked with a heavy accent. 'Are they the landless refugees from up the big mountains?' I asked myself. But before I could find an answer a young man had limped out from the crowd and asked Uncle Pan, pointing to Mao Mao, 'You know this man, don't you?'

Uncle Pan rolled his eyes at this young man, who had no red badge on his arm and whose clothes had been torn into tatters. He had scratches on his face, too, but the wounds had clotted.

We seemed to know him. Having stupidly scrutinized him for a few minutes, Uncle Pan suddenly jumped up, taking his hand from his bald head asking, 'Haven't you been hanged? Uncle Peifu told me that you were to be hanged this morning!' This young fellow was the false woman!

He did not answer the question, but went on asking in a very serious tone, 'Don't you know this man, old Uncle? Tell us quickly, because we are very busy.' He pointed again to Mao Mao.

Uncle Pan started, recognizing the bruised face of Mao Mao. 'Yes, I know him,' Uncle Pan said quickly. 'He is Mao Mao, our neighbour. What's wrong with him?'

Mao Mao suddenly broke out in a weeping voice, 'Uncle Pan, they want to hang me instead. They said that I was the *running-dog* of Landlord Chumin. I'm not a dog, Uncle Pan, am I? I am a grown-up man as you can see.'

'Shut up!' the false woman shouted. Then he turned to Uncle Pan, asking again, 'Is he a good man or not?'

'He is a good man, *officer*,' Uncle Pan answered respectfully, in a stuttering voice, realizing that this young man must have something of military rank about him.

'Then why should he become a member of the Order Preservation Corps?'

'Because he had nothing to eat, officer. We had a drought, you see? Nothing came up from the soil. And his wife, She-crow, has a big stomach. She consumes twice as much rice as a man. So Mao Mao had to get a job in order to feed her. Mao Mao loves her like a goddess, you see?'

The false woman could not help smiling at the statement. But he tried to conceal the smile by making a grimace, which, on his scratched face, looked ugly. 'Is that true?' he asked.

'Absolutely true,' Uncle Pan answered, assuming a serious look. 'I saw She-crow eating once. She finished four bowls of rice at one go while Mao Mao managed only two. She needs two husbands to feed her, believe me.'

'Right, I rely on your words,' the false woman said. Then

153

turning to the peasant volunteers, he added, 'Free him, comrades. We forgive him this time. We'll *hang* him if he tries to work for his landlord again!'

The peasant volunteers undid the ropes, setting Mao Mao free, and then left him to Uncle Pan. Before they went away, the false woman said to Uncle Pan again, 'I believe you, Uncle. One of our comrades who had taken refuge in your house one evening told me everything about you. Mao Mao is a poor peasant, we know. But he is at the same time our enemy. He should be our friend, because fundamentally he is landless. Keep an eye on him and see that he is good.' After that, he departed with the members of the Revolutionary Volunteer Brigade hurriedly for the town.

Mao Mao and Uncle Pan stood face to face, as though they had been strangers, a heap of ropes piled up idly at their feet. Mao Mao looked as pale as stone, and was covered all over with goose-flesh and his legs were shaking fitfully. Suddenly his knees gave way and he fell to the ground in a kneeling position. Both corners of his mouth were stretched downwards while his lips puckered up. With a tearful voice he murmured, 'Uncle Pan, you are really a god. You're much more benevolent than my God of the Kitchen – he doesn't look after me at all! I will try to buy a pound of pork and tell She-crow to make a bowl of delicious soup with it for you. I will watch her so that she doesn't consume it herself. I will, believe me!'

'Stand up! Stand up!' Uncle Pan shouted in great panic. 'I am not a god. Don't compare me with your God of the Kitchen, or else he will become jealous of me and bring me misfortune. I don't want your meat soup either. Do please stand up and tell me what it is all about!'

And Uncle Pan lifted him up by force.

'Uncle Pan, you cannot imagine how dreadful it is!' Mao Mao muttered, his lips still puckered up like a pig's snout. 'The false woman is not a burglar, but an underground leader or some-thing of a spy for the farm-hand brigade. He was organizing the refugees into troops – he confessed it to Wang the Lion the

154

other night. He has a large number of peasants under his command and gets his weapons from his headquarters, which are now in the county city. Oh! I did not know that he was such a powerful man, otherwise I would not have dared to take him to Wang the Lion.'

'How dreadful!' Uncle Pan said, widely opening his naive, old eyes. 'So the false woman is an army officer? I am glad I did address *her* – Oh, no! God forbid, *him* – rightly. Tell me what happened last night in the town. Did he take any part?'

'He did! And it was all because of this false woman that the riot took place. You know, Wang the Lion had personally tortured him to confess about his plot and had found on him a list of his men's names. He immediately made it public that he would hang the false woman and punish all his followers, so his men got scared. They stormed the town in the darkness, and, taking us unprepared, broke through the city wall. They were so many, Uncle. I think every refugee we saw wandering in the countryside took part in it. We were taken so unawares that even Wang the Lion and Landlord Chumin themselves were captured alive. Oh! Uncle, I am afraid. They bound Wang the Lion and Landlord Chumin in ropes as tightly as they did me. Very taut you see, as though they were binding up pigs. Oh, I am afraid, Uncle.'

'Did they really dare to do that?' asked Uncle Pan in great alarm.

'Why, I saw that with my own eyes. They kicked Wang the Lion's bottom just as Landlord Chumin's steward used to kick mine. And they even slapped Landlord Chumin's face. Do you remember how tender and round and soft his face is?' Mao Mao paused to give Uncle Pan time to recall the image of Landlord Chumin's face.

'Yes, I can remember very well,' Uncle Pan nodded. 'It is as tender and round and soft as the buttocks of a new-born baby.'

'Right. You have an amazing memory, Uncle Pan. I admire you. But oh my! Just imagine! Such tender skin. Each time the sturdy peasant volunteer boxed his cheeks, he left the marks of his five stumpy fingers there, red and purple and blue like rainbows.'

'Is that true? It that true?' Uncle Pan asked repeatedly, scratching his ears, his eyes goggling, as though he could not believe that it was Mao Mao who was talking.

'If I tell a single lie, may Heaven fall on me!' Mao Mao swore. And seeing Uncle Pan still in doubt, he suddenly clenched a fist and pounded his own bottom with it and said, 'You see, they kicked Wang the Lion like this, but much more heavily, of course.' Then he lifted the other hand and slapped his own face. 'See? Like this, just like this! Of course I cannot leave such bright marks on my cheeks. You know, my skin is coarse and thick!' And he raised the other hand.

'Stop! Stop!' Uncle Pan shouted. 'I believe you! I believe every word you say.' And he lowered his voice to a murmur and continued to himself, 'I imagine that the dynasty has changed again, things being so upside down. I wonder what new ways they are going to tell us to follow in the new dynasty. In any case I can't grow a pigtail again.' And instinctively he scratched his bald head.

'Oh, no! You don't have to,' Mao Mao said hopefully. 'I saw none of the volunteers had a pigtail. I wouldn't like to have one either. It is such a nuisance in the summer, don't you think so?'

'Let's hope so,' Uncle Pan said. Suddenly he seemed to remember something, so he added, 'I wonder if they will send the same people like Chumin's steward to the village to collect land rent.'

Mao Mao immediately grew pale. The hopefulness that had flashed on his face disappeared entirely. 'I don't know. It may be the steward again,' he murmured. 'He can change a master in any case, but he will always do the same job, I am sure. You can give yourself such airs, you see? Bad luck! Bad luck, indeed!'

'What do you mean by bad luck. Mao Mao? Did he strike you again recently?'

'Oh, no. I simply mean that he managed to escape from the town last night in the darkness with a few of Wang the Lion's men. I wish he had been *captured alive*, too. He also deserves a little spanking on his face; his face is as tender and soft and round as Chumin's.'

Uncle Pan stared at him curiously and did not make any comment. Mao Mao suddenly felt something queer in Uncle Pan's eyes and started with fear. He added quickly,

'Don't mind what I said, Uncle Pan. I was simply joking. I did not mean it. Please be kind, Uncle Pan, don't tell anybody about what I said of the steward. I was really happy about his escape. It is not *bad luck*, but good luck, very good luck.'

Uncle Pan heaved a sigh, throwing another glance pitifully at Mao Mao, saying, 'I do hope he won't come to the village again.'

Mao Mao had already started trembling, possessed by the fearful shadow of the steward.

Everybody in our village waited for the proclamation of the new dynasty, for the instructions about the new ways of life, the new manners, the new taxes, the new magistrate and the new taboos. Several days had passed, but nothing exciting happened. Only on the walls of a roadside shelter outside our village appeared posters of various colours. But they could not possibly be issued by the new government, because they did not seem serious. They looked like children's drawings, grotesque and queer and ridiculous.

One poster depicted a fox with a long, bushy tail conversing with a tailless wolf, while eyeing a tame, grazing sheep. The title for this picture read 'The Landlord (fox) and his steward (wolf) plotting together to suck the blood of the poor peasant (sheep).' The funniest part of it all was that the fox had a pipe in his mouth and was holding it with a front leg. Another poster was the picture of a hunter with a gun, which he was aiming at an escaping fox. This time the peasant was the hunter, but he was a different farm-hand: he had revolutionary ideas and was a member of the Revolutionary Volunteer Brigade. All these caricatures were extremely amusing to look at and made many a spectator laugh and chuckle, but appeared too simple to be of any importance. All government documents used to be abstruse and difficult, so difficult that even such intelligent people as Benchin, our Taoist priest, and Lao Liu, our story-teller, sometimes could not make out the sense. No! The pictures were too funny, so funny that they must be school-children's work. but the captions were done in very good classical calligraphy. How was that? No one could give an explanation.

Not long after, however, a messenger from the town visited our village. He had a piece of paper as his identification card and the testimonial of his authority as some sort of civil servant. It gave his title as: *Comrade Messenger of the District Revolutionary Party*. He said, in a very loud but squeaking voice, that the 'Political Organizer' of the local Revolutionary Party was to come to the village the next morning and that this comrade had many things to talk to the comrade villagers and that all the comrade villagers should kindly be present at the ancestral temple in time. He added, before he left for another village, that this meeting was highly important, demanding the 'co-operation' of all, whether young or old, male or female. 'By "co-operation",' he explained, 'I mean all of you *must be* present, otherwise, well . . .' He suddenly fell short of words. 'Well, well . . . Oh yes, I must hurry, good-bye!' And he rushed away.

His sudden departure without finishing his words left behind a mysterious air, which suffocatingly enveloped our villagers now impatiently awaiting the instructions of the new government.

The next morning, without fail, everybody went to the village temple with awe and curiosity. Shortly after breakfast the Political Organizer from the local Revolutionary Party in the town arrived with his secretary. We had expected a grand old gentleman in a sedan chair carried by four coolies, and a young scholar for his secretary carried by two, like the mandarins in the old dynasty. To our great astonishment neither of them was like that. The Political Organizer looked hardly more than twenty-five, but his secretary was as old as his father, with a crooked back and a pair of thick glasses. And they came on foot! They must have hurried much of the way, for their foreheads were perspiring in spite of the chilly weather and their shoes were covered by dust. They went straight to the upper end of the hall and remained standing behind the table in front of the ancestral altar.

As the young man stood facing us, scanning the audience with his penetrating eyes, Uncle Pan, who was sitting next to me on the floor, began to nudge me and whispered, 'Look at the new officials!' I looked at their faces carefully, one old and the other young, with nothing particular about them. So they were the new mandarins, I thought. But upon closer examination both Uncle Pan and I were taken aback. Uncle Pan's face even went steadily paler. The faces of these two mandarins we seemed to have seen somewhere before, many, many times. 'They can't possibly be our old acquaintances,' Uncle Pan murmured to himself, puzzled. 'We never have friends in the official circles. But, were it not for the clean shaved chin, I would certainly take the old secretary for Uncle Peifu.' Uncle Peifu, the old schoolmaster! Certainly it was he, I said to myself. No one else could have such a crooked back. And both his hands were fidgeting all the time, too. He missed his old cane, no doubt. But how he had changed his appearance, now wearing the soldierly grey uniform of the Revolutionary Party! He gave us the impression of a clown in the traditional comedy rather than a secretary of the young revolutionary. As soon as we identified him, our curiosity disappeared. Instead, we wanted to laugh a helpless laugh. But we all managed to maintain strict silence, because the Political Organizer looked very serious. He alone remained a mystery to our villagers. But Uncle Pan had already found out who he was. He whispered to me, in a hardly audible voice, 'Doesn't he look like the young fugitive who took refuge with us one night?' I nodded. But I did not dare confirm it in public.

'Comrades!' the Political Organizer suddenly addressed us, breaking the silence. Meanwhile the old secretary seated himself on a low bench, took a notebook from an old briefcase and then bent over the table and scribbled down quickly what the young man was saying. 'You must know that we have overthrown the old regime together with its old institutions, thanks to the efforts of all our brave comrades. From now on we shall, again through our common effort, build up a new society, a society without classes, without injustice, without poverty, in a word a society of which we ourselves are the masters. To be plain, we shall have no more landlords, no more stewards to kick our bottoms, no more corrupt officials to raise all sorts of taxes!' He paused to look at the audience.

There was a shuffle among our villagers as though they were galvanized by an electric current. All eyes were wide open, staring at the young Political Organizer, who had made such a daring utterance. A sturdy peasant suddenly stood up and asked desperately.

'Sir! If there are no more landlords, where shall we get our land?'

'Don't call me "sir"!' the Political Organizer corrected him. 'Call me "comrade". We have no class distinction now. Haven't you heard my words? Well, we are coming to the point of land. The new revolutionary government has worked out a programme to confiscate the land from landlords. Each of you will receive three acres of land as your share. For the time being you can stick to the land you have farmed from Landlord Chumin. You don't have to pay rent now.'

'Are you sure that we don't have to?' an old farm-hand asked. 'Mind you, Landlord Chumin's steward is rather difficult to deal with.'

'You don't have to bother about him either,' the Political Organizer assured him. 'He'll never dare to bother you again.'

'Hurrah!' A unison of jubilation broke out from our younger villagers.

'Now you understand,' the Political Organizer remarked, 'what this new era means to you!'

Lao Liu our story-teller was excited by the new turn of events.

His face turned red and his eyes sparkled with fire. He asked, 'How about Landlord Chumin and his concubine and her chaperon? Can the revolution overlook them?'

'Don't get too anxious, comrade,' the Political Organizer explained. 'Revolution is not to be accomplished overnight. We have to carry it out step by step. We'll deal with that fox later, as he is locked up at present.'

As the interpolation went on, the air in the hall was getting tense and excited. Most people stood up with dilated eyes and burning cheeks, drinking in the words of promise uttered by the young Political Organizer. Even Uncle Pan was agitated, beating his knees with his huge stumpy hands as though he were expecting something extraordinary to happen. The only person who was not in the least perturbed was the old secretary Uncle Peifu. He was scratching noisily with a pencil in the notebook, taking down every word people said. And his old sight was so poor that he practically had to press his eyes on the paper in order to make sure what he was writing about, his crooked bony back protruding like a hill. There was no smile or anger or enthusiasm or excitement about his sunken face. The only expression he showed was an occasional frown between his sparse eyebrows. And this frown was nothing new. He had had it ever since I could remember him.

'Now then,' the Political Organizer continued, raising his voice, 'you have understood what the new regime is for. It is for the poor people and belongs to them. In order to stabilize the new administration we must strengthen ourselves. In other words, we must get ourselves organized into a strong force so that the reactionaries cannot come back to power again. To put it in a simple way, we must have a peasants' union in the village. All the farm-hands, old and young, ought to be members. Only when we have a union can we put all our ideas together and do something. Am I wrong or not?'

There was no answer. Never before in the village had we had any kind of organization. Only rich people could afford to do this kind of thing. The poor farm-hands had no time for anything but farming. Their reticence seemed to get on the nerves of the young Political Organizer, for his brows were knitted. He murmured to himself, 'All the peasants are as silent as stone over popular movement.' But no sooner had he finished the comment than he raised his voice again. 'We must have a peasants' union, whether we like it or not. It is the order from the Supreme Council of the Revolutionary Party. Do please think it over!'

There was still no response. No one could understand why the union was so necessary and must be organized right away, now that Landlord Chumin was done away with.

'Comrades,' the Political Organizer went on explaining, softening his tone a little, 'if you don't mind my criticism, I should say that you don't think politically. Of course you haven't suffered so much as the peasants up in the big mountains. They have not only organized themselves into unions, but also fought revolutionary battles. Had it not been for them, you would not be able to have free land now. You must organize yourselves as they do. You should start the activity straight away. May I provisionally suggest to you a man who can give you the lead? He is a good proletarian and came from the north as a refugee. Our Research Committee has made a thorough investigation of him and kept a good record of him. I am sure he will have your confidence as well as our party's.'

He took out a small notebook from his pocket and lowered his eyes to it. After a moment of perusal he raised his head and said, 'His name is Uncle Pan. Uncle Pan he is called. Uncle Pan! Will you stand up, please?'

Uncle Pan stood up, completely confounded by the unexpected announcement. He was shaking all over with nervousness. He babbled, 'Sir, I am too old, too old for anything!'

'Don't say that, comrade!' the Political Organizer said. 'I know you very well. You're a good peasant. I've never forgotten you since that night when I took refuge at your house. Do you remember that night? Had I been arrested and killed then, things might have been slightly different in this district. Only a good proletarian can help his comrade at the risk of his own life. You saved not only me, but also the revolutionary movement in this region.'

This revelation puzzled all our villagers in the hall. All eyes were directed at Uncle Pan, who now went terribly pale. Even Uncle Peifu tried to straighten his crooked back and have a look at him. Unable to stand the stare that was concentrated on him. Uncle Pan seated himself on the floor again without a word.

'Good!' the Political Organizer said in a cheerful tone, taking his silence for consent. 'Uncle Pan is going to be responsible for the village union until a chairman is elected. Well then, the other thing we have to do immediately concerns our women comrades. We have suppressed them and forgotten that they are human beings ever since the beginning of our history. Rich people buy up girls as concubines just as though they were commodities; and bad husbands kick out their wives like old shoes when they no longer need them. We must now have equality for both sexes. Do you want this equality or not, women comrades?' He turned to the womenfolk who stood at the end of the hall.

There was no reaction at first. But after a few minutes a beautiful, resounding voice broke out: 'Certainly they want it!' It was the familiar voice of our story-teller, Lao Liu. He was standing upright, his eyes shining, one of his hands held high up in the air. All eyes focused on him, but he was not in the least perturbed by the stare. He kept his posture, quiet and composed, like a statue of the guardian of the fair sex.

'Who are you, comrade?' asked the Political Organizer, who was amazed by Lao Liu's calmness and determined attitude towards the womenfolk, as well as by his firm gesture. 'Do you speak on behalf of the female comrades in the village or simply on behalf of your own wife?'

'I am the village story-teller, *comrade*,' Lao Liu replied, using the new title he had picked up literally on the spot and letting his raised hand down. 'I have no . . .'

'I see! I see!' the Political Organizer said quickly, interrupting

163

him all of a sudden, and at the same time turned the leaves of his notebook. 'I see! I see! I find your name here. You're comrade Lao Liu, aren't you? I've heard so much about you! Here is a note about you our Research Committee has worked out.'

'Comrade Political Organizer!' Lao Liu hastened to complete his statement, interrupting the revolutionary, 'I have no wife! I've never managed to get a wife! The woman I loved was taken away by Landlord Chumin as a servant to a poor wretch of fifteen, whom he called his concubine. I can't help it, see? Because I am a poor story-teller. It's just like that: beautiful creatures are humiliated and ruined by the unscrupulous rich while the ugly ones are kicked about like tattered rags. We have just had a sad case in the village. A very good and energetic girl, whose face happens to be disfigured by smallpox . . .'

'Enough, comrade Lao Liu!' The Political Organizer stopped our story-teller, 'I understand you. I know you're a champion of the weak, of the oppressed and of the down-trodden. I just want to get in touch with you. We want you to work for the publicity board of the local Revolutionary Party. But you should get yourself acquainted with the revolutionary theories. Mere sympathy is not enough. We are going to have a training class for revolutionary personnel in the town. I strongly advise you to join it! Will you come to our headquarters tomorrow for an interview? Yes, do please come!'

Before Lao Liu could make an answer, a wail suddenly burst out and disturbed the air. It was sharp and long, interspersed with fitful sobs. Everybody turned their gaze in the direction of the door, where, in a shady corner, O Ran was in tears and screaming heart-rendingly. She was touched by Lao Liu's sympathy for the unfortunate females like herself and moved by his daring description of her face. No one in the village had ever paid the slightest attention to her even when the news of my brother's engagement to another girl was broken to the public. She had been completely forgotten. Lao Liu was the only person who spoke of her as a case, a member of the village community, before such a large gathering. As all the eyes were attentively fixed on her, her cry became louder and sharper, making the air tremble.

Lao Liu rushed to her like a protector of the weaker sex and lifted her up on his arms, bringing her more to the front and said to her in a soft voice, 'Don't weep, O Ran. I understand you and the grief that is hidden inside you. I know your heart is pure and beautiful and capable of elevated emotion as well as passionate love, although your face is unfortunately spoiled by a fatal disease, which is the property of the poor. But what does it matter if the heart is beautiful? O, how many a time have I been cheated by the material appearance which we call good looks. O! how much youth have I wasted on this deceitful delusion . . .'

Lao Liu went on with his monologue as though reciting the aside of a hero in one of his stories, completely disregarding the audience which had shifted its attention from O Ran to him. O Ran, soothed by the easy flow of his rhetoric, gradually closed her eyes, and clinging to him by crossing her arms around his neck, she soon stopped weeping. There was a great silence, a general stupor in the hall. The only sound that vibrated in the air was the rhythmic, even murmur of Lao Liu's story-telling voice, praising the beauty of O Ran's heart.

'Comrades!' the Political Orgnaizer suddenly shouted, calling the attention of the audience back from Lao Liu to the meeting, 'you should get your Union organized at the earliest date possible. The activities in other villages are under way. Yours must not lag behind. I am sure Comrade Uncle Pan will give you all the assistance you need. I must go now, but I hope to meet you next time in the new office of your Union.' And he stood up. Uncle Peifu also got up, lazily rubbing his dreamy old eyes, and heaved a sigh of relief.

But no sooner had the Political Organizer started moving, than he came to a halt. He thoughtfully fumbled in his pocket for his notebook again and perused a page. 'Oh, here is something about Comrade Benchin,' he said, raising his head. 'Who is Comrade Benchin?'

Our Taoist priest stood up in the crowd and replied, 'Yes, sir!' He held his pale, wizened face upwards so that his thick eyeglasses would not fall – his nose was almost too flat to support them.

'Don't call me "sir"! It's a feudal idea, understand?' the Political Organizer corrected him. 'There is a note about you in my notebook, put in by the research committee of the party. You are a Taoist priest by profession, aren't you? You must give it up! It is a feudal profession that serves to fool the masses for the benefit of the ruling class. Besides, you spread superstition that way. The local government has decided to give you three acres of land – you can choose it from Landlord Chumin's property in the valley. From now on you must engage in farming. Do you understand, Comrade Benchin?'

'Yes, sir, oh no, Comrade, yes, yes,' Benchin muttered. 'But I have never been used to farming . . .'

'You must learn it now. Every useful member of the community must engage himself in productive work!'

Benchin had no courage to speak further. The Political Organizer made for the door, followed meekly by his old secretary. And the crowd began to disperse. We threaded our way hurriedly to Uncle Peifu in order to give him our best regards. We got hold of him just outside the door.

'I could hardly recognize you in that grey uniform and without your cane,' Uncle Pan said apologetically. 'Tell me what you are really doing. You look terribly tired, old man.'

'I'm working for the local Revolutionary Party as a scribbler.'

'Going about with the young Political Organizer to take down the notes of what people like me and Lao Liu and Benchin babble about?'

'Not always. Sometimes I have to write captions for posters.'

'What? You mean you have to do your beautiful calligraphy for the schoolchildren's sketches, such ridiculous things as a fox with a bushy tail and a wolf without a tail at all?'

'Yes, exactly,' Uncle Peifu said, slightly blushing.

'How can you, an accomplished scholar, do such childish things?'

'A new dynasty, so new ways, my dear Uncle! What can I do? They have closed down my school, saying that I was preaching feudal ideas to the children. But I can't teach revolutionary theories, can I? I can't take up three acres of land, either, like Benchin. Too late, you see? I have no strength for farming. All my old hands can do now is writing and copying, copying and writing, or whatever you call it.'

The Political Organizer had already walked to the edge of the village. Seeing that his secretary was still chattering away in the village, he shouted out, 'Comrade Peifu! We must hurry up. We have got to finish the job in the next village before it gets dark!'

'Yes, Comrade Political Organizer, I'm coming!' replied Uncle Peifu feebly. Then turning to Uncle Pan, he went on, 'Goodbye, Uncle Pan. May God bless you!' and he caught up with the young revolutionary. In a minute they disappeared into the distance.

As soon as the Political Organizer was gone, Benchin walked up to Uncle Pan. His face was sullen and downcast as though he had just been to a funeral. In a weeping voice he said, 'Uncle Pan, you must help me to get rid of the three acres of land. I am not a born farmer. I don't want land.'

'But it is given to you by the Revolutionary Government. I can't do anything about it,' Uncle Pan said, spreading both his hands out in a helpless gesture.

'Have you no pity on me, Uncle Pan? Look what I've got!' And he also spread out his hands and rolled up his sleeves, showing two slender sticks of arms in shrunken pale skin. 'I can't even lift up a hoe. How can I farm land?'

'Well, it is not me who gives you the land,' Uncle Pan said, puckering up his lips in a hopeless smile. 'So I can't withdraw it from you!'

'Ah, ah,' our Taoist priest stuttered indistinctly. 'Ah, ah . . . ah, ah . . .' It sounded as though he were invoking the name of some god to exorcize ghosts.

The village square was now empty. The pale sun had reached the top of the sky. It was lunch-time.

CHAPTER 10

Lao Liu had taken the Political Organizer's advice and gone to the town to interview the officials of the local branch of the Revolutionary Party. Since then, he had disappeared from the village for about three weeks. Later on, it was found out that he had been receiving a revolutionary education at the political training class, which was being held in the town. When he returned to the village, he was entirely a new man. He seldom smiled. He did not even care to chat with our villagers. There was always a thoughtful frown above his eyebrows. Most of the time he shut himself in his cottage, studying some pamphlet. When he occasionally appeared on the village square he was always in a hurry.

One day Uncle Pan saw him coming out of his cottage with a pile of pamphlets under his arm hastening to the public earthern closet to the east of the village. 'Lao Liu, I haven't chatted with you for ages,' Uncle Pan called out. 'How are you keeping?'

'I am sorry, Uncle Pan,' Lao Liu said, 'I can't talk with you. I am frightfully busy.'

'What are you busy at?'

'Reading. You see, I must start my new job soon. Before that, I must do a lot of reading in order to master the revolutionary theories. I am afraid, until I start my new work, I can't spare a single minute to chat with you.'

'What new work is it?' Uncle Pan asked curiously. 'Is it story-telling or anything? You see, we have missed your stories very much.'

'Yes, well . . .' Before our story-teller could finish his sentence he had already vanished into the closet. And he remained there in a squatting position for some hours, so absorbed was he in his reading, while a long queue of busy farm-hands outside kept growing in length, unable to relieve themselves.

Three days later we were told by a messenger from the town that Lao Liu had been made Assistant Commissar of Publicity for the local Revolutionary Party. After that, our story-teller began to appear more often in the village square, and no longer with a pile of pamphlets under his arm. He had digested them. Early one morning when Uncle Pan was taking out the young cow, he saw Lao Liu again dashing away. Uncle Pan stopped him, and asked, 'What are you rushing about for, Lao Liu?'

'I am going to tell stories again,' was the concise reply.

'But haven't you always been telling stories?'

'Ah, but these are going to be new stories, stories about revolution that will wake the poor people up from ignorance and stupidity.'

'Aren't your old stories good?'

'No! They are no good at all. They are absolutely nonsense, feudal in character and poisonous in influence. I wish I had never told them. They are only good as an instrument for the rich to cheat the poor.'

'How can you say that!' Uncle Pan protested. 'All your stories were so interesting and moving that few of us could withhold our tears.'

'I'm sorry that you should have shed tears over them. It's a sheer waste of energy and emotion.'

'What words! I don't believe what you're saying, Lao Liu!'

'You must believe me, Uncle Pan, because you're now also doing revolutionary work for the village peasants' union. You must believe! From our revolutionary point of view all the old tales are only good for the rich. I'm sorry I have been a tool for them.'

'Well, well . . .' Uncle Pan murmured in a confused note,

170

scratching his bald head uneasily. Then his words fell into a monologue: 'Strange world! People change so quickly.'

'You should go to the political training class, Uncle Pan,' Lao Liu advised. 'You should, as a revolutionary.'

'I am not a revolutionary, Lao Liu, I don't understand revolution.'

'How can you say that? You ought to learn about it. Then you will believe in it. And when you believe in it you will have strength and be able to act. And through action you will understand more.'

'What are you talking about, Lao Liu? It is so unlike you! Have you gone in for the Confucian classics? All you've said sounds exactly like a quotation from some classics!'

'My uncle! It is a revolutionary theory! We must talk it over some day. I must hurry up now. I must go to the headquarters of the Revolutionary Party for instructions. Good-bye for the time being!'

And he darted off, as fast as the wind.

In the afternoon, a slender man was seen hurrying along the highway in the direction of our village, kicking up a cloud of dust about him. As he approached we could make out that it was Lao Liu, the newly appointed Assistant Commissar of Publicity. He was panting and his forehead was perspiring, in spite of the cold weather. Under his arm there was a big bundle of posters. He laid it on the wall of Mao Mao's open pigsty. Then, having gasped for a while, standing on the square, he shouted at the top of his voice to our villagers:

'Comrades! Comrades! Come out and listen! I have important news for you.'

Everybody recognized that it was Lao Liu's voice, although it now sounded courser than when he was telling a story and the title 'Comrades! Comrades!' rang rather strangely in our ears. People never failed to come to his call. He was still a favourite in the village, in spite of his new political interest which had so far remained a puzzle to all of us. People streamed out from their cottages. And O Ran was the first to run out and meet him. She had grown very fond of him of late as he had praised her many a time for the pock-marks on her face, which, he said, were the very marks of a miserable, unreasonable life in the old society, and the symbol of being a genuine proletarian. And many a time O Ran had been moved to tears by the argument.

After all our villagers had gathered about him on the square, Lao Liu jumped on to a big stone and said,

'Comrades, male and female comrades, old and young comrades! . . .'

'Just a minute!' Benchin our Taoist priest suddenly interrupted him. 'Tell me where you have learned all these queer words. Did you pick them up from some old books? Somehow they grate on my ears!'

'Silence! Silence!' Lao Liu shouted, making a sweeping gesture with both his hands. 'I beg you to remain silent, Comrade Benchin!'

'I'm not your comrade, Lao Liu! I am a Taoist priest!' Benchin protested.

'You feudal devil!' Lao Liu somehow could not keep his temper and raised his voice to the highest pitch. 'Your words sound seditious. How can you be like this? Have you forgotten that the new government gave you three acres of land?'

'Take away the land, please!' Benchin said, but his voice became much softer and friendly. 'Lao Liu, I shall regard you as my best friend if you can help me get rid of the wretched land.'

A fit of laughter burst out from the crowd, which drowned our Taoist's voice entirely. But Benchin was serious, for his face wore an austere look as though he were about to officiate at a service. He stared at Lao Liu earnestly, waiting for a reply. But our story-teller had something more urgent on his mind. Already his face looked impatient: he wore a frown and his ears were red. He said quickly, beating the air up and down with his hands to impose silence:

172

'I have no time to discuss the land with you. I must go to another village straightaway. This is the news that I want to tell you. Now that this country of ours is cleared of all the reactionary forces, we are going to have a mass meeting of all the people in the district to celebrate the establishment of the revolutionary local government. All of you are asked to be present tomorrow on the sandy beach before the town, where the meeting is to be held, all of you!'

Then he undid the bundle of posters he had brought with him, and gave it to Uncle Pan and said, 'Uncle Pan, please distribute them to all the comrades who go to the meeting tomorrow.'

Uncle Pan took them with a frown, but he did not say anything. The posters were of various colours, inscribed with slogans that we had never heard of in the village before, such slogans as 'Down with Landlord Chumin, the fat pig!' 'Cut the running-dog Wang the Lion's head off like a melon!' 'Land must be possessed by those who work on it!' 'Concubines must be married again to good people!' 'Nuns should find husbands and monks wives!' et cetera. People who could read a few words gathered about Uncle Pan and tried to make out the significance.

'They sound funny, don't they?' someone commented.

Benchin put on his thick eyeglasses, blinked for a good while, then scrutinized the characters like a scholar and finally shouted out like a master of calligraphy, 'Ha! Ha! They are beautiful ideographs. I know who did them. No one but our schoolmaster Uncle Peifu could have achieved them. I know his style. It can't possibly cheat my eyes, no matter how short-sighted they may be.'

'A pity that the slogans are not poems. They spoil the nice handwriting. I am sorry!' another man remarked.

'Silence! Comrades! Silence, comrades!' Lao Liu said loudly. 'Don't debate on such useless questions! We don't bother about calligraphy nowadays. So long as it expresses our ideas, it is all right, whether it is bad or good. Do you understand? Be sure to go to the meeting tomorrow, all of you! You'll see a very important man there. He is the delegate from the provincial capital and will come to make a speech specially for the occasion. He has crossed thousands of miles of land and water and speaks a foreign English. You know that pidgin English sounds like music performed by a crooked tongue. It's very amusing to hear. It takes you three years to learn the sentence "How do you do?" See?'

'Is he a mandarin?' someone asked.

'Of course not!' Lao Liu replied. 'How can we have mandarins nowadays! They represent the feudal society. Now we are having a revolutionary social order, so we have no more mandarins. He was a poor man. He was a worker!'

'Then how did he manage to travel thousands and thousands of miles? How did he manage to learn foreign English? We cannot travel beyond our country, and we cannot even learn to read our own language!'

'Well, that is another story which has nothing to do with revolution,' Lao Liu explained. 'Anyway, he is an important man. You ought to see him. You can meet such a man only once in a lifetime. He comes simply to give the speech and then goes back to the provincial capital straightaway. Don't miss the chance if you want to see a revolutionary leader!'

'Will he speak the foreign English to us?' asked a young farm-hand.

'I don't know,' answered Lao Liu. 'He may or may not. It all depends. Anyway, it has nothing to do with revolution, so I cannot tell. Well, I'm very busy. I must go to another village. I really must be going. Be sure to come to the meeting tomorrow. Good-bye!'

And he pushed his way through the crowd and then hurried away. At the turning of the highway outside the village he disappeared into the gathering afternoon mist.

The next day, with curiosity and enthusiasm, our villagers proceeded to the town, the line stretching on the highway like a long, crawling snake. We had stuck the posters on sticks and were now waving them as flags. They streamed in the air and clattered noisily like wings. O Ran had one in her hand but I had none, so we made an agreement to wave it by turn. We liked to hear the clap and to feel the sensation of its existence in our hands, which meant revolution. Everybody was in high spirits. The march went on joyfully and in great excitement, as though we were attending the Dragon Festival after New Year.

On other roads that converged to the town, similar lines of human beings with bright banners were moving on, slowly but with full force, rising like great waves that were racing to reach the common goal. After a misty night the sky was exceptionally clear. The sun was smiling. And this smile created a particular atmosphere of felicity hovering above the forest of flags that clattered above a sea of human heads. The various waves gradually flowed together on the sandy beach in front of the town, where a high platform, like a stage, had been erected for the meeting. A storm now broke out: a gigantic man standing on the platform. like a pillar, was shouting at the top of his voice:

'Down with landlords and their running-dogs!'

Immediately a great echo, a thousand times as great as the voice, roared up from the human masses that were winding about the high platform. The air was trembling. The earth seemed to be shaking all over with the explosion. The valley that lay hidden not far off in the mountains, seemed to be bursting with some kind of explosion, for it sent up a cloud of mist that darkened half the sky: our eyes were getting hazy and our ears were ringing with the thunder. No one had ever before heard such a voice. No one had ever before dreamed that the farm-hands could produce a roar. For centuries they had had almost no voice.

'Long live our revolution!' the gigantic fellow on the platform shouted again.

Another roar of thunder passed over the sky. The city wall seemed to be falling away, for we heard distinctly a continuous collapsing thud after the cry. And the quiet stream in the river seemed to be rising, too, agitated by the sound. I felt something itching in my throat. A blast of air burst from my lungs and flew out: 'Long live our revolution!' O Ran also sent out a high-pitched squeal. Uncle Pan croaked like a frog, low and heavy: 'Long live our revolution!' And then he fell into a stupor. He stared at the shouting masses like an idiot. It was only when the storm was over that he came to himself and turned to me and asked, 'Did I shout anything?'

'You were shouting, "Long live our revolution!" ' I said.

'I was mad! I was mad!' he reproached himself and beat his own head.

'Why, Uncle?' I asked, puzzled by his self-scolding. 'Everybody shouted the same thing.'

'Because I don't understand the slogan. I don't because I did not go to the political training class.'

Just then a small group of young people in revolutionary uniform walked up to the platform. The gigantic fellow retreated and seated himself on a bench. So there was no more shouting. The sudden hush made the time seem eternal and primitive. This in turn gave me a strange feeling. Just a moment earlier it was such a wild uproar. And now the earth seemed dead. The farm-hands seemed as voiceless as ever before.

The people in uniforms on the platform scanned the crowd down below, without a word, their observing eyes intensifying the silence. They certainly did not look like mandarins, in spite of their smart clothes. But they did not look like peasants either, because they were physically fragile, their faces pale. Their eyes were sunken. It seemed that they had not slept for nights. After a little while, a young man stepped forward and, waking us up from our reverie, announced that the meeting was on. He was the Political Organizer.

All our attention shifted to him as soon as he started speaking. His voice was at first very mild and even. But as he embarked on the topic of revolution his bony hand began to rise and went up and up in proportion with the volume of his voice. Gradually his fingers began to clench together into a fist. His voice broke out like thunder.

'The immediate purpose of our revolution is to right the wrong, to raise the downtrodden and to tread on the high-ups! Comrades! Take this opportunity to pour out your grievances against the old society!'

His voice came to a sudden stop, but his raised hand still remained high above his head. He was waiting for the people to speak up.

'Don't be afraid to speak, comrades, your landlords and their running-dogs are under lock and key,' he added.

We did not know what to say. We observed one another, without a word. Not a single villager had ever spoken in public. And it was not for speaking in public that people had come. We came in order to see the delegate from the provincial capital, the new mandarin, who spoke a foreign English.

Having waited for the voices from the crowd in vain, the Political Organizer urged: 'Comrades! You must not miss your opportunity to make your complaints openly. We have now Comrade Fei Lun with us. He has come on behalf of the provincial headquarters of our party to listen to your voices. He will take back your ideas so that the Revolutionary Government can work out a better programme for the improvement of your lives.' Meanwhile he pointed to a man of medium height, who stood in the middle of the platform.

There was still no response from the audience. But the focus of attention had now been shifted from the Political Organizer to the Provincial Delegate called Comrade Fei Lun. He was rather stout and his head was bald on top. In spite of the grey uniform he appeared like a schoolmaster rather than a revolutionary fighter; and the pair of thick-rimmed dark glasses made him look very much so.

'He doesn't seem in the least different from us,' Uncle Pan murmured. 'I don't think Lao Liu was right in saying that he speaks foreign English.'

'Don't murmur to yourself, but speak up to me!' Comrade Fei

177

Lun stood up and said in a loud voice. 'Speak up, I say, so that everybody can hear!'

His voice carried far, because all maintained a strict silence while he was speaking; and it stunned us. This Comrade Fei Lun was certainly a strange man, for he talked with a local accent. His intonation sounded exactly like Mao Mao's or Benchin's or Lao Liu's. But our village had never produced such a great man as to be a delegate from the provincial capital. He could not possibly be a local man.

'Speak up, comrades!' Comrade Fei Lun urged the audience again. 'I know you have a thousand grievances to pour out of your hearts, because I once *lived* among you. Don't be afraid. We are simply your servants. But we must know your trouble before we can do you service!'

There was a stir in the crowd. People stared at one another with confused eyes. The Comrade Fei Lun had warmed us, not with his kind words, but with his local accent, the accent of the peasants, the accent that spoke of sincerity, of friendship, of common misery.

'Don't you have anything to say about Landlord Chumin, for instance?' Comrade Fei Lun reminded us.

This very remark touched the heart of many a farm-hand. All the faces suddenly grew red and all the eyes sparkled with fire. There had been much to say about him, but no one had ever dared. Now this mandarin from the provincial capital openly persuaded us to comment on him. It was just like a dream. It could not possibly be true. It might be a trap to sound the opinion of the poor farm-hands and then punish them for their seditious thoughts. The stir continued, but there was no voice. All the eyes were glaring with resentment, but their profound, dark pupils reflected a ray of suspicion.

But the suspense did not last long. A voice shot up from a corner, breaking the brooding silence. 'Comrade Provincial Delegate, may I speak a few words about Landlord Chumin?' It was Lao Liu who startled the crowd with his courageous question.

178

'Certainly! Are you a peasant?' the Comrade Fei Lun asked.

'I'm a revolutionary, but also a local man!'

'Good! Do speak, comrade!'

'I thank you, comrade! What I want to say is that Landlord Chumin is the most lecherous person in the district. He bought a girl of fifteen as his concubine not long ago. And yet his appetite was not satisifed. He went further, he even took Aunt Chrysanthemum away from our village. She is a beautiful woman, believe me, comrade, although she hasn't got many brains. We are sorry for her, indeed, But we are also very indignant over the matter. You see, many of us cannot get married for life. Chumin has taken away all the chances!'

'Well said!' was a thunderous roar from the audience.

Now the stir began to get infectious. Lao Liu's words had now the function of a fuse that starts an explosion as soon as it is ignited. The bird of hesitation that had brooded on the mind of the people was now scared away. Hundreds of voices shot up like fire-crackers, blasting the age-old sombre tranquillity about the town.

'Landlord Chumin is a vampire!'

'Chumin can kill a thousand people without blinking his eyes!'

The Comrade Fei Lun remained motionless on the platform, watching the people shout and wave their fists in the air. The roar rose up like a gigantic tide, causing a resonant explosion each time it beat the shore. Then a brief spell of quietness; and then another explosion. Gradually everybody got hot with anger, eyes stood out, bloodshot, and veins twitched on foreheads. The dike of the river of suppressed discontent was broken. And the revolutionaries on the platform, who caused the break, stood with idle hands watching the waters rush and flood.

'We quite agree with you, comrades!' said the comrade Fei Lun at last. 'What are we going to do with this enemy of the people, then? You must think it over. It's up to you to make a decision upon him!' Then he turned to the gigantic man, who had led the people to shout slogans at the beginning of the

179

meeting, and said, 'Will you fetch Chumin and Wang the Lion over here, comrade, please?'

This giant went down the platform and made for a thatched shed a few hundred yeards away. After a moment he came up again with four armed guards – peasants from the big mountains with red badges of the Revolutionary Volunteer Brigade – and two men in chains. They left the prisoners in the middle of the platform, facing the audience. One of the captives was of small build, but fattish, with deep-set eyes and a grotesquely large bushy moustache under his flat nose. The other was a mammoth with a mass of flesh hanging on his brown face.

'What do you say of this man?' asked the comrade Fei Lun, pointing to the short man, but looking at us. 'You know very well what sort of a man he has been.'

We knew this man very well, indeed. He was 'the overlord, the benefactor, the patron of education and the richest man' of the district. It was his land that most of our villagers worked on. It was his shops from which we bought our salt and vegetable oil. It was in his discarded house that Uncle Peifu had set up a school. But it was strange to see him here in chains and huddled up like a rat pulled out of the water. He used to come into the dreams of many a peasant, especially at New Year, when new contracts had to be signed for his land, and cause them to wake up with shudders in the middle of the night, with a chill running down their spines, no matter how thick the quilt they were covered with. It was unbelievable that he looked so mild and gentle now, as quiet as the voiceless farm-hards. However, his small, glittering eyes under the bushy brows were full of life, searching nervously over the crowd. They did not mean much now. Still, they were frightening: no one dared to say a word against him.

Waiting for a reply, the Comrade Fei Lun turned from the small man to the mammoth and pointed at him while asking the audience: 'You must have something to say about this fellow. He is the most active enemy of the people. I understand he organized the Order Preservation Corps and drove many poor people to practical starvation by hoarding the grain in order to corner the market. What shall we do about him? Comrades, speak up frankly! You don't have to be afraid of him now!'

All the people stared at the Provincial Delegate in awed silence. He seemed not a real man, but a spirit who dared to judge this mammoth. Wang the Lion was the name of this prisoner, a name which our villagers used to invoke to frighten crying children. It must be simply a vision that he was in chains. He could free himself at any time. Then he would come to the villages with his men and burn down the cottages and kill all those who had dared to scold him and brand him as the enemy of the people. He had done such things before.

In face of the great silence the young people in uniforms on the platform stared inquisitively at one another. They did not seem to believe that these two prisoners could have so much magic as to hold the masses in such primitive suspense. The Comrade Fei Lun walked to the short man, known as 'Landlord Chumin', and stooped over him and looked into his eyes, like a dentist examining a patient. The Political Organizer stood beside him, scanning the landlord with a puzzled air. In the midst of the hush Comrade Fei Lun suddenly straightened his back and shouted at the prisoner:

'Confess to the people what you have done to them. This is a public trial for you. There is no escape. You have to face public judgement.'

His voice sounded so loud in the dead stillness that it practically shattered the whole audience. This was a trial, the platform was the court and the peasants the jury! 'So this is the new dynasty!' someone murmured. 'At last we have to change sides!' another said. Once one started, many other comments followed, all made in low voices, and there was a general buzz.

The landlord raised his head slowly and gave a glance at us. The buzz was quelled for a second as Chumin's sharp eye swept over us. But soon the collective noise rose again and grew steadily into a hubbub. 'I've committed no crime,' Chumin said quietly to the Provincial Delegate. 'I have always been kind to the people. During the famine last year, for instance, I did not even demand a single grain from them for rent. You can ask them.' And he gave another squint at us as he spoke the last sentence.

The Provincial Delegate kept measuring him with his eyes as though he were studying a curio. Then he made a sign to the Political Organizer, who seemed to be reminded of something. The young man walked to the front of the platform and asked the people down below: 'Have you heard what Chumin said, comrades? Is what he said true?'

The hubbub died down of its own accord as the question was asked. 'No. It's untrue! He has signed away our cottages!'was a strong protest from among the crowd.

'He has signed away my daughter, who is only fifteen!' was another protest, provoked by the first protest.

'He also took away Aunt Chrysanthemum, who has a husband!'

'His men in the Order Preservation Corps beat my brother to death for stealing a bowl of rice!'

The charges went up into the air like the explosion of fire-crackers, deafening the ears. And the buzz that followed sounded like the heaving of the sea that filled the space with a roar of billows and provoked a gigantic echo from afar. The revolutionaries on the platform quietly watched the billows swell and then recede, and they waited for the hollow echo to sink, slowly and imperceptably, together with the sea. When silence was resumed at last, the Provincial Delegate turned to the two prisoners, who hung their heads, pretending to hear nothing, and asked,

'Have you heard what the people said of you?'

Chumin lifted his eyes, turned his head obliquely upward, and asked back: 'Do you take the peasants' words for truth?'

'I do!' the Provincial Delegate said.

'Just think. I could have starved them to death by withdrawing the land,' Chumin said quietly, 'if I were hard on them.' He turned his gaze to us and looked at us intently and raising his voice, added, 'Their words did not come from their consciences, I am sure.'

'Hang him!' was the deafening chorus from a corner of the crowd.

'Hang him together with his henchman Wang the Lion!' was another uproar echoing the first.

'Comrades, be quiet!' the Provincial Delegate shouted, waving both his hands. 'We must keep quiet now. You must hear what he says.'

So there was silence again, but a formidable silence that brewed another storm, a silence that sent a chill to the bone. Chumin started trembling on the platform and Wang the Lion turned pale. The landlord gave a nervous stare at the Provincial Delegate and asked naively, 'Do you believe their words? They are such ignorant people. They don't know even how to distinguish white from black.'

'Yes, they are ignorant, because they never had a chance to go to school,' the Delegate said.

'Now you understand!' Chumin said, with a tinge of hopefulness in his tone. 'If you were with me for some time, you would know me. You would know that I am kind and considerate to them . . .'

'I know you very well!' the Delegate said, interrupting him. 'I have known you since my childhood! Look at me!' He took off his dark glasses, and, thickening his voice, he continued in our peculiar, heavy local accent: 'Your Lordship, I've just heard that you took away my ex-wife. Is that true or not?'

Chumin was taken aback by the sight, goggling at the delegate like a man of stone. There was a shuffle in the crowd, a general stir. A wave of murmurs rose again. People looked at one another as though they had not been able to recognize their familiar faces. A voice finally broke out from the hum and brought all the bustle to stillness. It was Lao Liu who was speaking, standing on his tiptoes: 'Mintun! Mintun! You have cheated my humble eyes! Hurrah for our Mintun! Hurrah for our village which has produced a great man at last!'

All the people from our village craned their necks and, throwing up their arms, shouted simultaneously: 'Hurrah for Mintun! Hurrah for our village!' It was a miracle. Perhaps it was a dream. No one had ever thought that Mintun could become a mandarin of the new dynasty.

'Be quiet, comrades!' the Delegate called out, beating the air with both his hands. 'Your hails smell of feudal ideas! I am not a great man! I am only a proletarian as you are! I knew you would be startled. That is why I put on dark glasses . . .'

'Hurrah! Hurrah for our Mintun, the great man!' The cheers continued to thunder and many peasants from other villages joined in the chorus, having realized that the mandarin from the provincial capital came from among themselves. Never before in the history of the district had the peasants produced a man beyond the rank of village head.

'Silence, comrades! Silence, comrades!' the Delegate shouted at the top of his voice. 'We must use our reason to judge the case of Chumin and his running-dog Wang the Lion first! Think over what we are going to do about them!'

'Hang them!' came a unison.

'Are you sure?' the Delegate asked.

'Sure!'

'All right!' the Delegate pronounced. 'Then their imprisonment by the Revolutionary Volunteer Brigade is justified and therefore legal. But we have no right to pass the sentence. The verdict has to be pronounced by the People's Judicial Commissars at the magistracy. So they shall be delivered to the people's court at the county city.'

A thunder of applause split the air.

'Comrade Political Commissar!' the Delegate turned to the Political Organizer and said, 'Will you see to it that the prisoners are removed to safe custody?'

The young commissar signed to the peasant guards to come. They climbed up to the platform and led the condemned away. Both the prisoners hung their heads low, their faces deadly pale, as they laboriously dragged their steps in chains. The fetters clanked heavily as they moved along. A great silence was imposed again by the metallic noise, rhythmical and monotonous, only broken now and then by a high ringing chink produced by the iron rings.

'Mintun! How can you do such a thing against Lord Chumin!' A female voice went up sharply into the air, shaking the funereal stillness into pieces.

A woman was pushing her way towards the platform. 'Mintun! You can't do such a thing!' The crowd was flabbergasted by her violent advance. Many a young farm-hand tried to stop her, pulling her back by the edge of her garment. She struggled vehemently to free herself. But her strength failed her and she collapsed. Uncle Pan and O Ran and I rushed to the spot to help her sit up. She was our Aunt Chrysanthemum, who had been among the crowd without our knowledge.

Upset by the incident, the Delegate came down from the platform to investigate. As soon as he realized that it was Aunt Chrysanthemum who had made the scene, he turned pale, but gradually a cloud of crimson crept up his neck to dilute the pallor. By this time Lao Liu had also arrived in a great hurry. Both stood face to face over Aunt Chrysanthemum, and stared at one another inquisitively as though they had come from two entirely different planets. Frowns appeared on their brows, and their lips were drawn. Aunt Chrysanthemum's dull, glassy eyes swept from one to another. Both men seemed to have much to say, but none could open his lips. It was a strange situation. Indeed, it was grotesque. None of us had ever dreamed that they, the three of them, would meet for the first time after many years on such an odd occasion and in such an odd locality and amidst such an odd crowd.

'How can you do such a dreadful thing to such a person as Landlord Chumin, Mintun?' Aunt Chrysanthemum said at last, her voice very quiet.

'No, I shouldn't,' the Delegate replied, also very quietly, with a touch of sarcasm. 'From *your* point of view I shouldn't.'

'No, you're mistaken,' Aunt Chrysanthemum corrected the

Delegate. 'Not from *my* point of view, but from *your* point of view.'

'What do you mean? I don't understand you,' the Delegate said.

'Why, aren't you going to live in the village? You have been absent for so many years. Your ancestors up in Heaven long to see you, long to receive your filial offerings from the altar. If you are going to be back home, Mintun – I am sure you are – how can you afford to offend such an important man of the district as Landlord Chumin?'

The Delegate's forehead wrinkled up in folds, and he said, 'Are you talking sense, Chrysanthemum? Haven't you been slightly affected by the revolutionary movement of the peasants? What do you expect me to be? A reactionary?'

'I don't understand a word of what you say, Mintun. You sound like a classical scholar, talking only in classical language. But do tell me, aren't you going to live in the village, now that you have become a great man? I have been waiting for you all these long years, these long days and long nights.'

'What? Hasn't Chumin made a concubine of you? From what I have gathered just now, he has . . .' The Delegate was ill at ease.

'You heartless man! What makes you speak like that? Ask anybody in the village if I haven't made an honest living by the sweat of my brows. No one ever dares to touch me, except you!'

'I am so sorry!' the Delegate apologized, lowering his voice, 'I didn't know that. You must forgive me for the mistake.'

Aunt Chrysanthemum suddenly beamed up. She tried to get up and spread out her hands to reach the Delegate. Meanwhile she said, 'I forgive you, Mintun. I forgive you everything. Let's forget the past lonely years. Let's go back home together.' And she closed her eyes and exclaimed with elation. 'O! my dreams have come true at last. I have had so many beautiful dreams and now they have become realities!'

The Delegate recoiled at her words and said quickly, 'No! I can't go back to the village. I no longer belong to the village. I belong to the revolution, to the masses! No, I must go back to the provincial capital right away.'

'What?' Aunt Chrysanthemum opened her eyes with fright and shouted in alarm. 'Don't you think of me? Didn't I come into your dreams sometimes?'

Instead of answering her questions the Delegate kept on repeating: 'I must go back to the provincial capital right away. I must! I have so many committee meetings to attend. Besides, she is going to deliver a child . . .' Then he fell into a soliloquy, 'I must be by her. She doesn't know much about this country. She can't do without me . . .'

'What? What? What . . . what . . . what . . .' Aunt Chrysanthemum's eyes grew wild and her voice terrifying. 'Have you got another woman?'

'Not another woman, but a comrade,' the Delegate corrected her, trying to soften the atmosphere by putting on a bitter smile. 'I met her while I was studying at Dr Sun Yat-sen's University in the capital of the Workers' Fatherland. She loves China and the Chinese people. She herself is also a proletarian . . .'

'Ah–' Aunt Chrysanthemum shrieked all of a sudden and threw her head back and fainted away.

We stood silently, staring at the scene without a word. We did not understand what it was all about. The situation looked so odd that it appeared like a dream. Embarrassed by the eyes that were now fixed on him from various directions, the Delegate broke the silence by talking to Lao Liu, 'Comrade Lao Liu, I was glad to hear from Comrade the Political Commissar this morning that you had given up the profession of telling the old-fashioned, feudal stories. Just look! What an effect those feudal ideas have on poor Chrysanthemum. Who told her to wait for me such long years? Take her home, Comrade Lao Liu, will you? And please enlighten her with the new ideas in your capacity as the Assistant Commissar of Publicity. I hope to see you more often. But I must go now.'

The crowd made way for the Delegate to pass through. He vanished into the city together with the young revolutionaries.

The gigantic man on the platform led the audience in shouting revolutionary slogans again. After that he announced that the meeting was adjourned. The audience began to disperse in various directions to the hills. We were the only people left watching over Aunt Chrysanthemum sitting on the ground with her head buried in her slender hands, which were now shaking in fits. As the beach was now empty we began to feel chilly. A gust of wind passed over, stirring up a cloud of sand, which enveloped Aunt Chrysanthemum's face. She gave a hysterical shudder and uttered a sigh. Then she slowly raised her head and opened her eyes only to see a vast, vacant space on the river. She had regained consciousness. She was listening absent-mindedly to the stream that murmured in the gale.

Lao Liu stooped over her affectionately and tried to lift her up in his arms. He whispered in her ears, softly and tenderly, 'Let me take you back home, Chrysanthemum. You have nowhere to go but home, I'm sorry that I've influenced you with my feudal ideas. Had you not been worshipping heroes, we might have . . . Well, it's not too late yet. Let me try to make up for it . . .'

'Get away with you!' Aunt Chrysanthemum shouted wildly all of sudden. 'Don't try to fool me with your sugary tongue. I hate you *men!* I don't want to see you *men* again! Get away, please!'

'Don't talk in such an impulsive way, Chrysanthemum,' Lao Liu said quietly. 'I mean what I said.'

'Get away with you! I don't want to see you *men* for a second!' Aunt Chrysanthemum screamed.

'Are you sure that you don't want to see men again?' Lao Liu asked naively like a child.

'Get away, please! Why should you trouble me like that? Haven't I suffered enough?' Aunt Chrysanthemum nearly burst into tears.'Ah, ah . . .' Before our Assistant Commissar of Publicity could finish his words, his face went deadly pale, his outstretched arms dropped down mechanically, and he himself became rooted to the spot like a stone.

Aunt Chrysanthemum struggled to get to her feet. She succeeded. Having stood for a while to steady herself, facing the wind, she dragged her steps towards the terrace in front of the city gate. But instead of going into the wall she turned right and took a zigzag path that led into the mountains. The sun was tilting towards the western horizon. Her shadow, cast on the plain of dying grass and yellow dust, appeared unusually elongated and lonely.

'Where are you going, Aunt Chrysanthemum? It is cold in the mountains!' Uncle Pan called out, trying to stop her.

'To the White Lotus Convent,' she replied half-heartedly, but there was a touch of resentment in her tone.

'What for? It is the place for nuns!'

'I want to forget this world and *men*!'

'I see . . .' Uncle Pan muttered to himself and scratched his head, trying to understand what Aunt Chrysanthemum meant. Then he raised his voice and called out again like an old father: 'But the White Lotus Convent is miles and miles away, deep in the wild mountains. How can you get there at this time of the day?'

'I don't mind,' Aunt Chrysanthemum replied, continuing on her way. In a minute she entered a ravine and disappeared.

'Strange, strange, indeed,' Uncle Pan murmured to himself, again madly scratching his bald head. 'I don't understand women. I don't understand women. They are absurd creatures.'

Lao Liu stared at the ravine, into which Aunt Chrysanthemum had vanished, his face vacant, his eyes hazy, as though he were dreaming of something. A fresh gale swept along in the direction of the gathering clouds that were sailing at full speed towards the north. Lao Liu started as the wind ruffled his hair. He heaved a sigh of relief, and soliloquized, looking at the setting sun, 'Now the day is breaking. My dream has come to an end!' He turned round and, with steps as light as a deer's, he marched to O Ran and took her in his arms.

'I love you, O Ran, from the bottom of my heart,' he whispered, his soft voice vibrating in the wind like reading a stanza of poetry. 'I have *decided* to love you, to love you with all my soul!'

O Ran gazed deeply at Lao Liu, completely confounded by the affection showered on her by our story-teller. Rays of tears began to shine in her eyes. As they remained silent, looking into each other's eyes, her tears suddenly rolled out and flooded her broad face, dotted with a myriad of pock-marks. 'There is nothing in me to deserve your kindness and sympathy, Mr Lao Liu,' O Ran said, still looking into the serious face of the Assistant Commissar of Publicity. 'I am a servant girl by birth. I am . . .' Her voice broke out into sobs.

'But you are beautiful! You are heavenly beautiful!' Lao Liu pronounced his words evenly and rhythmically as though he had been reciting a piece of verse.

'Do you really think so? . . .' A naive smile emerged on O Ran's messy face. She stopped sobbing, waiting seriously for the Assistant Commissar to answer.

'You are beautiful! Your *heart* is the most beautiful in the world!' the Assistant Commissar of Publicity confirmed his statement. 'You have the soul of the proletarian. Your heart beats in the proletarian way. I can feel that.'

'Have you nothing to comment on my face?' O Ran asked again.

Our Assistant Commissar hesitated for a second, staring at her gigantic pock-marks. Then he said decisively: 'It looks amazingly beautiful because it mirrors your beautiful soul.'

'Thank you. But don't you feel ashamed of my humble origin?'

'On the contrary, I am proud of it!'

'Ah, Lao Liu, ah, Lao Liu . . .' O Ran's tears poured out like torrents again, her body racked with sobs. But her arms gradually went up round Lao Liu's neck, and her eyes closed.

'Let's go,' Uncle Pan said to me. 'The sight makes my old heart beat faster.'

So we went back home, leaving them alone. When we told my mother what had happened, she did not make any comment. She only murmured to herself: 'So O Ran is not going to be my successor in the house.' Then she turned to me, still murmuring, 'I wish I could live longer. We can't leave our ancestral house to fall to pieces in the second generation. We must have a good housewife to keep it together.' Her voice suddenly broke up and left the sentence unfinished.

Neither Uncle Pan nor I could understand what she meant. But we detected something sad in her tone. So Uncle Pan tried to change the subject by saying, 'Do you know, ma'am, that Aunt Chrysanthemum has gone to the White Lotus Convent in order to be a nun?'

'Why? She has never been so religious as to devote her life to the meditation of Buddha,' my mother said with surprise.

'Well . . .' Uncle Pan paused as soon as he began. 'I can't tell you why. Women are queer creatures, that's all. Oh no! You're an exception, ma'am, the only exception.'

We never heard of Aunt Chrysanthemum from that day.

CHAPTER 11

On the day Landlord Chumin and the commander of the Order Preservation Corps, Wang the Lion, were to be delivered to the people's court at the county city for the final verdict, all our village was astir. Everybody was excited and yet everybody was afraid. In the old days Chumin's word was law. He could send any farm-hand who dared to offend him to prison. He could starve a family by withdrawing land from it. He could rule even such people as our schoolmaster Uncle Peifu, who did not farm his land at all. That he was now to be dragged away for a final trial by the destitute peasants who made up the Revolutionary Volunteer Brigade was something unthinkable. It could not possibly be a reality. We all wanted to see that our own eyes did not cheat us.

We got up very early that day. Quite a number of our young villagers had been up even before dawn. For it was said that the prisoners were to be removed from the town very early in the morning so that they could reach the county city before it got dark, the magistracy being far up in the west, hidden in the big mountains. We went to the top of the steep hill on the left of our village, which overlooked the highway leading up to the county city, in order to see the prisoners pass. Mao Mao was sitting beside me on a rock. He wore a huge blue turban so that he might not be recognized by Wang the Lion, of whom he was still afraid.

'He had a terrific voice, which seems still ringing in my ears,' he explained his fear.

Yet it was this voice that made him anxious to see his former commander in chains on his way for sentence.

The sun was climbing the sky slowly like a ball of fire from the dark peaks in the east, but the earth was still enveloped in the morning mist. And the ancient city wall of the market town in the distance, stretching out on the ridge of the low hill down to the river, looked like a giant reptile still deep in its slumber. It did not stir. It did not even seem to be breathing. A few weeks earlier when the peasant volunteers were stationed in the town there was always a bugle call early in the morning, indicating its return to life. But after the mass meeting on the beach they, being formed mostly of refugees from up in the west, were disbanded and sent back home to resume their farm work for the next spring. Now that the revolution in the district was accomplished with the condemnation of Landlord Chumin and the commander of his Order Preservation Corps, they were indeed unnecessary. Only a few guards were left in the town now and no reveille was needed to wake them up.

We watched with concentrated attention for the mist to lift and the city to revive. The sun rose higher and higher and became smaller and smaller. A vague smile broke through the dense saturated air of the morning and showered warmth on us. The sky appeared. It looked pale blue, as always. The veil of fog that had concealed the city was dispelled like vapour, revealing the grey, undulating, ancient wall on the hill. Right in front of us the sombre door of the gate, wrapped in galvanized iron, reflected the fresh sun with a thousand rays. We screened our eyes with our hands to see it open.

It did not seem to have quite wakened yet, although it radiated the shafts of the sun. We waited, straining our eyes to bear the strong dazzle. Gradually a patch of darkness emerged, crossing the field of reflection, first a narrow strip of shadow, then a rectangular space of profound hollowness – the mouth of the giant reptile. A human figure crept out of it. Then a second. Then a third. They lined themselves up in a row on a mound and sent up simultaneously a hasty urgent bugle call.

Immediately after that, more human figures threaded out, eight of them, with two limping in chains.

The sun was now shining very brightly and the view before us became clear. We could see the people moving down the slope to the highway. As they drew nearer and nearer to us, we could recognize their faces. The two men in chains did not seem to have slept well the night before, because there was a kind of weariness about their looks and their legs were reluctant to move. We heard a huge voice urging them, so huge that it reminded us of the impatient farm-hand driving an old plough cow in a cracked field: 'Lazy-bums! Do you expect sedan chairs for you?' The men in chains did not make any reply, hanging their heads dejectedly, just like the ever-silent old ploughing cows.

The highway twisted around the steep hill we perched on. When the group came to the first bend, our hearts began to beat hard. Mao Mao started shaking all over. He was a timid man by nature. The great poverty he had been in had deprived him of all his self-confidence. Sometimes he became afraid without any reason. His causeless fear rose to the highest peak, and made him start like a scared deer when a sudden uproar broke out in the neighbourhood. It darted into the air like a thunderbolt, its echo exploding in the valleys nearby like rockets. A number of strong men jumped out of the deep ditches and ricefields on both sides of the highway, all armed with swords and pistols. They pounced upon the peasant volunteers like wolves upon goats. We heard the firing of guns and then shrieks of pain. They were wrestling with one another in a tangled mess.

'I have a terrible chill in my back,' Mao Mao murmured. 'Let's go back to our cottages and bolt our doors. Didn't you hear the guns? They can pierce your chest and blow off your head. I know such weapons, believe me. I have been taught to use them in the Order Preservation Corps.'

Without waiting for any comment he hurriedly ran away into the village. The fighting on the highway made a terrific sight. The assailants had got hold of the peasant volunteers one by one and were pounding their ambushed victims with fists and the butts of their guns, producing hollow noises which gave out no echo. The two in chains were freed. Wang the Lion was offered a long sword. But he did not take part in the fight. He simply stood side by side with a fearful man, whom we later recognized as Chumin's steward, and gave orders to the attacking men, howling like an owl. This strange voice of Wang the Lion's frightened us much more than the fighting itself. We rushed down the hill and took refuge in our cottages, tightly bolting our doors. Even so, the strange howls seemed to be still ringing on our roofs.

It took us a good while to come back to ourselves, long after the hubbub had thinned out and finally died away. Uncle Pan, sitting against the wall, stared at my mother with his confused eyes like an out-and-out fool. He did not even scratch his bald head as he generally did under such circumstances.

'Don't day-dream, Uncle,' my mother said, waking him up. 'The din was over a long time ago.'

Uncle Pan rolled his eyes several times and his lips fluttered nervously. At last he babbled incoherently: 'I don't understand this new dynasty, ma'am. It seems that people concern themselves only with fighting. Can you tell me, ma'am, how I can shake off my responsibility to the Peasants' Union? I've done nothing for it and shan't be able to do anything. I am of no use to the new dynasty.'

Before my mother could make an answer, we heard hasty knocks at our door. Our watchdog Laipao was yelping furiously at somebody. Dead silence immediately reigned in the room. We had no courage to answer the knocks.

'Let me in, please! Let me in, please!' A voice called out from outside, and it sounded quite familiar to our ears. 'Let me in, please! Let me in! Laipao is tearing my clothes!'

'Quick, Uncle Pan!' my mother said in great haste, standing up. 'It's Uncle Peifu!'

Uncle Pan dashed to the door and lifted the bolt and pulled it open. Uncle Peifu was jumping and waving his hands threateningly at Laipao, who was barking fiercely at him. Seeing Uncle Pan, he heaved a sigh of relief and slipped inside the door as fast as he could. Laipao was locked out. But he kept on whimpering for a good while outside. When silence was resumed, Uncle Peifu threw himself in an armchair and sighed again. He had no cane with him, but his hands were still fumbling nervously for something by the leg of the chair. Apparently he could not forget the habit, although he had ceased being a schoolmaster.

'Dreadful! Dreadful!' he muttered. his eyes widening deliriously at us. 'I can't understand it! I can't understand it!'

'What is it?' my mother asked. 'I understand people are fighting on the highway. Is it a change of dynasty?'

'I don't know. I don't know,' Uncle Peifu said repeatedly. 'They not only fought on the highway, but also went into the town to fight the young Commissars. They literally beat the Political Organizer into a jelly. They killed him outright. And they wanted to kill me, too, but I managed to escape in the confusion.'

'Who are they?' Uncle Pan asked anxiously. 'Are they bandits? I saw them jump out from the ditches to pounce upon the guards. They must be robbers, judging by what they have done.'

'No, not at all!' Uncle Peifu replied. 'They are Wang the Lion's men who were disbanded by the revolutionaries. Chumin's steward, who escaped, has collected them together secretly and organized them into a band again. They came to free Chumin and Wang the Lion. And they succeeded!'

'Was the Political Organizer really killed?' my mother inquired with great concern.

'Why, have I ever told a lie? They dragged him out of his office to the market place. I was then in the lavatory, ma'am. Thank God, I've the habit of going there every morning. And once I get settled down on the stool, I cannot move away for at least half an hour. You see, ma'am, I like to read poetry that way. It's a bad habit, of course. But I can't help it. Got used to it, see? Thank Heavens, they missed me that way. I saw through the window how they killed the Political Organizer. Oh, it's shocking, ma'am. The Steward slapped his face first this way and that. Then Chumin kicked his loins, and finally Wang the Lion cut his head off with a big sword. You know what Wang the Lion looks like when he is killing a man. His eyes bulged out, his teeth clenched, his face turned blood-red, and his sword sailed across the neck like a razor across a piece of paper. It was as easy for him as to cut a melon . . .'

'Enough! Enough! Uncle Peifu, enough!' my mother interrupted him in great haste and at the same time buried her head in her hands. 'Poor Political Organizer! He was so young. When he came to us that night, he looked just like a boy. He was no older than my son . . .'

Uncle Peifu stared at my mother, his mouth wide open, completely dumbfounded by my mother's fright. 'Why, ma'am, have I frightened you? It's a true story, ma'am. I saw it only once in my life. It still flashes before my eyes. I can't forget it, and never shall.'

Uncle Pan broke into his monologue, asking, 'How about our Lao Liu? Was he also killed? He went to the town for a committee meeting last evening and did not come back.'

'No. I think he has escaped in the confusion, too. I saw him running away through the back door of the office when the Steward's men were pouring into the city.'

'Are they still searching for the revolutionaries?' Uncle Pan asked again.

'No, they left as soon as they killed the Political Organizer – I don't know where they have left for. Anyway, the town is now empty. By the way, talking of the Commissars, I remember something, Uncle Pan. You must help me out. I don't want to wear this dreadful revolutionary uniform again. I don't want to be a secretary to any political organizer even though I have to starve to death.'

And he got up. We began to notice that he looked really queer in the uniform made of grey nankeen. He had shaved off his respectable long beard when he became the secretary. But he did not look in the least young, with his bare, wrinkled chin, nor smart, in the boyish uniform of the new dynasty. On the contrary, he made a pathetic figure of a comicality and grotesqueness. He himself seemed to have also perceived this quality now, for he tore off the jacket with vehemence and determination, and threw it on the ground like rag and said to it, 'Get away with you! I don't want you any more!' Then he lifted his eyes and looked at Uncle Pan, saying imploringly, 'My dear old friend, give me a long gown, please! My size is almost the same as yours.'

'Are you sure that you want a long gown?' Uncle Pan asked, completely flabbergasted by his action and confused by his words. 'I mean, can I give you my long gown?'

'Why! From whom else can I get a gown? I've sold mine in order to buy this damn uniform.' He pointed at the discarded jacket, which lay piled up by his feet like a heap of rags.

'Don't misunderstand me, Uncle Peifu,' Uncle Pan explained. 'I can give you my gown easily, I simply meant: don't you have to ask permission from your revolutionary headquarters in order to change your revolutionary uniform into civilian clothes?'

'What permission? Haven't I told you that my boss, the Political Organizer, was killed in cold blood?'

'I know,' Uncle Pan nodded, 'What are you planning to do then? Do you really mean that you don't want to be a revolutionary secretary any more? Or, to put it simply, to change your profession?'

Uncle Peifu said, wildly opening his eyes, 'You've got it, my old man. That is exactly what I want the long gown for. If Chumin comes back to power again – which is very likely, judging by the present turn of events – I will try to reopen my school. Teaching is my life-long career, you see. No matter what dynasty comes and goes, children must have education. By the way, can you find me a nice birch twig? I lost my old cane in the horrible revolution.'

'I can't find you a birch twig just now,' Uncle Pan answered. 'But I'll get you a long gown first, if you have really made up your mind to go back to teaching again. It is my New Year dress. I hope you find it respectable.'

And he went into his room. In a moment he returned with the garment. Uncle Peifu put it on instantly. It fitted him very well. He looked back and forward, and seemed to be satisfied with it. Then he let out a long sigh of relief as though he were at last freed from a nightmare, and became a schoolmaster again.

'Do you think Chumin will let me be a teacher again when he comes back to power? You see, I must earn a living, revolution or no revolution.'

'I don't know,' Uncle Pan answered.

'Perhaps he will, if I grow my old beard in time. I am sure he can't find a cheaper teacher then me. I'll try to reduce the fees a little, if he insists . . .'

Uncle Pan maintained strict silence, for he knew nothing about education.

In the afternoon, when order in the town was restored with the arrival of fresh revolutionary guards from the county city, Uncle Peifu went back home. At the moment of departure he reminded Uncle Pan again. 'Do look out for a nice birch twig for me, Uncle Pan. I may need it at any time.'

'Well, I'll try,' Uncle Pan said, gazing with great confusion at the old school-teacher's shaky figure vanishing into the falling dusk.

The next day there was no morning mist. The sun shed its warmth exorbitantly, making our backs itch. Uncle Pan took the young cow out to the village square for a sun-bathe. He held that she needed it more than anything else: her beautiful, golden hair needed it to get glossy and her heart wanted its warmth to be cheerful. He always thought that she had been unhappy since her mother was stolen the previous autumn. In a way she looked as lonely as an orphan. Although Uncle Pan tried to talk to her now and then like a grandfather, she was too young to understand his language.

Uncle Pan was now sitting by her side in the sun, smoothing her flank with his large hand. Just as he was about to begin a mimic conversation with her, she suddenly gave a kick. She was starting with fright, for the watchdogs flocked to the end of the village and barked furiously at a group of people, all in army uniform. These strange visitors made us start, too. They all carried rifles. Unlike peasant volunteers, they wore, in addition to smart uniforms, military caps each with a design of a sickle and hammer as the frontal badge. We could hardly imagine where they came from. It was only when they marched with military steps to the middle of the square that we began to realize that they must be the regular soldiers from the county city, where there was a detachment of the Revolutionary Army. One of them, a short, smallish fellow with a pistol at his waist, walked right up to Uncle Pan and asked: 'Uncle, please tell me where Mao Mao lives.'

Uncle Pan was completely taken aback by this abrupt question, his hand immobile on the flank of the cow. It was strange that this man should know Mao Mao, who never had a friend outside the village. And the queerest thing of all was that this man's voice sounded so familiar. But Uncle Pan was not sure where he had heard it. He stared at this smallish man with the pistol, like a fool.

'What are you looking at me for, old Uncle?' the man asked. 'Don't you recognize me? Your beautiful cow ought to remind you of me.'

Uncle Pan perused this man's face. Suddenly he jumped up and shouted with surprise: 'Say! Are you the false woman? Certainly I remember you!'

'I am not a *false* woman – the disguise was only an expedient during the period of *white terror*,' the man said loudly with several stresses in his sentence. 'I'm a *real* man.'

'I beg your pardon!' Uncle Pan apologized repeatedly. 'You are a revolutionary officer. I remember. I remember. You brought Mao Mao back to the village early in the morning on

200

the second day of the revolutionary dynasty. I remember! I remember!'

'Good! Tell me where Mao Mao lives.'

Uncle Pan suddenly turned pale at the words, feeling something wrong with the request. He hesitated and began to scratch his bald head. 'Well, well. I . . . I . . .'

'Tell me at once, please! You must know where Mao Mao's cottage is. Don't you remember that morning I handed over Mao Mao to you? You're responsible for him. We want him now!' The man's voice was threatening.

'Well, well . . .' Uncle Pan stuttered, eyeing the pistol on which the man had laid his hand. 'Well, I don't know whether he is in or not.'

'Take us to his place. I beg you!' the man shouted.

'All right, then,' Uncle Pan murmured, on the point of weeping.

Unwillingly he moved in the direction of Mao Mao's house. The strange visitors followed him with heavy steps.

Mao Mao was in, busy at preparing a meal for his wife in the kitchen. For a long while he did not come out, for he must wait till the food was well cooked. She-crow had been pregnant for several months and her belly bulged up like a small hill. She refused to do any work before the delivery. She said that any kind of physical exertion would damage the health of the baby in her womb or disfigure its shape. She said that she must bear the most beautiful child in the world, the most healthy, so that he would make a first-rate farm worker – and she was sure as a pikestaff that it would be a 'he' and not 'she'. Mao Mao believed in her words, so he did everything for her, including the cleaning of her night stool. And she refused to eat hard food. So Mao Mao must see to it personally that every dish was cooked 'as soft as cotton', to use She-crow's own words.

The officer became impatient, waiting in the room for Mao Mao to come out. Finally his patience wore out and he shouted angrily: 'Mao Mao, are you planning to escape?'

These words frightened She-crow. She realized something

must be wrong and this officer should not be offended or else he might do something unpleasant to Mao Mao. So she called out to the kitchen: 'Mao Mao, come out to see these gentlemen! I give you the order to come out! Don't bother about the food. I say, don't bother.'

'Yes, my dear,' Mao Mao replied from the inner room. And in a minute he appeared.

'So you are here!' the officer said, walking up to him. 'Do you recognize me?'

Mao Mao scrutinized him and immediately started trembling. He certainly recognized the officer, once a false woman he had beaten up, who had kept him a prisoner immediately after the capture of the town by the Peasant Volunteer Brigade and who had threatened him with death by hanging if he had anything to do with Wang the Lion again. These words were still fresh in his memory. Mao Mao was now covered all over with goose-flesh. His whole body shook violently as though in a fit of malaria.

'You are under arrest,' the officer said quietly.

As soon as the words were spoken, the other soldiers walked up to Mao Mao and put him in handcuffs.

'What for? What for? Your Lordship?' Mao Mao babbled hysterically like a lunatic.

'Aren't you one of Wang the Lion's men?' the officer questioned him.

'I was. But I have nothing to do with him now.'

'But his men started a riot yesterday and killed the Political Organizer. Weren't you informed of that?'

'I was not, your Lordship. I was not, your Lordship.' Mao Mao wanted to weep. 'I was then trembling in my cottage behind the bolted door. My wife, She-crow, can prove it.'

'That it not my business; I myself don't want your proof,' the officer said. 'You will explain it for yourself at the People's Court in the county city. Let's go. This is my job.'

The soldiers dragged Mao Mao out of the cottage by the handcuffs. Mao Mao refused to move, like a reluctant pig, but in vain. A soldier was beating him behind with the butt of his rifle and shouted at him: 'You traitor of your class! How can you avoid the verdict of your people!'

Mao Mao did not understand the words, but he had a vague feeling that he must go with them. So he at last gave up the idea of resistance and moved meekly between them in the direction of the highway leading to the county city up in the mountains. But when he was about to jump over a narrow ditch that separated the village from the highway, he called back to She-crow: 'Dear wife! Go to the kitchen quickly and see that the food is not burned in the frying pan!' Then he crossed over the ditch and disappeared from view into the hazy distance.

Mao Mao's wife, She-crow, stood on her doorstep, agape, as silent as a stone. Uncle Pan stood a few yards away from her and stared at the empty highway like an idiot.

'What does that mean? What does that mean?' She-crow suddenly broke the silence by asking Uncle Pan, with a touch of anger and surprise in her voice. 'What are they going to do to my Mao Mao?'

'I don't know, Mrs Mao Mao,' said Uncle Pan politely, his voice faltering. It was the first time he had called her by the title 'Mrs'. Ordinarily he generally referred to her as 'Mao Mao's greedy boss.'

'You ought to know, Uncle. You ought to know!' She-crow shouted, raising the volume of her voice progressively with the flow of her words. 'You must know, for in the first place you sent them to my cottage and in the second place you are the Chairman or something or other in that Union – in other words, you are something of a village head in the . . . what do you call it? Oh yes, in the revolutionary dynasty. And in the third place . . . well, well . . . anyway, you must know!'

Uncle Pan was completely dumbfounded by the shower of words that knocked on his eardrums like thunder. And while she was speaking her eyes bulged out, as round as balls, as if she wanted to swallow him up alive. His old face went pale, and his lips started quivering fitfully. After a long while of stupefaction a few words came out of his convulsive mouth intermittently: '*Madam* Mao Mao, *Madam* . . . Mao . . . Mao . . .'

'I don't want you to call me *Madam* or even *Lady*!' She-crow interrupted him all of a sudden. 'I just want you to tell me plainly and frankly what it is all about. You revolutionaries are ever so secretive. I know your ways. Don't think I am foolish!'

'No, you're not foolish. You're very clever, *Madam* Mao Mao . . .'

'Ahem!' she interrupted Uncle Pan again, pointing her index finger right at the forehead of the old uncle, 'don't try to flatter me. Tell me right away the secrets of your revolution!'

Uncle Pan's face went as pale as wax. He babbled nervously, '*Madam* Mao Mao, you must give me a chance to explain if you want to know what it is all about . . .'

'All right! All right!' She-crow interrupted Uncle Pan again, her arms now akimbo. 'Tell me the secret of your revolution. Now then, one, two, three . . .' And she glared at him like an eagle.

'*Madam* Mao Mao,' Uncle Pan began as ordered, 'I've no connection with the revolutionaries. But I presume they take Mao Mao to the county city for investigation in order to find out whether he has any connection with the organized riot yesterday. You see, he was a member of the Order Preservation Corps. And unfortunately it was that Corps again which started the disturbance yesterday.'

'I see.' She-crow nodded. 'How long do you think the investigation will take?'

Uncle Pan's eyebrows went up. 'It may take ten days or half a month, I cannot say exactly how long. You see, official business is always done at a very slow pace. In the old days a case took even three years!'

'So long!' She-crow shouted. But her eyes were staring blankly at the vacant space before her. She was thinking of something. Suddenly she burst into a fit of tears, screaming, 'How shall I go on living? How shall I go on living? I am so used to the food

Mao Mao cooks for me: I am so used to his service, which is always so prompt. Oh my mother, I cannot go on living without him. Besides, it is so cold at night. I can't sleep without him. Oh, my dear mother, those revolutionaries simply want to put me to death! No, they want to put your grandchild to death!' And she began to finger her bulging belly tenderly. After a few minutes, while still screaming heart-rendingly, she suddenly beat the belly in a fit of madness.

'*Madam* Mao Mao, you shouldn't do that! It will hurt the baby! You must be reasonable, *Madam* Mao Mao. You must be careful, otherwise the baby will . . .' Uncle Pan started to sweat. He was panicky and afraid.

'I want it to die! I don't even want to live myself! Oh, my dear Mao Mao! Oh, my sweetest Mao Mao! How can I live while you are kept in jail!' She proceeded from screaming to mournful lamentation, which, with a woman like her, would as a rule take three to four hours to come to an end. Uncle Pan turned as white as a sheet of paper, madly scratching his head. But unexpectedly She-crow paused for a while in her sobbing, and started to wipe the gushing tears with the edge of her garment. Meanwhile she murmured with groans: 'Uncle Pan, if you want to save my life and the life of my baby, you must go to the county city at once and tell the authorities that Mao Mao is a good man, the best peasant in the world. Then they will release him at once. They believe your words, I know, because you are all comrades. You saved Mao Mao once when the revolutionaries first took him to you for evidence. You must go to the county city at once, Uncle Pan. You're the revolutionary village head, I know. Don't think that I am foolish.'

'Yes, I will, I will,' Uncle Pan said as fast as he could manage, without refuting a single word she uttered. 'But you must rest yourself. You must not hurt the baby. I certainly will do my best to speak for him!'

He left her with a sigh of relief.

*

After having cut two days' ration of soya-bean cake for our young cow, Uncle Pan left for the county city in the afternoon. The day was well spent. The sun had already tilted towards the west. My mother advised him to start the journey the next morning, but Uncle Pan insisted that he must go right away. He said that after Mao Mao had been arrested he began to imagine things, not only about him, but also about his wife and the baby in her womb; and that these imaginations made his old heart painful, without knowing why. So he left, taking with him half a dozen rolls of bread as his food.

He did not come back the second day. One the third day he still did not turn up. She-crow began to get impatient, and called on us once every three hours. She related with gestures and sighs, while tears streamed incessantly out of her swollen eyes, that she had dreamed terrible things about Mao Mao, had dreamed that Mao Mao had escaped on the way and was sheltered by a young widow living in the hills; that Mao Mao's soul was immediately captured by this witch and did not want to come back to the village again; that such things were quite possible for Mao Mao who could easily fall into the hands of women, especially young widows, just like a mouse into the clutch of a cat; and that Mao Mao would forget her once he was out of her control. Each time she finished her dream-tales, she would burst into a fit of sobs and started to bewail her hard fate. And she refused any kind of consolation from my mother. Nor would she go away. She just sat in our living-room till her tears were exhausted and her voice grew dull. Then she would cry, 'Ah, my mother! My dear mother! The baby is moving inside me again!' Then she would hold up her belly with both hands carefully and walk home, with my mother's support, to sleep.

On the fourth day, in the afternoon, She-crow stayed in our living-room for another three hours, lamenting about her sad destiny and complaining about the cold spell at night, which made her sleepless till daybreak. Then after another customary burst of sobs at the conclusion of the visit she tottered home, holding up her womb with both her hands. As soon as she disappeared from view a shaky old man ducked in with furtive steps. It was Uncle Pan. He looked thinner and his eyes were ringed with black patches. He must have been sleepless all these nights.

'Uncle Pan! So you're back! You should have come in a moment earlier. She-crow is just gone,' my mother said.

'Yes, I saw her going home,' Uncle Pan said.

'Didn't you tell her the news about Mao Mao?'

'No. As a matter of fact I was hiding myself behind a maple tree till she was away.'

'Why? I don't understand you.'

'I heard her lamentation when I first came to the door. I couldn't bear it, because it breaks my old heart. So I avoided her and retreated to the tree. I've no courage to face her, ma'am.'

'What do you mean? You've done nothing wrong to her?'

'But I showed the soldiers to her cottage, where Mao Mao was arrested.'

'But they would have found out Mao Mao's cottage in any case. Besides, you didn't know that they were going to arrest Mao Mao.'

'I don't think that way, ma'am.' Uncle Pan tried to put on a wry smile in order to soften his contradiction of my mother. But the smile looked like a tearful grimace, 'I don't think that way, ma'am. I'm a simple-minded farm-hand. so I think about things in a very simple-minded way . . .' Suddenly his voice broke and he lowered his head.

'What's the matter with you, Uncle Pan?' my mother asked in surprise. 'You look so weak. Are you hungry?' Then she called out into the kitchen: 'O Ran! Cook a bowl of hot noodles for Uncle Pan! He is hungry.'

'No, ma'am,' Uncle Pan stopped her, his voice trembling. 'I'm not hungry, ma'am, although I haven't had anything to eat for some time . . .' He paused. After a while, in a low voice, he went on, 'Ma'am, Mao Mao is dead!'

'Dead!' my mother shouted with horror.

'It's a sad story, ma'am. I never expected it. You know Mao Mao was arrested by the false woman, whom he had beaten badly after our burglary case and whom he brought to the head-quarters of his Order Preservation Corps for torture. He was very afraid of this false woman, ma'am, I know, because the fellow is a revolutionary spy and once threatened to hang Mao Mao alive if he did anything against the revolution again. So Mao Mao became terribly nervous on the way to the county city, thinking he would be tortured for information, of which he had none, and then hanged. One of the soldiers whom I met told me that Mao Mao was shivering all the way with fear. When they were nearing the city, Mao Mao had no longer any strength to move his steps. Then they dragged him by force to the city gate. Just as they were crossing the bridge over the moat, Mao Mao suddenly threw himself into the water below. The water was very deep there, ma'am, you know.'

'Didn't they pull him out?'

'They did. But it was of no use, because Mao Mao was already dead. His hands were bound together by the handcuffs, so he couldn't struggle. He fell into the water like a stone, so the soldier told me.'

'Are you sure that the story is true?' My mother's eyes became dilated with horror.

'Absolutely true, ma'am, because I saw Mao Mao with my own eyes. It is a ghastly sight, I can assure you. His corpse was exposed on the mound not far from the city gate. It was all swollen, worse than a man dead of dropsy. Poor Mao Mao, no one bothered about him. He was altogether forgotten by the world. The revolutionaries were very busy. All the soldiers were engaged in military manoeuvres. When I went to the county government and asked for a coffin to bury Mao Mao, they said they had no time for that at the moment. I said it was not fair to a poor man like Mao Mao. They said that they couldn't help, that the right wing people, headed by a military lord called Chiang Kai-shek, had separated themselves from the revolutionary forces in the provincial capital and were launching offensives at various points against the revolution; that their reactionary movement seemed to be spreading out into this district because they were very powerful, being supported by both foreign powers and rich landlords; and that they were terribly busy setting up defences in this district. In a word, ma'am, they could not give a coffin, nor send people to bury Mao Mao. So I had to bury him myself without a coffin. His corpse was terribly heavy. I could not possibly believe that he was one of our villagers, one of my fellow farm-hands. But his shabby clothes told everything. Poor Mao Mao has never worn a new garment since he got married to She-crow, as you know, ma'am.'

My mother remained silent, staring out through the window, where a few sparrows were chirping and fighting over some food, as usual. Uncle Pan put his head in both his hands and scratched his scalp madly with his fingers. O Ran at that moment emerged from the kitchen holding in her hands a bowl of hot noodles, the steam from which spiralled up into the air like a dragon. Uncle Pan said in a low, but heavy, voice, 'Thank you, O Ran, but I don't want to eat anything. I am not hungry.'

'Do eat some, Uncle. I did my best to cook it,' O Ran said, like a grown-up woman. She had been of late most of the time with Lao Liu, and had learned to behave like a guest in the house rather than a member. Seeing that Uncle Pan was irresponsive, she added, 'Do please eat some, Uncle. I may no longer have an opportunity to cook for you, just as you may no more have a chance to taste my cooking. Things in the world are changing so terribly fast!' And she put the dish on the table and then vanished into the kitchen again.

My mother started at her words and turned her gaze from the window to the old, familiar dining-table. 'Things are changing terribly fast, indeed!' she soliloquized. Then turning to Uncle Pan, she added, 'Do eat something, Uncle, otherwise you will be exhausted.'

'I can't, ma'am,' Uncle Pan said, lifting his head. 'Mao Mao's corpse keeps haunting my imagination. It's queer, it's very queer, indeed. The moment I close my eyes I see Mao Mao.'

'You'll forget about it in time. It will not take us long to forget a dead man.'

'I've forgotten many a fellow farm-hand, but I think I can never forget Mao Mao, who died in such a horrible way and whom I buried in that strange place with my own hands. You see, ma'am, when I was digging the grave, my hands were trembling like leaves in a storm.'

'Ow . . .' My mother echoed thoughtfully.

After a moment of silence Uncle Pan began again, in a childish tone, with an artificial, childish smile, 'Ma'am, I think I ought to go back to my native village up in the north. I've been thinking of it all these days.'

My mother started, her eyes suddenly growing wild and fixing on Uncle Pan, and asked, 'What makes you think of this? You have never thought of your war-torn birthplace before.'

'Many things make me think of it now, ma'am.'

'May I hear about them?' My mother grew nervous.

'Death, in the first place. When I was young I did not think of death. But now I do. I want to be buried near my ancestors, ma'am. And She-crow, in the second place. I can't possibly face her. If I break the news to her she might give herself up to a fit of madness and beat her belly violently as she usually does under such circumstances, so as to cause the premature birth of her baby. She must have a healthy, good baby in order to continue Mao Mao's family line. It is the only thing poor Mao Mao left in this world. I cannot bear seeing it damaged.'

'But this is your home, Uncle.' My mother pointed to the ground. 'You've helped build up the household. Without you it no longer would be a household.'

'I know, ma'am. But everything is now so different. The village seems so strange to me now. So does the town. Even O Ran . . .'

'I understand what you mean,' my mother interrupted him. 'But *we* are the same. Only the younger people change. Soon we shall have nothing to do with them. We are of the old time, you see. Yunchi will soon get his *bonus*, I expect. Then we shall retire. We shall shut our ears and eyes to the present world.'

'But I am a lonely old man, ma'am. I can't retire.'

'You'll have the young cow to distract you. She will bear your grandsons and grand-daughters. Her family will keep you busy.'

'Yes, perhaps you're right, ma'am. But the circumstances are so different now!' Uncle Pan heaved a sigh. His old eyes grew dim and vague and dull. He stared blankly through the window at the trees and the highway beyond and the undulating hills beyond the highway. Then he resumed in a dreamy voice as though speaking to himself, 'When I was approaching the village on my way back from the county city, I could hardly recognize the familiar sight of the shining tiles, the sandstone walls of our cottages and the blue sky over the village square, where Lao Liu's golden voice used to ring. I only felt something chilly about the village, something dark and cloudy hanging over the roofs, and something like the swollen shadow of Mao Mao's corpse towering before my eyes.'

'That is only a momentary vision caused by Mao Mao's death,' my mother explained. 'Don't think about it any more, Uncle. Try to think about something else, about your beautiful cow, for instance. Try to think of the day when, as all of us old people retire with a big *bonus*, you and the young cow and her children will do nothing but gambol on the green hills . . .'

'Sounds very nice, ma'am. But tell me: are you sure that you'll give me the cow?'

'Why, she is your cow. She has always been your cow. You saw her come into the world, nursed her and have brought her up to her present shape. She is yours! She is absolutely yours!'

'Do you really mean it?'

'Of course I mean it. To whom does she belong do you think? When you were away, she did not even sniff at the food I gave her. She recognizes only one person in the world, that is you.'

'Thank you, ma'am. I'll keep the cow. She will be the companion to my old age. She will remind me of the fertile earth

211

I've worked on, of the green sea of rice I have planted, of the golden waves of wheat I have sown. Ma'am, I like to think of such things. They make my old heart warm and smile . . .' Suddenly his voice snapped. Nameless tears welled out from his delirious, dark-ringed old eyes.

'Oh, Uncle Pan! Uncle Pan! You are too tired. You need some rest.' My mother dashed to him and helped him to stand up from the low bench he was sitting on. Then she signed to me to come near. We supported him into his room and laid him in his bed. Uncle Pan was as weak as an old invalid. But he was sobbing fitfully like a child.

After we came out to the living-room my mother murmured, with feeling and sadness, 'He *is* old. I've never thought of that. Time does fly very fast! He *is* old. We are *all* getting old!'

The next day Uncle Pan did not turn up for breakfast. We thought he was too tired. My mother warned O Ran not to wake him up and disturb him as he needed more sleep. But when the sun moved almost to the zenith Uncle Pan still did not appear in the house. My mother began to be curious. So she went to his room. To our surprise he was not there. We thought he might be in the next room feeding the cow. So we went to the cowshed. It was empty too. The cow was gone.

My mother stood in the middle of the room, trying hard to think what was the matter. 'Can it be that he took the cow out to pasture? No! There is no grass in the valley this time of the year.'

Hesitantly my mother went back to Uncle Pan's room again. She struck a match and lit the oil lamp on the table beside the bed, for it was dark in the room. There, on the table, we found a slip of paper, inscribed with a few scratchy characters. They were Uncle Pan's handwriting, looking very childish and without style. And, as Uncle Pan had not learned enough words to express himself, the sentences read also very clumsily.

Ma'am – I could not sleep a wink last night. Mao Mao kept on appearing before my eyes and his wife's lamentation ringing in my ears. I don't feel well, ma'am. I think of my birthplace in the north, of my parents and their graves which must have remained unrepaired since I was away. I have decided to start the journey back home before dawn with my daughter the cow, whom you promised to give me. I am sorry, ma'am. I am sorry at heart. I wish you good health, that Yunchi gets the *bonus* and your sons become great men. And give my love to O Ran, ma'am.

   Your servant,
    Old Pan.

My mother darted into the living-room like a madwoman and remained standing by the window, stupified, with the slip of paper in her hand. For a long while she kept silent, staring at the scratchy, shapeless characters. Then suddenly she called out to the kitchen: 'O Ran! Uncle Pan sends you his love.' But there was no answer to her call. After having waited a few minutes she shouted again, with a much louder voice: 'O Ran! Uncle Pan sends you his love!' There was still no answer. O Ran recently was in the habit of going to Lao Liu. They were now frantically in love. She did not like to stay in the house. Whenever there was an opportunity she would go to cook or do mending for the Assistant Commissar of Publicity.

'Perhaps she has gone to the story-teller's cottage, mother,' I said, still referring to Lao Liu by his old profession.

'I thought so,' my mother said quietly, her eyes becoming glassy and dull. And she let her stretched hand fall, the note slipping out of it and sailing gently down to the floor.

Her eyes followed the piece of paper, and as it settled down on the ground, they fixed on it as though it were something strange. Then, suddenly she lifted her head and sent out a peal of hysterical laughter. The echo kept ringing in the room like a bell. For a long while it lingered in the air.

CHAPTER 12

A few days after Uncle Pan's disappearance Lao Liu called on us. His visit to our house appeared like a great event, for he had seldom come to see us since he had become the Assistant Commissar of Publicity, not even for the sake of O Ran. It was always she who went to meet him. He was always busy with his work, which had to be done mostly at the headquarters of the local Revolutionary Party in the town. He came back to the village only in the evenings, and he always had a huge bundle of posters and notices under his arms to be looked over at night.

'I have only a few minutes to stay, ma'am,' he said to my mother, laying the bundle of propaganda materials on the table. It unrolled itself, displaying a set of new caricatures, which I had not seen before. The first picture showed a wolf in an army commander's uniform with its bushy tail curled up like a hook and a long sword dangling at its waist. A long file of troops were marching behind him. The caption read: *Chiang Kai-shek has betrayed the revolution. The landlord is coming back to restore his lost prestige and liberated serfs.* My mother gave a glance at it without a comment. Our ex-story-teller added, 'I'm leaving, ma'am, leaving perhaps for a long while. I come to tell you news which you must be interested to hear.'

'What is it?' my mother asked him both with alarm and surprise, for Lao Liu's face had an exceptionally serious air.

'News about Uncle Pan,' Lao Liu said quietly, but his voice grew heavy.

214

'Uncle Pan!' my mother shouted, her face went pale. 'What news? Good or bad?'

'Don't get excited, ma'am. It's not altogether bad news . . .'

'Is he coming back?' my mother interrupted him.

'Listen, ma'am. I've heard from O Ran that he disappeared at night with his cow. As a matter of fact I have been worried about him. He didn't know, ma'am, how serious the present political situation is. The reactionaries in the provincial capital have started an offensive against us, and, supplied with modern arms from foreign countries, have defeated the revolutionary army at several strategic places. Chumin, Wang the Lion and the steward who escaped have been made advisers to an "expeditionary force", which is soon to come to this district and to take the county city as its first objective.'

'But how about Uncle Pan? Tell me about Uncle Pan only!' my mother asked anxiously, interrupting him again. 'I don't want to hear about Chumin and his army.'

'Listen quietly, ma'am. I'll come to that,' Lao Liu said in an unperturbed voice, as quiet as when he was telling a story. 'In the face of this extraordinary *white terror*,' Lao Liu stressed this new terminology with a cough and then went on, 'you know what this means of course, we have to be on the alert. So the HQ of the newly reorganized Peasants' Volunteer Brigade decided to post patrols secretly on various roads in the district at night, just in case the reactionaries tried to sabotage and send spies to sneak in . . .'

'You mean Uncle Pan . . . ?' my mother interrupted him again, and her face became livid.

'Be quiet, ma'am, I'll come to him soon. It won't take a minute,' Lao Liu reassured her, still as quiet and unperturbed as a story-teller. And he went on with his preamble: 'Look here, this is the point that made me worry, as soon as I heard from O Ran the news about Uncle Pan's departure. Suppose he came across one of the patrols and was mistaken for a saboteur or a spy . . .'

'What?' my mother cried out.

'Do be quiet, please. I am coming to the point,' Lao Liu said. 'So I tried my best to find out if anything had happened to him. You see, I am in no way less concerned about him than you. My relationship with O Ran has brought me much closer to this house. He is no less my uncle than O Ran's. I inquired of my friends at the HQ of the Peasants' Volunteer Brigade in the county city about him. They told me that they had captured an old peasant with a cow one night recently. The patrols nearly killed him, mistaking him for a thief or a spy for Chumin. He had very bad luck, ma'am. He might have got through the district successfully, had it not been for the cow. You see, the cow made a terrific noise with its hoofs on the gravel path, which provoked great suspicion in the dead of night. It was only after severe interrogation at the HQ that they found out that the captive was the provisional chairman of the peasants' union in this village. It is Uncle Pan, of course . . .'

'Did they accuse him of being a spy or saboteur?' There was alarm in my mother's voice and her eyes wildly enlarged.

'They did! But I went to see them as soon as I heard about it. I guaranteed to them in my capacity as the Assistant Commissar of Publicity for this district that Uncle Pan was a good and honest peasant in the village. I also explained that Uncle Pan had lately grown homesick about his native place and wanted to get back as soon as possible and that was why he started the journey before dawn.'

'Do they believe what you said?'

'Of course they do! Do you expect them to believe in the words of the reactionaries?'

'Very good, Lao Liu. I'm most grateful. When do you think they will send Uncle Pan back to the village?'

'That is rather a problem, ma'am.' The sparse brows of the ex-story-teller knitted. 'Uncle Pan's position is different. He is the provisional chairman of the peasants' union in the village, as you know. It is against revolutionary principle at the present moment to desert one's post for another district, homesick or not. It shows lack of understanding of revolutionary theory on his part. So he is to be reformed. They have put him in a reformatory, which is newly set up in a secluded village specially for political deserters.'

'Oh, oh . . .' my mother exclaimed with weariness. Her alarmed eyes became vague and misty. She was confused by what Lao Liu said. 'But Uncle Pan has never been political, still less is he revolutionary,' she murmured as though to herself, staring blankly at the floor. Then she raised her voice: 'How about the cow? Can he take the cow with him to the reformatory? You see, he's a lonely old man . . .'

'What has the cow to do with politics?' our story-teller asked with surprise. 'She was confiscated for public use. It is already a bad gesture for Uncle Pan to take this piece of *private property* with him on his way home.'

'You don't understand, Lao Liu, what the cow means to his life.' My mother tried to explain to the Commissar, but her voice soon dropped with a sigh. 'No one can understand that. But do tell me, when will they let him go back home?'

'When he is thoroughly reformed and an active revolutionary.'

'Active revolutionary! Can he be one?' My mother's inquisitive voice lapsed into a murmur: 'Ah, if he really becomes one then he will never come back home.'

'I am afraid so. He would then devote his life to revolution. On the other hand, if he fails to reform himself he will hardly be able to get out of the institute.'

'I see . . .' my mother mumbled to herself, looking down thoughtfully. After a moment she lifted her eyes and asked quietly, 'Can't you use your influence to get him exempted? You see, a reformatory is supposed to be a place for young people, as far as I can gather. But he is so hopelessly old . . .'

'I can't, ma'am. It is a matter of revolutionary *discipline*. I simply can't!' Lao Liu said, frowning, and became rather impatient. Then, looking out through the window, he suddenly shuddered and exclaimed, 'Oh, my! I meant to come here for a few minutes. Now I've spent half a day. I must hurry up!' Then turning to my mother he added in a low voice: 'Ma'am, I want to ask your permission for something.'

'What permission do you have to ask from me, Lao Liu?' my mother said, surprised. 'You're now a revolutionary *official*. You can do anything you like.'

'No, ma'am. I can't do things blindly. Revolutionary officials are different from the old-fashioned bureaucrats. We must do things according to order and discipline.'

'What is it, then?'

Lao Liu gazed at my mother's stunned face for a while. Then he said calmly, 'I want to take O Ran away with me.'

'Away?' My mother started, fixing her dilated eyes at Lao Liu as though he were a stranger. 'What do you mean? I don't understand you, Lao Liu.'

'Listen! Chumin and Wang the Lion have been made advisers to a big expeditionary army, as I have told you. They are coming to this district at any time. As this place is strategically indefensible we have been instructed to withdraw to the high mountains in the west and build up a revolutionary base there around the county city. You see, it is going to be a long-term struggle. I may not be able to come back in the near future. So I want to take O Ran with me: I shall marry her as soon as possible. Ma'am, I may have to leave for the mountains any time within these three days, because our intelligence men have reported that Chumin's troops are already on the move.'

'Are you sure?' my mother said doubtfully. But her face had already turned pale.

'I'm quite sure.'

'Then even if Uncle Pan becomes thoroughly reformed, he wouldn't be able to return to us even for a visit . . .'

'It all depends. But do tell me, can I take O Ran away with me?'

'Well,' my mother paused as soon as she began. She lowered her head thoughtfully. Her eyes were blurred by a veil of tears that reflected glaringly the dull light from the window. She could not speak.

'Do tell me, ma'am. I want a word from you,' Lao Liu pressed and began to roll up the posters that lay on the table.

My mother said, her head still held low, 'I have no authority whatever over her now, Lao Liu. I am no longer her mother-in-law as you know, not even her guardian, since she is now grown up. You've got to ask her herself. Shall I call her?'

'Yes, please.'

'O Ran! Come out for a minute!' my mother called to the kitchen.

'Yes, *mother*!' O Ran answered.

In a minute O Ran came out from the kitchen. She still wore the old apron, the old blue nankeen robe which my mother had made for her for the New Year; and she still wore the old pigtail, slender and long. She stood in front of us, as innocent, obedient, hard-working and devoted as ever, except that she looked much taller now, with a pair of large hands and big shoulders.

My mother said to Lao Liu, 'Now ask her yourself.'

Lao Liu walked up to O Ran and performed a profound bow in front of her like a knight before his mistress in one of the stories he used to tell us in the old days. And in a low, even voice, he said, 'O Ran, I'm withdrawing with my comrades to the big mountains up in the west. I want to take you along, because I love you and want to marry you. What do you think about it?'

'Are you sure of what you say?' O Ran asked sternly like a mature woman.

'One hundred per cent sure,' replied Lao Liu, with another bow.

'When are you going, then?' O Ran asked again in a firm voice.

'In one or two days.'

'Good! I'll go with you.' Her answer was simple and concise. Her voice was simple and concise, too.

Lao Liu straightened up and was all smiles. I expected O Ran would burst out into tears over the departure to an unkown region and for sentimentality about this house in which she was brought up. On the contrary she looked surprisingly happy, her sullen, pock-marked face brightened up, and a smile was hovering about her lips and eyebrows. She was not only cheerful, but proud. My mother raised her head slightly and stole a glance at her, but immediately lowered her eyes again.

Lao Liu put the bundle of posters under his arms again and said to my mother, 'Thank you, ma'am, for your motherly care for O Ran all these years.' Then turning to O Ran, he went on, 'I will be seeing you soon, O Ran. I must go now. Be ready to start the journey at any time.' And he went out as hurriedly as he had come in.

My mother threw her head on the back of her chair. Her chest began to heave up and down and the tears shone brightly in her eyes. But she succeeded in restraining them. She was always like that: she never actually wept.

Lao Liu and O Ran left the village for the big mountains together with the commissars of the local Revolutionary Party just a few hours before the arrival of the new, regular troops under Chumin and Wang the Lion's direction. They came as quietly as the revolutionaries went away. There was not a single shot. In fact our villagers hardly perceived their presence in the town, had it not been for the new proclamations, stamped with the huge red seal of the new administration.

The document was pasted on the wall of our ancestral temple at the end of the village, facing the highway. It was first discovered by Benchin our Taoist priest early in the morning. He was greatly excited, shouting at the top of his voice in the village: 'The dynasty is again changed! This new one is the real, permanent dynasty! At last the day breaks!' He mingled his shouting with sighs and cheers. It was the first time since the arrival of the revolutionaries that our villagers had seen him in such an active mood. He seemed to have become younger and more vigorous. And this vivacity of his stimulated not only curiosity, but also a new hope for life and future. Many people went to the temple to read the official notice of the new local government.

The document consisted of three paragraphs, under three different headings, all written in classical language without caricatures like foxes or wolves. The first item dealt with the new regime, which was qualified as legal, representing the nation: it was the real government of the country, and consequently everybody must take orders from it, whatever they might be. Its present task was the suppression of the revolutionary bandits and the restoration of order. The second paragraph stipulated that the people should cleanse themselves of all the poison injected into them by the young bandits and return to the old way of living exactly as it had been before the bandit revolution. Under the third heading a case of crime and punishment was defined. Anybody who believed in any doctrine other than the instructions of the new government was a traitor punishable according to the act of treason. To illustrate this statement, a concrete example was given. Uncle Peifu the old schoolmaster was to be executed in public on the beach before the town tomorrow morning for his adherence to the bandit party as a secretary.

The three paragraphs themselves attracted very little attention because our villagers could hardly understand them. But the example itself caused a general stir. All stood agape, staring at one another, and maintained a dead silence. No one had ever suspected that Uncle Peifu was a traitor. This old school-teacher had always been on the verge of starvation, and because of this he had developed into the most ridiculous figure of a skeleton, short-sighted and hunchbacked. He was always laughed at behind his back for his comical looks, although highly respected at the same time for his ability to read and to write. Now this pathetic figure seemed to be wavering unsteadily before our eyes. Somehow we felt sad.

'It's a pity! It's a pity!' Benchin said with a sigh. 'That a pillar of education should have committed treason against the state!' He used as many elegant words as possible in order to impress our illiterate farm-hands on the spot. Then he went on, suggesting himself as the successor of the unfortunate schoolmaster in the field of teaching. 'It is a great loss for the parents indeed. Who is going to teach their children? I am rather worried, because I can't do two jobs at one time. If they ask me to be a teacher than I must give up preaching, which I am rather unwilling to do.'

And he looked round for response. As none of our villagers could afford to send their children to school, the mournful silence continued. Disappointed by the general apathy for education, Benchin dragged his steps away from the crowd and headed for our house. He wanted to tell the news to my mother, for Uncle Peifu was our family friend. My mother was sorting out all the things that O Ran had left behind, and dusting them and packing them carefully into a souvenir case. It seemed as though a very valuable member of the house was dead, for my mother was sobbing as she fingered the old objects with care and tenderness. Without much greeting Benchin selected a comfortable armchair by a corner and seated himself. He was ready for a long chat.

He described the new dynasty in a calm voice, but with great enthusiasm and animation, interpreting the proclamation as the golden decree issued by the 'Court of the new Emperor', who was sent down by the King of Heaven to restore to the ancient middle kingdom all the old virtues and institutions that had been destroyed by the 'revolutionary bandits'. Then he closed his eyes, heaved a sigh of relief and went on in dreamy tones: 'Oh, I wish the new Emperor would pay a little more attention to education and the *spiritual life* of the people!' Then he opened his eyes and stared at my mother and asked, 'You know, ma'am, what caused the downfall of the revolutionary bandits?' Without waiting for a reply he made the answer himself with great emphasis: 'The contempt of the Taoist priest! That is why they cannot hold on. But on the other hand if the priest does not value himself by drifting into the tide of bandit uprising as the pitiable old schoolmaster Uncle Peifu did, then . . .' He could

222

not find proper words to finish the statement, but sighed repeatedly. After a while he raised his voice again, and gave a full description of Uncle Peifu's condemnation as a revolutionary bandit by the new government.

'Are you sure Uncle Peifu is going to be executed?' my mother asked, as her hands started to tremble.

'Have I ever told a lie?' our priest retorted. Then he started to swear by the names of ghosts, holy and unholy.

'All right, all right, I believe you,' my mother said repeatedly, panic-stricken. 'But what are we going to do for this old friend of ours, then? We all know that the poor schoolmaster is an innocent man.'

'Absolutely nothing,' said Benchin firmly, putting on a serious face. 'The proclamation was issued by the Court of the New Emperor through the office of Chumin and Wang the Lion. The Emperor himself may change his mind by some sort of appeal. But do you think people like Chumin and Wang the Lion would alter the decision? They are men of iron will, ma'am. They do not swerve half an inch even over such small matters as land rent. I know them well, although I have never farmed their land.'

'I see,' my mother said to herself thoughtfully. 'You are perhaps right. But we must do something for our poor Uncle Peifu.'

'Certainly! I'm thinking of continuing his school after his death, which has been his life-long career. Do you think I'd make a good schoolmaster? I'm not particularly keen on teaching, but in view of my long standing friendship with Peifu I must do something to continue his career. By the way, ma'am, if somebody suggests the idea, would you support me . . . ?'

'How can you think of such things, Benchin!' my mother said, depressed and sad. 'He hasn't died yet. Aren't you his friend?'

'I'm sorry! I'm sorry, ma'am!' our priest apologized repeatedly, his face blushing, his conscience aching. 'I was simply expecting a job, ma'am, to be frank. I've been starved. I'm not interested in anything else, new Emperor or old, if you want the truth. Look at my bones. I'm sorry for Uncle Peifu, but . . .'

'But you must do something for him as an old friend,' my mother interrupted him and looked into his helpless, starved eyes.

'Tell me what I can do, ma'am,' our priest nearly cried out. 'I am ready to do anything for the poor man.'

'Go and chant the sutra before he is executed so that his innocent soul can go up into heaven. He has suffered too much in this world. He shouldn't get reincarnated into a human being again, at least not into a schoolmaster. Do try your best to elevate his soul, Benchin.'

'I will, ma'am. Since the revolutionaries came I've been forbidden to do it. I shall enjoy doing it again.'

'Please do it properly,' my mother said. 'Here is some money to buy incense and paper.' She took from her purse a handful of copper coins and handed them to Benchin. As our priest took the money she murmured, 'It seems as though Uncle Peifu were already dead.'

'I've the same feeling, ma'am. I feel unhappy, too, without knowing why,' Benchin remarked dejectedly.

And he left, walking unsteadily like a ghost.

The next day, towards noon, Benchin tottered into our house again, much weaker and more shaky than before. It seemed as though he had not slept a wink. His eyes stood out deliriously and stared straight like a pair of glass eyes, dull and stupid. His lips were twitching fitfully right and left, emitting some kind of sound, incoherent like murmur, but even like a prayer. He remained at the door, leaning against the doorpost like a beggar. As my mother and I went near to greet him, we began to make out what he was muttering about.

'Uncle Peifu, I won't take up your job. Be sure, I won't . . .'

'What's the matter with you?' my mother asked, looking into his delirious eyes.

The priest went on murmuring, 'Uncle Peifu, I won't take up your job. Be sure, I won't . . . I want to stick to my old job: preaching. Uncle Peifu, I won't . . .'

'What's the matter with you, Benchin?' my mother asked again.

The priest went on murmuring as though he had heard nothing: 'Uncle Peifu, I swear I don't want to be a schoolmaster . . . I swear by the name of the sainted ghosts . . .'

'Are you mad, Benchin?' my mother shouted in his ears. 'What are you talking about?' And she began to shake him by the shoulder. 'You must be mad.'

'I'm not mad, ma'am. They are mad. They killed Uncle Peifu with a sword early this morning, ma'am, a long sword, two feet long, no, three feet long; no, a hundred feet long. They cut Uncle Peifu's neck three times, but his head did not come off: too bony, ma'am. It's an old neck; the bones were too hard to cut. And the blood spurted out, a hundred feet high, like a fountain. It's strange, ma'am, the old bony fellow should have had so much blood. Um . . . da . . . da . . . da . . . um . . . hai . . .'

My mother turned to stone. Her hands that had rested on the priest's shoulders fell mechanically. Her eyes became as delirious and dull and stupid as Benchin's. A string of disconnected words fell slowly from her lips: 'So Uncle Peifu was executed . . .' But suddenly she started as though waking up from a nightmare, and asked the priest again: 'Did you pray for him? Did you pray to God not to reincarnate him into a schoolmaster again?'

'I don't know. I don't know. Ha! Ha! Uncle Peifu is there. There he is!' He pointed at the highway, on which two strangers were coming along in the direction of our village. 'There is Uncle Peifu, see? Uncle Peifu comes with Chumin's steward to ask me to take up his job in the school. No! no! I won't take it. Uncle Peifu! How are you, my old man?' He shouted at the two people and simultaneously dashed to them.

They met in the middle of the village square, where Lao Liu

used to set up his drum-stand and tell stories in the good old days. One of the newcomers asked Benchin: 'Are you the Taoist priest of the village?'

'I am, my old man,' the priest answered incoherently. 'Do you want me to teach? No, thank you!'

'We don't want you to teach,' one of the men said, and showed him a pistol that he carried at his belt. 'Come along with us. We're from the new local government. We were watching you murmuring prayer at the execution ground this morning. You birds of a feather!'

'What is that?' my mother asked the visitors in great panic.

'He is under arrest,' one of the plain-clothes detectives said.

'What for?'

'For trial! Don't you know that he is a revolutionary bandit?'

'But he is a great supporter of the new dynasty,' my mother said. 'He confessed that not a long time ago.'

'Then how do you account for the fact that he received three acres of Lord Chumin's land from the revolutionary bandits? He is not an ignorant peasant, you know. He is a priest capable of reading and writing, just like his accomplice the schoolmaster.'

'Don't argue with a village woman, pal,' the other detective said. 'Let's go. We have so many other jobs to do these days!'

And they put Benchin in chains, and dragged him away in the direction of the town. The priest did not offer any resistance, but kept saying: 'I don't want to teach, mind you! Thank you, no! My profession is to preach, to preach, to preach! I would not change it for gold, real, heavy gold! I won't.'

The plain-clothes men did not care a fiddle about what he was saying, but pulled him away by the chain like a donkey. Benchin went on babbling, as he moved his feet heavily: 'No, I don't want to teach. No, thank you! You had better find another man for the school!' His voice became inaudible as he was dragged further along the highway. In a moment all of them disappeared at a turning of the road.

*

Many days passed. We began to hear now and then rumblings of cannons from the mountains in the distance. It was rumoured that battles were engaged frequently between the revolutionary Peasant Volunteer Brigade and Wang the Lion's troops up in the west. Sometimes in the depth of the night we were wakened by explosions. My mother would start and could not sleep any more. Then she would stare at the window till it grew opaque outside and then bright, and finally the sun rose.

The village gradually began to get active and nervous. Sometimes our villagers would throw away their bowls during meals and rush out of the village and climb up hills and listen hysterically to the mysterious explosions, of which no one knew the source. No one could guess how far away they might be. But everybody was afraid. The clouds above seemed to hang low as if they would fall at any moment, crushing the village as well as the people. Sometimes when a sudden big explosion sounded somewhere in the west, the cows would jump up and our villagers would dash helter-skelter like a host of mice at the fall of a brick. The earth was boiling. Our village was boiling, too.

But our house seemed to be cold and quiet. My mother sat most of the time by the window, looking blankly now at the kitchen, where O Ran used to be bustling about, now at the tiny patch of ground outside the door, where Uncle Pan used to squat smoking a pipe or poking fun at Mao Mao or brushing our ploughing cow. She would maintain a dead silence, contemplating these old familar places. She did not seem to bother much about the explosions afar or about the hubbub made by our villagers.

One morning, however, she became a little talkative, when our watchdog Laipao came in from outside. He walked around and round the room and then went to my mother and sniffed at the edge of her gown repeatedly and finally pulled at it vehemently, whimpering as though he were saying something. My mother patted his head and said sympathetically, 'Poor thing, you have been starved. Half of the household have disappeared. Nobody cooks for you and nobody keeps you company.

My poor Laipao!' Then she raised her head and said to me, 'Son, I remember a dream I had last night. I dreamed Laipao was carrying a letter in his mouth from your father. Perhaps the messenger in town has resumed his errand-running to 'The Big City' down the river, now that landlord Chumin has come back and opened his shops again. Will you go and see if there is any message from your father? He ought to have written to us a long time ago.'

'Yes, mother,' I said.

And I went into town. I found the old messenger, Sweet Potato. He had really just started his job again and had made a trip to the big city down the river, and in his mail bag there was a letter from my father. I asked him how my father was getting on and whether he had got his big bonus. He would not say a word. He simply said that he himself was very busy owing to the fact that apart from carrying business letters for the merchants he had also sometimes to spend some time tracing the recipients who had disappeared during the disturbances. He gave me the letter and told me to go.

When I came back and showed the letter to my mother, she smiled, saying, 'Strange that the dream has come true. Our souls are now in communication with that of Laipao's at night. Laipao has now really become a regular member of our family. Poor thing, we shouldn't let him do night-watching anymore. We have no more cows to be stolen.' She paused for a while. Then she said again, 'Read the letter to me, will you, son?'

I tore the letter open and read. 'I've heard what happened to our native district,' the letter said. 'It is nothing particularly shocking to me. Much worse things have happened in this big town. Hundreds of young people and students have been shot. But I think and hope that our eldest son is still all right, although I haven't heard from him for ages. As to my business, it hasn't gone so smoothly as we expected . . .' Suddenly I felt a black patch shifting right and left before my eyes, and I could not continue reading.

'Go on, son!' was my mother's anxious voice.

I rubbed my eyes for a while, then I went on. My voice grew a little faltering. I did not understand why. 'The foreign businessmen to whom my boss sold his cargo are said to be suffering from general economic depression at home and refused to buy any more raw materials. The result is the drastic fall of prices and my boss has therefore to close down his firm for some time. The big bonus has to be postponed. But in view of my long service in the firm my boss has promised to look after me till the business is started again – Let's hope this won't be long, for my age does not wait for me. Meanwhile he offered me the job of coaching his children as a means of earning a living during the depression. It is not so bad as in our native town. In fact it is much better than Uncle Peifu's job: it enables me to keep a family. Will you come out to join me? I long to see you. And our younger son ought to start learning a trade or go to a modern school, too, now that farming as a profession is out of the question. Besides, I understand the village is now in a mess. Perhaps it is better for you to live here for some time. I can't possibly get back home to fetch you because of the children I have to look after every day. You may leave the house to the care of Uncle Pan and O Ran – send my love and best greetings to them.'

My mother secretly let out a sigh as I was folding up the letter. 'So he has to become a schoolmaster again at this time of his life!' she said in a low voice. 'Poor man. He doesn't know what has happened to his old colleague Uncle Peifu. He hasn't the slightest idea about Uncle Pan and O Ran, either.'

'But his teaching job is much easier than that of poor Uncle Peifu, the boss being totally different,' I remarked, trying to comfort her. Meanwhile I had a vision of the exciting life in the big town, of the modern school to which I might go. My heart had in fact already flown to the big city. I asked naively, 'Shall we go to join him, mother?'

'Oh no!' my mother said decisively. 'How can we leave our ancestors' home?'

*

A few days later the rumblings of guns sounded nearer and nearer. Rumour had it that the revolutionaries had built up a strong base in the big mountains and had gathered many more peasant volunteers to fight battles. Big casualties had been inflicted on Chumin's and Wang the Lion's men. We could see long lines of stretchers carried down to the highway from the mountains in the distance. And one afternoon a company of soldiers from Wang the Lion's headquarters came to conscript our villagers in order to replace their losses. Many young farm-hands were herded away by force. Through the window my mother watched them vainly struggle to escape on the highway and finally disappear in the hazy distance.

'Son,' she turned to me and said, 'I am afraid we shall have to take your father's advice. They may come to conscript you at any time, because you are no longer a small boy. I can't give you up to that kind of fighting, whose nature I don't understand.'

'Yes, mother,' I said. I was only too glad to leave my native village for a new life in a big town, although my mother appeared unspeakably sad about it.

Early next morning we quietly locked up our door and left the village. We carried with us only the necessary clothes and a bundle of letters which my father and elder brother had written home during the past few years, and the ancestral tablet. When we walked out of our village my mother looked back several times, but she did not say anything, nor utter a sigh. The village had not changed a bit. Its cottages, its trees, its black-tiled roofs, everything looked exactly as I could remember it. But there was a kind of gloominess, a kind of cloudiness hanging over it in the sky. Perhaps it was the morning mist.

We went across the river by the foot-bridge. The transparent water sailed down calmly as of old. I liked the sand at the bottom that was fine and white and glittering with the first rays of the sun. I tried to linger by the railing of the bridge for a while, just to have a good look at the sand, which I used to play with when I was a small child. But my mother urged me on. She did not want to look at the sand. She avoided seeing anything that we knew. I saw her staring intentionally straight at the other side of the river, with which we were not familiar at all.

When we got to the other side of the river, we came on to another highway, which led to another world, the world of 'The Big City' down the river. It was a long road. It covered a distance of over one hundred miles. We extended our gaze along the stretch of this lengthy, dusty, yellowish, ancient highway, and began to realize how immeasurably lonely we were. My mother suddenly stopped and said, 'Oh, we've forgotten our Laipao! We must take him with us. Son, try to call him. We're not very far from the village yet.'

I went to the top of a hill nearby and called out as far as my voice could reach: 'Laipao! Laipao!' The echo rang on the river like a bell. Suddenly a whitish animal dashed out of our village from between the trees, and rushed at full speed in the direction of my call. As it came to the stream and then plunged into it I could recognize it was our Laipao. For he never took the bridge, but always swam in the water, in spite of the cold. In a minute he reached me. He scampered about me like a pup, licking my hands and my chin. I led him down to the highway. He became almost mad when he saw my mother. He leapt and frolicked about her as though he had found a treasure, a home. I had never seen him so cheerful before.

My mother tapped his head gently and wanted to say something to him. But as soon as she opened her lips, her voice quivered and her eyes became veiled with tears. Somehow I felt my heart heavy at the sight. So I turned my head away, pretending not to see. In front of me stood a huge, ancient tree. I caught the sight of a poster stuck high up on its trunk. It was left behind by the revolutionaries. In order to appear natural, I read out the words as though trying to enjoy myself:

WE SHALL COME BACK AGAIN

My mother seemed to have perceived my intention. And certainly she had heard what I was saying. So she secretly dried

231

her tears with her sleeve and tried to look strong, saying in an artificially natural tone in response to what I murmured, 'I doubt it!' Just at that moment, some naive cowherd in the hills not far away tuned up the old, familiar song. As it was not sung in chorus as it used to be, the note had a rather sad touch:

> Aiyu, ai-yu, ai-aiyu, ai-yo-ho-o, ai-ho . . .
> Aiyu, ai-yu, ai-aiyu, ai-yo-ho-o, ai-ho . . .
> This yellow earth gave us rice in spring
> And in autumn, soya beans and sweet potato.

My mother remained attentively silent till it was finished. And she waited for a few minutes more, till the ringing of the echo vanished in the air. Then, with a deep sigh which she could not suppress, she added, 'Son, you're right. WE SHALL COME BACK AGAIN. This is the place of our birth, a place of our ancestors and of our kind.'

'Yes, mother,' I said while my eyes still rested on the poster: 'WE SHALL . . .' Before I could finish the sentence a sudden explosion of cannonballs rumbled in the distance, interrupting me and breaking the centuries-old tranquillity of the country morning.

'Let's hurry,' my mother said in great haste. 'Let's hurry on our way.'

So we started out. I went in front, my mother behind me; and Laipao behind my mother, innocently wagging his tail. He did not know that it was going to be a long journey.